JOHN

Meet God Face to Face

Gary M. Burge
Mark L. Strauss
Sean A. Harrison, General Editor

Tyndale House Publishers, Inc.
Carol Stream, Illinois

Visit Tyndale's exciting Web sites at www.nltstudybible.com, www.newlivingtranslation.com, and www.tyndale.com

NLT Study Series: John

Copyright © 2009 by Tyndale House Publishers, Inc. All rights reserved.

Cover photograph copyright © by Rosemarie Gearhart/iStockphoto. All rights reserved.

The text of John is taken from the *Holy Bible,* New Living Translation, copyright © 1996, 2004, 2007 by Tyndale House Foundation. All rights reserved.

Designed by Timothy R. Botts and Dean Renninger

Edited by Sean A. Harrison

This Bible portion is typeset in the typeface *Lucerna,* designed by Brian Sooy & Co. exclusively for Tyndale House Publishers, Inc. All rights reserved.

TYNDALE, New Living Translation, NLT, the New Living Translation logo, and Tyndale's quill logo are registered trademarks of Tyndale House Publishers, Inc.

NLT Study Bible is a trademark of Tyndale House Publishers, Inc.

ISBN 978-1-4143-2196-7 Softcover

Printed in the United States of America

15   14   13   12   11   10   09
7   6   5   4   3   2   1

The purpose of the *NLT Study Series* is to call individuals and groups into serious conversation with God and engagement with his word.

We have designed these studies to provide you and your group with a complete, new Bible study experience. Our aim has been to help you engage seriously with the Bible's content, interacting with it in a meaningful and deeply personal way, not just regurgitating rote answers to fill-in-the-blank questions or producing purely subjective opinions. We also hope to encourage true community study with the honest sharing of different perspectives and experiences. Most of all, we want to help foster your direct communication with God, encouraging you to tell God what is on your mind and heart. We want to help you understand what God is teaching you and apply it to the realities of personal and community life.

To this end, each study in the *NLT Study Series* includes twelve weeks of individual and group studies focusing on understanding the meaning of the text of Scripture, reflecting on it personally and with others, and responding actively to what God is saying to you through it.

Each volume of the *NLT Study Series* can be used by itself, with no other resources, but you can also use it with your Bible of choice. Each volume of the *NLT Study Series* includes, along with the twelve-week study, one book of the *NLT Study Bible*, with both the text of Scripture and all of the study aids alongside it. The *NLT Study Bible* was designed to open up the world of the Bible and to make the meaning and significance of Scripture clear, so it makes a great personal and small-group study resource.

It is our hope and prayer that these studies will help you and those in your group to understand God's word more clearly, to walk with God more fully, and to grow with one another in relationship with our God.

> *Open my eyes to see*
> *the wonderful truths in your instructions.* PSALM 119:18
> *Come . . . let us walk in the light of the* LORD! ISAIAH 2:5

Sean A. Harrison
General Editor

CONTENTS

Gospel of John Study

JOHN'S GOSPEL is one of the most beloved books in the Bible and may well be the most often read. This is because the Gospel so clearly states the good news of salvation and the way to an eternal relationship with our Creator God. The most famous verse in the whole Bible, John 3:16, comes from this Gospel: "For God loved the world so much that he gave his one and only Son, so that everyone who believes in him will not perish but have eternal life." This sentence says it all: what motivated God to save us, how he did it through the gift of his Son, how we must respond in faith in order to be saved, and what the result of our salvation will be—eternal life with God.

John's Gospel is written in a simple style and with simple vocabulary. Certain words occur again and again: believe, remain, send, life, truth, word, love, light, the way. Yet beneath this simplicity lies profound spiritual truth. The Gospel's prologue (John 1:1-18) summarizes its central theme: Jesus the Son of God is the "Word" or "Message" (*logos*), through whom God reveals himself to human beings. The Word was with God from all eternity and the Word *was* God. God created all things through him. The Word became a human being, but the world that he created rejected him. Yet those who believed in him and accepted him became children of God and received eternal life. Those who believe in the Son come to know the Father, while those who reject the Son also reject the Father. The Son's purpose is to do the Father's will and to reveal him to a lost world. We can know God the Father because Jesus the Son, who is fully divine, became a human being and came to earth to suffer and die as the Passover lamb to pay the penalty for our sins.

As you read this Gospel, keep this central message in mind. Notice how often Jesus speaks about his relationship with God the Father and the truth about God that he is bringing. Every conversation Jesus has, every miraculous sign that he performs, every conflict or debate in which he engages, contributes to this central theme. The purpose of the book, as the author himself states, is "that you may continue to believe that Jesus is the Messiah, the Son of God, and that by believing in him you will have life by the power of his name" (John 20:31).

Mark L. Strauss
San Diego, California
March 2009

How to Use This Study

THE PRIMARY WAY we recommend using this Bible study guide is for personal daily meditation and study, along with weekly fellowship and discussion.

The introductory session (p. A11) is designed to launch the group study. Group participants need not prepare for this session, but the leader is encouraged to work through it in advance in order to be able to guide the group effectively. The introductory session provides orientation to the Gospel of John, and gives a taste of what the daily and weekly study will be like for the following twelve weeks.

Each week, there are five personal daily studies plus a group session. You can use the daily study guide for your personal daily conversation with God, or you can use it around the table with your family.

You don't need to participate in a weekly group meeting in order to use this study guide. For instance, you can just do the study individually, working through the daily studies and then using the weekly group session as a time of reflection.

Similarly, you don't have to use the study on a daily basis in order to benefit from using it in a group setting. You can just do the study with the group each week by reading the passages, thinking about the discussion questions, and participating in the group discussion.

Ultimately, it's between you and God how you use this study. The more you put into it, the more you will get out of it. If you are meeting with a group, we encourage you to decide together what your level of commitment will be, and then encourage each other to stick with it. Then keep up your part of your commitment to the group.

RECOMMENDATIONS FOR DAILY STUDY

Each daily study is designed to be completed within 15 minutes, but optional "Further Study" is usually provided for those who want to go into greater depth.

Start the daily study by reading the passage recommended for each day. Reflect on what it means, and write down your questions and thoughts about it.

You can use the space provided in the book to write thoughts and answers to questions. If you find that you need more space, we recommend purchasing a small blank book with lined paper to use as a Bible study journal. Use the journal to write your answers to the reflection questions, your own thoughts about the passage, what you think God is saying to you, and your prayers to God about what you have studied.

The NLT Study Series is designed to be used with the *NLT Study Bible*. The Gospel of John from the *NLT Study Bible* is included for your reading and study. You can also use the *NLT Study Bible* itself, either the print edition or the online version at www.nltstudybible.com. The included section of the *NLT Study Bible* retains its page numbering, so the study guide can be used to refer to either the included section or the *NLT Study Bible* itself.

It can be helpful to highlight or mark the Bible text and study materials where they answer your questions or speak to you in some way. You can:

- underline, circle, or highlight significant words and phrases,
- put brackets around sections of text,
- write keywords in the margin to indicate a topic,
- write page numbers cross-referencing the study guide,
- write dates cross-referencing your journal entries.

Finally, talk with God about what you are learning and how you are responding to it, but also take time to listen to him and hear what he might be saying to you through it. Cultivate your relationship with God day by day.

RECOMMENDATIONS FOR GROUP STUDY

When the group comes together, read the entire passage for the week together, then spend some time letting each person share their own dialogue with God and the Bible that week: insights they've gained, questions they have, and so on.

Then use the discussion questions to stimulate the discussion for that week. You don't have to do all of the questions—you can pick just one.

When the discussion is winding down, spend some time reflecting on what God is saying to you as a group, and how you are going to respond to what God is saying. Spend some time praying together about these things.

Finally, take a look at the passage for the coming week, and make sure everyone understands what they will be doing in preparation for the next meeting of the group.

Orientation to John and Prologue

SESSION GOALS
- Get oriented to the Gospel according to John.
- Discuss what members hope to learn and how we hope to grow in this study.
- Introduce how we are going to be studying together.
- Answer any questions about how to begin.
- Commit ourselves to the Lord and to each other, to participate to the best of our ability.

GETTING ORIENTED TO THE GOSPEL OF JOHN

Answer the following questions, either individually, or in discussion together with your group.

What do you know about the apostle John? Can you recall any events from John's life?

What do you know about the Gospel of John? Can you recall any key verses from it?

What do people in the world today think about who Jesus was?

How do you hope to grow spiritually from your study of the life of Jesus as presented in the Gospel of John?

INTRODUCTION TO THE GOSPEL OF JOHN

Read the "Setting" in the Introduction to John's Gospel, pp. 1764–1765. What kinds of debates were going on in Ephesus at the time John wrote his Gospel? How might the Gospel be a response to these debates?

Read the "Meaning and Message" section of the Introduction, p. 1767. What aspect of the meaning and message of John's Gospel are you most interested in exploring?

READING: JOHN 1:1-18

Read this passage aloud; if you're in a group, choose one reader. Read slowly, clearly, and thoughtfully. What questions or observations do you have after reading this passage?

STUDY

Jesus is identified as the "Word" (Greek, *logos*) in John 1:1-2. What does this mean?

Make a list of things we learn about the "Word" in this passage (1:1-18). What do you think is the most important?

John 1:14 states, "The Word became human . . . ." Also read John 1:12-13, 16-18. Why did the Word become human?

What, according to John 1:18, does Jesus do for us?

FURTHER STUDY (Optional)

Read "The Word," p. 1769. What was stunning about Jesus being "the Word"?

REFLECTION

John 1:12 says that we have become "children of God" because Jesus came to save us. What does it mean practically to live in this world as God's children?

What is this passage saying to you? What might God be saying to you through this passage?

QUESTIONS

Do you have questions about doing the daily study or preparing for the next meeting?

PRAYER

Take turns praying about this Bible study and the next twelve weeks. You can tell God what your thoughts and questions are, and ask him for his help, strength, and insight. You can thank him for this Bible study and for the Bible itself. You can ask him to speak to you and to the others in the group. The leader, in closing, can also commit this study to God.

WEEK
ONE

Testimonies about Jesus and Cleansing the Temple

JOHN
1:19–2:25

OUTLINE

DAY **1** ◆ John 1:19-28

....

READING: **JOHN 1:19-28**

> Begin with prayer, asking God to give you insight, understanding, and an open heart to listen to and follow his word.

> This section is identified in the *NLT Study Bible* as the beginning of the "Book of Signs" (John 1:19–12:50). Throughout this section Jesus' identity is being revealed: through the testimony of others, through Jesus' miracles (called "signs"), and through his teaching.

STUDY

> When John the Baptist is asked about his identity, what does he deny, and what does he affirm, about himself and his role?

> In 1:22-23, John quotes from Isa 40:3 to describe his role. Why did John consider himself "a voice"? How did John fulfill that role?

> Read the study note on 1:24. What were the Pharisees' expectations for the Messiah?

FURTHER STUDY (Optional)

> Read the study note on 1:27. Why would John consider himself a slave?

> Read Isa 40:1-11. How does the prophet Isaiah described relate to the coming of Jesus?

REFLECTION

> John the Baptist downplays his own importance and exalts Jesus as the Messiah. In what practical ways can we turn attention away from ourselves and toward Jesus?

> What do you think God is saying to you through your study of this passage?

PRAYER

> Talk to God about what you have read, any questions or concerns you might have, and what you think he might be saying to you today. You can write your prayer here if you wish.

DAY 2 ◆ John 1:29-34

READING: **JOHN 1:29-34**

Begin with prayer, asking God to give you insight, understanding, and an open heart to listen to and follow his word.

This episode describes John the Baptist's testimony about Jesus and his description of Jesus as the "Lamb of God who takes away the sin of the world."

STUDY

John calls Jesus the "Lamb of God." According to the study note on 1:29, what are the possible backgrounds for this title? What did John realize about Jesus to have used it?

John the Baptist describes what happened at Jesus' baptism (1:32-34). Also read Matt 3:13-17. What is the significance of John's testimony about the Holy Spirit descending?

In 1:34, John calls Jesus "the Chosen One of God." Read Isa 42:1-4 for background. What do you think it means that Jesus is given this title? Why would John use this title? (See study note on 1:34.)

FURTHER STUDY (Optional)

Why do you think the Holy Spirit descended on Jesus at his baptism (1:32)?

Read Luke 3:22; 4:1, 14, 18. What role did the Holy Spirit play in Jesus' life?

What role(s) does the Holy Spirit play in our lives?

REFLECTION

This passage relates to John's testimony about Jesus. In what ways can you testify about Jesus in your daily life?

What do you think God is saying to you through your study of this passage?

PRAYER

Talk to God about what you have read, any questions or concerns you might have, and what you think he might be saying to you today. You can write your prayer here if you wish.

DAY 3 ◆ John 1:35-51

READING: JOHN 1:35-51

Begin with prayer, asking God to give you insight, understanding, and an open heart to listen to and follow his word.

This episode repeats the testimony of John the Baptist about Jesus and tells about Jesus' call of several disciples. Following Jesus in discipleship is central to the Christian life.

STUDY

Again John calls Jesus the "Lamb of God." See Isa 53:7 for background to this title. What is Isa 53:7 about, in the context of Isa 52:13–53:12?

Read the study note on 1:41. What is the significance of applying the title "Messiah" to Jesus? What does it mean for Jesus to be the "Anointed One"?

Read the study note on 1:46. Nathanael assumed that Nazareth could not be the origin of "anything good." What changed his mind about Jesus (read 1:47-48)?

FURTHER STUDY (Optional)

"Cephas" means "rock" in Aramaic, the language Jesus and his disciples spoke. "Peter" (petros) is a Greek translation of this word. Why do you think Jesus called Simon "Rock"?

In John's Gospel Jesus often begins important sayings with the phrase "I tell you the truth." According to the study note on 1:51, what is the significance of this phrase?

See the study note on 1:51 for the background to the title Son of Man and the allusion to Jacob's ladder in Gen 28:10-22. What was Jesus saying about himself? What would the disciples have understood from Jesus' statement?

This passage recounts how the new disciples brought friends to Jesus. Identify someone you would like to introduce to Jesus and write out one way that this might happen.

What do you think God is saying to you through your study of this passage?

PRAYER
Talk to God about what you have read, any questions or concerns you might have, and what you think he might be saying to you today. You can write your prayer here if you wish.

DAY 4 ◆ John 2:1-12

READING: JOHN 2:1-12
Begin with prayer, asking God to give you insight, understanding, and an open heart to listen to and follow his word.

At a wedding in Cana of Galilee, Jesus turns water to wine, the first of seven "miraculous signs" Jesus will perform in John's Gospel. It not only reveals his glory, but also symbolically shows that he is bringing the "new wine" of messianic salvation that will replace the waters of Jewish ritual.

STUDY
Locate Nazareth on the map at the introduction to the Gospel of John (p. 1764). Cana was a small village just north of Nazareth. Read John 4:43-54 to learn about another miracle that occurred there. Is there any connection between these two miracles?

When asked to help, why did Jesus tell his mother that his time had not yet come? What did Jesus mean by "his time"? (Read study note on 2:4.)

Why do you think Jesus went ahead and created more wine for the wedding feast?

FURTHER STUDY (Optional)
Read the study note on 2:6. The water jars were used for Jewish ceremonial washing. What might this symbolize about Jesus' ministry?

Read "Miraculous Signs," p. 1772. How is a "sign" different from a "miracle"? What does this difference tell you about the purpose of Jesus' supernatural acts?

REFLECTION

This passage climaxes in the claim that Jesus revealed his glory and the disciples believed in him (2:11). Can you identify a time in your life when you saw God's glory and this experience increased your faith in him?

What do you think God is saying to you through your study of this passage?

PRAYER

Talk to God about what you have read, any questions or concerns you might have, and what you think he might be saying to you today. You can write your prayer here if you wish.

DAY 5 ◆ John 2:13-25

READING: JOHN 2:13-25

Begin with prayer, asking God to give you insight, understanding, and an open heart to listen to and follow his word.

Jesus' "cleansing" of the Temple was actually a symbolic act of destruction. By judging the Temple this way, Jesus showed that his sacrificial death on the cross would end the need for animal sacrifices in the Temple and would provide a new and perfect way to God.

STUDY

Read the study note on 2:13. In Matthew, Mark, and Luke, Jesus attends only one Passover celebration in Jerusalem—at the end of his ministry. What is the significance in John of Jesus attending three Passover celebrations throughout his ministry?

How had the religious leaders in Jerusalem turned religious activity into commerce?

What is the significance of the objection Jesus raises against the sellers in 2:16?

What does Jesus mean in 2:19 when he says, "Destroy this temple, and in three days I will raise it up"? Compare 2:21-22 and the study note on 2:19.

FURTHER STUDY (Optional)

The study note on 2:14-17 explains that a similar episode appears near the end of the Synoptic Gospels (Matthew, Mark, and Luke). What is the significance of Jesus referring to himself as the temple? What does this say about where God was dwelling at that time?

REFLECTION

Jesus "cleansed" the Temple because many of God's people had forgotten that the Temple was to be a place of prayer and worship. Can you identify an area in your life that needs to be cleansed and once again made into a place that honors God?

What do you think God is saying to you through your study of this passage?

PRAYER

Talk to God about what you have read, any questions or concerns you might have, and what you think he might be saying to you today. You can write your prayer here if you wish.

GROUP SESSION

READING: JOHN 1:19–2:25

Read John 1:19–2:25 together as a group.

DISCUSSION

You can use the following questions to guide what you share in the discussion. Give each person at least one opportunity to share with the others.

What did you learn from John 1:19–2:25? What was one thing that stood out to you as you studied this passage? How did John 1:19–2:25 surprise you? Do you have questions about this passage or the study materials that haven't been answered? What does God seem to be saying to you through what you have studied?

TOPICS FOR DISCUSSION
You can choose from among these topics to generate a discussion among the members of your group, or you can write your thoughts about one or more of these topics if you're studying solo.

1. What role does John the Baptist play in the ministry of Jesus?

2. What is the role of "Miraculous Signs" in John's Gospel?

3. Why did Jesus cleanse the Temple? What is the significance of this event for John's Gospel?

GROUP REFLECTION
What is God saying to us as a group through this passage?

ACTION
What are we going to do, individually or as a group, in response to what God is saying to us?

PRAYER
How should we pray for each other in response to God's message to us in this passage?

Take turns talking to God about this passage and about what he is saying.

NEXT: JOHN 3:1-36 (Nicodemus and More Testimonies from John the Baptist)

WEEK
TWO

Nicodemus and More Testimonies from John the Baptist

JOHN
3:1-36

OUTLINE

DAY **1** ◆ John 3:1-8

READING: JOHN 3:1-8

Begin with prayer, asking God to give you insight, understanding, and an open heart to listen to and follow his word.

Jesus' discussion with Nicodemus, a respected leader among the Jews, demonstrates the inadequate understanding the religious leaders of Israel had and the spiritual significance of Jesus' coming.

STUDY

Who did Nicodemus think Jesus was?

Read the study note on 3:3. Why is it necessary to be born again to enter the kingdom of God? What does this tell us about God's kingdom?

What does it mean to be "born of water and of the Spirit" (3:5)?

FURTHER STUDY (Optional)

Read the study notes on 3:6, 8. What is the relationship between "wind," "spirit," and "Spirit"?

REFLECTION

Identify something in your life today that is characteristic of your old life without Christ. What steps can you take to change this and to live out the new life Christ has given you?

What do you think God is saying to you through your study of this passage?

PRAYER

Talk to God about what you have read, any questions or concerns you might have, and what you think he might be saying to you today. You can write your prayer here if you wish.

DAY 2 ◆ John 3:9-15

READING: **JOHN 3:9-15**

Begin with prayer, asking God to give you insight, understanding, and an open heart to listen to and follow his word.

As the conversation between Jesus and Nicodemus continues, Jesus rebukes Nicodemus for not understanding spiritual things and explains that Jesus, the Son of Man, must be "lifted up" in the same way that Moses lifted up the bronze snake in the wilderness.

STUDY

To be "lifted up" (3:14) means not only that Jesus will be lifted up on the cross to die, but also that he will be exalted to heaven after the victory of his resurrection. Why are both his death and his resurrection important for our salvation?

Read the study note on 3:13. What makes Jesus different from all other human beings?

Read the account of Moses lifting up the bronze snake in the wilderness in Num 21:4-9. What analogy is Jesus making between that event and his crucifixion?

FURTHER STUDY (Optional)

Read "Believing," p. 1775. What is the significance of John's use of the verb *believe/trust* instead of the noun *belief/faith* throughout the Gospel of John?

REFLECTION

Even though Nicodemus was a religious leader, he did not truly understand spiritual things. In what ways can our "religion" sometimes get in the way of an authentic relationship with God?

What do you think God is saying to you through your study of this passage?

PRAYER

Talk to God about what you have read, any questions or concerns you might have, and what you think he might be saying to you today. You can write your prayer here if you wish.

DAY 3 ◆ John 3:16-21

READING: JOHN 3:16-21

Begin with prayer, asking God to give you insight, understanding, and an open heart to listen to and follow his word.

Jesus explains to Nicodemus the way of salvation and the reason he came to the world.

STUDY

Read and meditate on John 3:16. What is the message of this verse?

How does the message of this verse sum up the whole message of the Bible?

John 3:18 reads that there is no judgment against anyone who believes in Jesus. Why, according to 3:19, are people who do not believe judged by God?

FURTHER STUDY (Optional)

John 3:16, 18 say that Jesus is the "one and only Son." This phrase has traditionally been translated "only begotten Son," but most New Testament scholars now agree that the Greek word *monogenēs* means "one and only," not "only begotten." Read the following definition from the *NLT Study Bible* Greek-Hebrew Word Study Dictionary:

> *monogenēs* (3439): *unique, one and only.* This word indicates something that is the only representative of its kind, with the implication that it is special or extraordinary in some way. It can refer to a unique child, special to the parents, whether or not the child is an only child.

Also read other examples of *monogenēs* in the New Testament: Luke 7:12; 8:42; 9:38; John 1:14, 18; Heb 11:17; 1 Jn 4:9.

What does it mean that Jesus is God's "one and only Son"? What does this say about the uniqueness of the Christian faith?

God loved the world by sending his Son to save us. His love motivated this extraordinary act of self-sacrifice. What does your love for God and for the world motivate you to do?

What do you think God is saying to you through your study of this passage?

PRAYER
Talk to God about what you have read, any questions or concerns you might have, and what you think he might be saying to you today. You can write your prayer here if you wish.

DAY 4 ◆ John 3:22-26

READING: JOHN 3:22-26
Begin with prayer, asking God to give you insight, understanding, and an open heart to listen to and follow his word.

In John's Gospel, John the Baptist bears important testimony about Jesus. He constantly exalts Jesus and takes a second place to him.

STUDY
Although this passage says Jesus was baptizing, John 4:2 clarifies that it was actually his disciples who were doing the baptisms. What is the significance of this point?

What was the purpose of John's baptism? Read also Luke 3:3.

What concern do John's disciples express to him about Jesus (3:26)? What was motivating them?

John says these events happened before John the Baptist was thrown in prison. Read
Mark 1:14; 6:14-29 for an account of John's arrest and execution. Why did Herod have
John arrested?

REFLECTION

If some other person or group is doing better than you or your group, what attitude do
you have? What attitude *should* you have?

What do you think God is saying to you through your study of this passage?

PRAYER

Talk to God about what you have read, any questions or concerns you might have, and what
you think he might be saying to you today. You can write your prayer here if you wish.

DAY 5 ◆ John 3:27-36

READING: JOHN 3:27-36

Begin with prayer, asking God to give you insight, understanding, and an open heart
to listen to and follow his word.

In these verses, John the Baptist makes an important statement about his role as
forerunner of the Messiah: "He must become greater and greater, and I must become less
and less." This statement is a fundamental perspective for all followers of Jesus Christ.

STUDY

Was John envious of Jesus' success?

What images did John use to describe his relationship to Jesus?

How was Jesus superior to John?

FURTHER STUDY (Optional)

In 3:29, John identifies Jesus as the bridegroom and himself as merely the "best man." Read other references to Jesus as the bridegroom: Matt 9:14-15; Rev 19:7; 21:2. What do you think this means about the nature of Jesus' ministry? Who is the bride?

REFLECTION

John says in 3:29 that he is filled with joy because of Jesus' success. Sometimes we are not joyful because of other people's success, but jealous. Can you think of such a time?

What do you think God is saying to you through your study of this passage?

PRAYER

Talk to God about what you have read, any questions or concerns you might have, and what you think he might be saying to you today. You can write your prayer here if you wish.

GROUP SESSION

READING: JOHN 3:1-36

Read John 3:1-36 together as a group.

DISCUSSION

You can use the following questions to guide what you share in the discussion. Give each person at least one opportunity to share with the others.

What did you learn from John 3:1-36? What was one thing that stood out to you as you studied this passage? How did John 3:1-36 surprise you? Do you have questions about this passage or the study materials that haven't been answered? What does God seem to be saying to you through what you have studied?

TOPICS FOR DISCUSSION

You can choose from among these topics to generate a discussion among the members of your group, or you can write your thoughts about one or more of these topics if you're studying solo.

1. Jesus talks to Nicodemus about being "born again." What does this mean, according to this chapter, and what role does the Holy Spirit play?

2. John 3:16 is perhaps the most famous verse in the Bible. Reflect on and discuss its importance as a summary of the Christian faith.

3. John the Baptist makes statements to emphasize his role in relationship to Jesus. What does he always say about his role? Why is this a model for all true disciples?

GROUP REFLECTION

What is God saying to us as a group through this passage?

ACTION

What are we going to do, individually or as a group, in response to what God is saying to us?

PRAYER

How should we pray for each other in response to God's message to us in this passage?

Take turns talking to God about this passage and about what he is saying.

NEXT: **JOHN 4:1-54 (The Samaritan Woman and Healing an Official's Son)**

WEEK
THREE

The Samaritan Woman and Healing an Official's Son

JOHN
4:1-54

OUTLINE

DAY **1** ◆ John 4:1-15

READING: **JOHN 4:1-15**

Begin with prayer, asking God to give you insight, understanding, and an open heart to listen to and follow his word.

Jesus' encounters a Samaritan woman, breaks down traditional barriers of race, gender, and social status, and reveals the truth about God's love for all people everywhere.

STUDY

John 4:4 states that Jesus "had to go through Samaria." Jesus could have gone around Samaria, as many Jews did. Why do you think John says Jesus "had" to go?

What did Jesus mean when he offered the woman living water in 4:10? What did the woman think the living water was?

In 4:14, what does Jesus say his "living water" will do for a person?

Read "Living Water," p. 1777. What was Jesus offering the woman?

FURTHER STUDY (Optional)

Read the study note on 4:4-6. What was the relationship between Jews and Samaritans in Jesus' day? Can you think of any modern parallels?

REFLECTION

Jesus breaks down social and religious barriers by talking to a Samaritan woman. In what ways could you break down a social, cultural, or racial barrier in order to share God's love with someone?

What do you think God is saying to you through your study of this passage?

PRAYER

Talk to God about what you have read, any questions or concerns you might have, and what you think he might be saying to you today. You can write your prayer here if you wish.

DAY 2 ◆ John 4:16-26

READING: JOHN 4:16-26

Begin with prayer, asking God to give you insight, understanding, and an open heart to listen to and follow his word.

Jesus' conversation with the woman from Samaria reaches a deeper level as he demonstrates divine knowledge about her life. This leads to a discussion about the nature of true worship and Jesus' self-revelation as the Messiah.

STUDY

In 4:16, Jesus changes the subject. What was the purpose of his request?

The woman perceives that Jesus is a prophet, and so she asks him a theological question in 4:19-20. Do you think she was trying to change the subject? If so, why?

What do you think Jesus means by the statement "salvation comes through the Jews"? See study note on 4:21-22.

What does it mean to worship God in Spirit and in truth? See the study note on 4:24. What kind of worship is the opposite of worshiping in Spirit and truth?

FURTHER STUDY (Optional)

What was the significance of Mount Gerizim for the Samaritans? See study note on 4:20.

The Greek of 4:26 is ambiguous (see also study note on 4:26). Jesus may be saying he is the Messiah (the coming king who would bring salvation). Or, this may be a claim to be God. Which do you think is most likely in this context, and why?

REFLECTION
Jesus addresses this woman's personal needs and religious convictions. How could you share Jesus' love with someone by doing the same thing?

What do you think God is saying to you through your study of this passage?

PRAYER
Talk to God about what you have read, any questions or concerns you might have, and what you think he might be saying to you today. You can write your prayer here if you wish.

DAY 3 ◆ John 4:27-38

READING: JOHN 4:27-38
Begin with prayer, asking God to give you insight, understanding, and an open heart to listen to and follow his word.

When the disciples return, they are puzzled to find Jesus speaking with a woman who is a Samaritan. But they are about to find that his priorities are different from theirs.

STUDY
Why do you think the disciples were shocked to find Jesus talking to the woman?

What does Jesus mean that he has food that they know nothing about (4:32)? How was Jesus nourished by God? See study note on 4:32-34.

What does Jesus mean that the fields are already ripe for harvest? See 4:35 and study note.

FURTHER STUDY (Optional)
Who are the "others" that Jesus refers to in 4:38?

In what ways are the fields ready for harvest today?

Do you have negative feelings about any particular groups of people? How could you share God's love more effectively with them?

What do you think God is saying to you through your study of this passage?

PRAYER

Talk to God about what you have read, any questions or concerns you might have, and what you think he might be saying to you today. You can write your prayer here if you wish.

DAY 4 ◆ John 4:39-42

READING: JOHN 4:39-42

Begin with prayer, asking God to give you insight, understanding, and an open heart to listen to and follow his word.

By breaking down barriers and speaking with this Samaritan woman, Jesus not only leads her to the truth, but many others in her village believe as well.

STUDY

Why did the Samaritans believe in Jesus, according to 4:39?

Based on what you have gleaned about Jewish and Samaritan relationships, what is surprising about 4:40?

What is the significance of the title "Savior of the world" that the Samaritans gave to Jesus?

REFLECTION

What does this passage teach us about sharing with others what God has done in our lives?

What are some ways you might break down ethnic, social, or cultural barriers to make the good news of salvation available to others?

What do you think God is saying to you through your study of this passage?

PRAYER
Talk to God about what you have read, any questions or concerns you might have, and what you think he might be saying to you today. You can write your prayer here if you wish.

DAY 5 ◆ John 4:43-54

READING: JOHN 4:43-54
Begin with prayer, asking God to give you insight, understanding, and an open heart to listen to and follow his word.

Back in Cana in Galilee, Jesus performs the second "miraculous sign" of the Gospel by healing a government official's son, again revealing his glory and provoking faith.

STUDY
What had previously happened in Cana (2:1-11)? What was the significance of that previous miracle?

In what way did the official demonstrate his faith in Jesus?

How does the timing of the miracle prove Jesus' amazing healing power (4:52-53)?

Do you see any similarity or connection between 2:1-11 and this passage?

FURTHER STUDY (Optional)
Jesus returns to Galilee and receives a positive welcome from the Galileans, despite his claim that a prophet is not honored in his hometown (4:44). How is being "welcomed" different from being "honored" as a prophet? See also study note on 4:44-45.

Why does Jesus criticize the Galileans in 4:48?

Read Matt 12:38-40 for an example in Matthew's Gospel of a request for a sign. Who asked for this sign and what was Jesus' response?

REFLECTION

John 4:50 says that the man believed in Jesus even though he had not yet seen the miraculous healing. God wants us to trust him even if we don't yet understand what he is doing in our lives or cannot yet see the results. Can you identify a situation in which at first you did not understand God's purpose, but later you came to understand?

What do you think God is saying to you through your study of this passage?

PRAYER

Talk to God about what you have read, any questions or concerns you might have, and what you think he might be saying to you today. You can write your prayer here if you wish.

GROUP SESSION

READING: JOHN 4:1-54

Read John 4:1-54 together as a group.

DISCUSSION

You can use the following questions to guide what you share in the discussion. Give each person at least one opportunity to share with the others.

What did you learn from John 4:1-54? What was one thing that stood out to you as you studied this passage? How did John 4:1-54 surprise you? Do you have questions about this passage or the study materials that haven't been answered? What does God seem to be saying to you through what you have studied?

TOPICS FOR DISCUSSION

You can choose from among these topics to generate a discussion among the members of your group, or you can write your thoughts about one or more of these topics if you're studying solo.

1. What contrasts do you see between Nicodemus and the Samaritan woman (see study note on 4:1-42). How do these two passages reveal God's heart for the humble and insignificant?

2. Jesus told Nicodemus he had to be "born again." In what way is our salvation like a new birth? What happens to us when we are born again by God's Spirit?

3. The Samaritans and Jews hated each other, yet Jesus reached out to a Samaritan woman. Can you identify some similar relationships of anger and hatred between groups today? What would need to be done to break down the barriers of suspicion and hatred? How does our faith in Jesus compel us to do so?

GROUP REFLECTION

What is God saying to us as a group through this passage?

ACTION

What are we going to do, individually or as a group, in response to what God is saying to us?

PRAYER

How should we pray for each other in response to God's message to us in this passage?

Take turns talking to God about this passage and about what he is saying.

NEXT: **JOHN 5:1–6:71 (Jesus as Fulfillment of Sabbath and Passover)**

FOUR

Jesus as Fulfillment of Sabbath and Passover

JOHN
5:1–6:71

OUTLINE

DAY **1** ◆ John 5:1-15

. . . .

READING: **JOHN 5:1-15**

Begin with prayer, asking God to give you insight, understanding, and an open heart to listen to and follow his word.

In the next six chapters, Jesus attends various Jewish festivals and uses their imagery to portray himself as the fulfillment of Judaism (see study note on 5:1–10:42). This first episode (5:1-47) portrays Jesus as the Lord of the Sabbath, healing on the Sabbath day.

STUDY

Why did so many sick people gather at the pool of Bethesda? See study note on 5:3.

See study note on 5:8-9. Why did the religious leaders object to the healing of the man (5:10)?

Why does Jesus tell the man to stop sinning? See study note on 5:14.

FURTHER STUDY (Optional)

A number of similar Sabbath controversies occur in the other Gospels. Read Mark 2:23-28 and 3:1-6 for two examples. What does Jesus do on these occasions, and what does he teach when the religious leaders object?

REFLECTION

The Jewish leaders object to the man carrying his mat on the Sabbath and miss the greater fact that he has been healed. In what ways might we let our own religious traditions blind us to the greater reality of what God is doing in the world?

What do you think God is saying to you through your study of this passage?

PRAYER

Talk to God about what you have read, any questions or concerns you might have, and what you think he might be saying to you today. You can write your prayer here if you wish.

DAY **2** ◆ John 5:16-30

READING: **JOHN 5:16-30**

Begin with prayer, asking God to give you insight, understanding, and an open heart to listen to and follow his word.

In the context of debating the Jewish religious leaders about healing on the Sabbath, Jesus teaches about his authority and his relationship with the Father.

STUDY

Jesus justifies healing the man on the Sabbath by saying that his Father is always working and so is he (5:17). According to the note on 5:17, what point was Jesus making? And why did the Jewish leaders try to kill Jesus (5:18)?

Jesus says he can do nothing on his own (5:19-20a, 30). What does he mean?

Jesus claims that God, his Father, "sent him" (5:23, 24). What are the two primary tasks that God gave to Jesus?

What will the Son of Man do at the end of this age?

FURTHER STUDY (Optional)

Read "The Jewish Leaders," p. 1779. Is John's Gospel anti-Semitic? Is the translation "the Jewish leaders" better than simply "the Jews" in these passages?

REFLECTION

Jesus said he can do nothing by himself, but only does what the Father directs him to do. He lived a life of complete dependence on the Father. In what ways do you sometimes try to live in your own power? How can we live a life of greater trust and dependence on God?

What do you think God is saying to you through your study of this passage?

Talk to God about what you have read, any questions or concerns you might have, and what you think he might be saying to you today. You can write your prayer here if you wish.

DAY 3 ◆ John 5:31-47

READING: JOHN 5:31-47

Begin with prayer, asking God to give you insight, understanding, and an open heart to listen to and follow his word.

In his response to the Jewish religious leaders, Jesus now turns to the issue of the testimonies that confirm the truth of who he is and what he has come to accomplish.

STUDY

According to the study note on 5:31-40, Jesus introduces a series of witnesses to testify on his behalf. Read these verses. Who or what are the five witnesses Jesus points to?

John the Baptist is the second witness testifying on Jesus' behalf (5:33-35). Read 1:15, 29-34; 3:27-36. What did John the Baptist say about Jesus?

In 5:36, Jesus' teachings and miracles are the third witness. What are some examples you have already seen of this witness in John's Gospel?

Read 5:37-38. In what ways has God himself testified on Jesus' behalf in John's Gospel?

Scripture is the fourth witness to Jesus (5:39-40). Read the study note on 5:39-40, and read Luke 24:25-27. What are some examples of the Old Testament testifying about Jesus?

REFLECTION

Jesus says the greater witnesses about himself are his teachings and his miracles (5:36). Can you think of any of Jesus' teachings in the Gospels that are so significant or life-changing for you that it confirms for you that he is who he claimed to be? Can you name a miracle in your own life that confirms for you that Jesus is indeed the Son of God?

What do you think God is saying to you through your study of this passage?

PRAYER

Talk to God about what you have read, any questions or concerns you might have, and what you think he might be saying to you today. You can write your prayer here if you wish.

DAY 4 ◆ John 6:1-21

READING: JOHN 6:1-21

Begin with prayer, asking God to give you insight, understanding, and an open heart to listen to and follow his word.

The stories in ch 6 use images from the Passover festival to communicate about Jesus. The feeding of the 5,000, the only miracle of Jesus that is recorded in all four Gospels, takes on special significance in John as Jesus goes on to teach about himself as the bread of life.

STUDY

Having returned to Galilee, Jesus feeds a great multitude. According to the study note on 6:1-15, what is the Old Testament background to this miraculous sign? What is the significance of that connection?

How was Jesus testing Philip in 6:5-7? What response was he looking for?

What is the people's response to the miracle? What do they say about Jesus and what do they want to do with him? Why does Jesus slip away?

How do Jesus' actions and words in 6:16-21 reveal his deity?

FURTHER STUDY (Optional)

At the end of the miracle, the people say, "Surely, he is the Prophet we have been expecting!" Who is this Prophet? Look up the references cited in the study note on 6:14 for possible answers.

What does Jesus' miracle of the feeding of the 5,000 teach us about his ability to meet our daily needs? What are some areas you need to trust him more (health, finances, relationships, etc.)?

What do you think God is saying to you through your study of this passage?

PRAYER

Talk to God about what you have read, any questions or concerns you might have, and what you think he might be saying to you today. You can write your prayer here if you wish.

DAY 5 ◆ John 6:22-71

READING: JOHN 6:22-71

Begin with prayer, asking God to give you insight, understanding, and an open heart to listen to and follow his word.

After feeding the 5,000 with a few loaves and fishes, Jesus teaches the people that he is the bread of life. His teaching, however, disturbs many of his followers, and many desert him. When he asks the twelve disciples if they are going to leave, too, Peter makes a strong statement that Jesus alone has the words that give eternal life.

STUDY

How does Jesus respond when the people ask for a miracle in 6:30-31? What does he offer them instead?

What does Jesus mean that he is the bread of life (6:35) and the bread that came down from heaven (6:41)? (What does bread do for people?)

What does Jesus mean when he offers his flesh as true bread and that people must eat his body and drink his blood? See study notes on 6:53-58; 6:60-61; 6:63.

FURTHER STUDY (Optional)

Why was Jesus' teaching hard for his disciples to accept?

How did Jesus' disciples respond to this difficult teaching (6:60, 66)? How did the Twelve respond (6:68-69)?

Jesus says in 6:63 that only the Holy Spirit gives eternal life. It is not a matter of human effort. (Cp. 6:29; Eph 2:8-9.) How are we saved, according to these texts?

REFLECTION

Jesus here calls himself the bread of life (6:35). In what ways does Jesus provide physical, emotional and spiritual sustenance?

What do you think God is saying to you through your study of this passage?

PRAYER

Talk to God about what you have read, any questions or concerns you might have, and what you think he might be saying to you today. You can write your prayer here if you wish.

GROUP SESSION

READING: JOHN 5:1–6:71

Read John 5:1–6:71 together as a group.

DISCUSSION

You can use the following questions to guide what you share in the discussion. Give each person at least one opportunity to share with the others.

What did you learn from John 5:1–6:71? What was one thing that stood out to you as you studied this passage? How did John 5:1–6:71 surprise you? Do you have questions about this passage or the study materials that haven't been answered? What does God seem to be saying to you through what you have studied?

TOPICS FOR DISCUSSION

You can choose from among these topics to generate a discussion among the members of your group, or you can write your thoughts about one or more of these topics if you're studying solo.

1. When Jesus was accused of breaking the Sabbath by healing, he responded in various ways. Here in John, Jesus reminded the people that God works on the Sabbath, so he can also. In the other Gospels, he points out that the Sabbath was made for human beings, and not vice versa, and that, in any case, he is the Lord of the Sabbath. See also Rom 14:5-6. Do you think Christians are required to rest on the Sabbath (which is Saturday)? If not, how do we respond to this Old Testament command today?

2. Jesus identifies himself as the bread of life. What principles for our Christian lives can we derive from this metaphor?

3. Simon Peter's confession (6:68-69) marked an important turning point at a time when many other followers found Jesus' teaching too difficult. Compare this passage to Peter's confession in Matt 16:13-20. Have you experienced any turning points like this in your relationship with God?

GROUP REFLECTION

What is God saying to us as a group through this passage?

ACTION

What are we going to do, individually or as a group, in response to what God is saying to us?

PRAYER

How should we pray for each other in response to God's message to us in this passage?

Take turns talking to God about this passage and about what he is saying.

NEXT: **JOHN 7:1–8:59 (Jesus at the Festival of Shelters)**

Jesus at the Festival of Shelters

JOHN
7:1–8:59

OUTLINE

DAY **1** ◆ John 7:1-24

READING: **JOHN 7:1-24**

Begin with prayer, asking God to give you insight, understanding, and an open heart to listen to and follow his word.

John 7–8 continues the theme of Jesus as the fulfillment of the Jewish Festivals. This time it is the Festival of Shelters, during which there were ceremonial water and light rituals. In this passage he arrives in Jerusalem and defends his message as coming not from himself, but from God. In the passages that follow, Jesus claims to be living water and the light of the world.

STUDY

Why did Jesus' brothers want him to go to Jerusalem for the Festival of Shelters (7:2-5)? What was Jesus' response? Why did he respond that way? Why do you think he eventually went? (See 7:10.)

What does Jesus say in 7:16-18 about his message?

Why do you think Jesus was accused of being demon possessed? What prompted this accusation?

FURTHER STUDY (Optional)

Jesus' brothers did not believe in him during his public ministry (7:5; see Mark 3:20-21, 31-35). After his resurrection, however, they became leaders in the church (see Acts 1:14). What must have happened between the time of Jesus' resurrection and the beginning of the church—a period of 40 days (see Acts 1:3)?

Jesus uses a lesser-to-greater argument in 7:21-22 to show that it is legitimate for him to heal on the Sabbath. What is the point he is making? See study note on 7:22.

What does Jesus mean when he says, "Look beneath the surface so you can judge correctly" (7:24)?

A46

REFLECTION

Jesus' own brothers did not believe in him, and his own people attacked him by saying he was demon possessed (7:20). Have you ever been attacked by those who are close to you? How did you respond? How could you respond in a way that is both loving and truthful?

What do you think God is saying to you through your study of this passage?

PRAYER

Talk to God about what you have read, any questions or concerns you might have, and what you think he might be saying to you today. You can write your prayer here if you wish.

DAY 2 ♦ John 7:25-52

READING: JOHN 7:25-52

Begin with prayer, asking God to give you insight, understanding, and an open heart to listen to and follow his word.

This passage continues the account of Jesus' time at the Festival of Shelters. It describes the people's speculation about whether Jesus is the Messiah, several failed attempts by the religious leaders to arrest him, and his claim to provide living water.

STUDY

Why do some of the people doubt that Jesus is the Messiah (7:27, 40-44, 47-49)?

Identify the attempts to arrest Jesus. What happens each time they try? What explanations are given for why this happens? What does this tell us about Jesus' mission?

Where did Jesus come from (7:28-29)?

Where was Jesus going to go (7:32-36 and study note)?

FURTHER STUDY (Optional)

What is the living water Jesus was offering people? When would it be available?

Jesus says that anyone who is thirsty can come to him for "living water"? In what ways are people spiritually thirsty? How does Jesus meet that need?

What do you think God is saying to you through your study of this passage?

PRAYER

Talk to God about what you have read, any questions or concerns you might have, and what you think he might be saying to you today. You can write your prayer here if you wish.

DAY 3 ◆ John 7:53–8:11

READING: JOHN 7:53–8:11

Begin with prayer, asking God to give you insight, understanding, and an open heart to listen to and follow his word.

Jesus teaches a powerful lesson about God's forgiveness and love toward sinful people.

STUDY

The law said that the punishment for adultery was stoning (Lev 20:10; Deut 22:22-24). Read the study note on 8:5. How were these religious leaders ignoring part of that law? What was their purpose in bringing the woman to Jesus (see 8:6 and study note on 8:5)?

What did Jesus mean when he said, "Let the one who has never sinned throw the first stone!" See also the note on 8:7. Why do you think the oldest ones left first (8:9)?

Jesus forgives the woman, but tells her to stop sinning. What does this say about God's forgiveness and personal responsibility?

REFLECTION

Can you think of a time when you condemned someone else's sin, but then realized you were guilty of something similar? How can we avoid this kind of hypocrisy?

What do you think God is saying to you through your study of this passage?

Talk to God about what you have read, any questions or concerns you might have, and what you think he might be saying to you today. You can write your prayer here if you wish.

DAY 4 ◆ John 8:12-30

READING: JOHN 8:12-30
Begin with prayer, asking God to give you insight, understanding, and an open heart to listen to and follow his word.

Jesus' teaching at the Festival of Shelters continues. Here he identifies himself as the light of the world, teaches about his authority, and warns the people of the consequences of their unbelief.

STUDY
What do Jesus' words about being the light of the world mean in the context of the Festival of Shelters (see study note on 8:12)?

The law required two witnesses for a conviction (Deut 19:15). Who are the witnesses in 8:17-18 that confirm Jesus' identity? Why is Jesus' testimony about himself a valid witness?

What did Jesus mean that his opponents were "from below" while he was "from above"? See the study note on 8:23.

FURTHER STUDY (Optional)
What does Jesus mean that when the Son of Man is "lifted up," then you will "understand that I Am he"? See the study note on 8:28. Go back and read the note on 1:51 for the background to the Son of Man.

Read "Misunderstanding," p. 1785. What does this tell us about people who do not have the Spirit of God in their lives?

REFLECTION

Jesus says he is the light of the world. Identify some of the darkest times in your life, when you experienced the most pain or loss or confusion. In what ways does Jesus bring "light" to you in dark places?

What do you think God is saying to you through your study of this passage?

PRAYER

Talk to God about what you have read, any questions or concerns you might have, and what you think he might be saying to you today. You can write your prayer here if you wish.

DAY 5 ◆ John 8:31-59

READING: JOHN 8:31-59

Begin with prayer, asking God to give you insight, understanding, and an open heart to listen to and follow his word.

Jesus' discussion and debate with his religious opponents continues to heat up. He accuses them of being children of the devil instead of children of God, and they accuse him of being an illegitimate child and a demon-possessed Samaritan. In the end, Jesus says, it is God who will vindicate him.

STUDY

What does Jesus say in 8:31 is the test of true discipleship? What promise does he give his true disciples (8:32)?

What important Jewish assumption does Jesus challenge in 8:39? See also the study note on 8:33.

In what way is the statement "We aren't illegitimate children!" in 8:41 both a defense of themselves and an attack on Jesus? What accusation was being made about Jesus' birth? See study note on 8:41.

Jesus states that "before Abraham was even born, I Am!" (8:58). What did Jesus mean by this? See the study note on 8:58. Why did his listeners try to throw stones at him?

FURTHER STUDY (Optional)

Jesus' language about being set free (8:32-33) is followed by an analogy about slaves and sons (8:34-38). What point is Jesus making?

In 8:48, Jesus' opponents accuse him of being a Samaritan devil. What do they mean by this? (Consider how the Jews viewed Samaritans.) How does Jesus answer?

REFLECTION

The people defend their actions in 8:39 by claiming that they are children of Abraham. What is the problem with this? How might we do something similar? Where should our focus be?

What do you think God is saying to you through your study of this passage?

PRAYER

Talk to God about what you have read, any questions or concerns you might have, and what you think he might be saying to you today. You can write your prayer here if you wish.

GROUP SESSION

READING: JOHN 7:1–8:59

Read John 7:1–8:59 together as a group.

DISCUSSION

You can use the following questions to guide what you share in the discussion. Give each person at least one opportunity to share with the others.

What did you learn from John 7:1–8:59? What was one thing that stood out to you as you studied this passage? How did John 7:1–8:59 surprise you? Do you have questions about this passage or the study materials that haven't been answered? What does God seem to be saying to you through what you have studied?

TOPICS FOR DISCUSSION

You can choose from among these topics to generate a discussion among the members of your group, or you can write your thoughts about one or more of these topics if you're studying solo.

1. Chapter 7 continues speculation about whether Jesus is the Messiah. Examine some of the prophecies about the Messiah in the Old Testament, including 2 Sam 7:11-16; Isa 9:1-7; 11:1-9; Jer 23:5-6. What were the Jews expecting?

2. What is the main message of the account of the woman caught in adultery? Does it teach that people should not judge others for their sin? Is judging ever appropriate? See the study note on 8:11 and discuss situations where judging is or is not appropriate.

3. The Jewish people considered their common ancestry with Abraham to give them a unique relationship with God. In what way was this true? In what way was it not true?

GROUP REFLECTION

What is God saying to us as a group through this passage?

ACTION

What are we going to do, individually or as a group, in response to what God is saying to us?

PRAYER

How should we pray for each other in response to God's message to us in this passage?

Take turns talking to God about this passage and about what he is saying.

NEXT: **JOHN 9:1–10:42 (Healing the Blind and Shepherding the Sheep)**

WEEK
SIX

*Healing the Blind
and
Shepherding
the Sheep*

JOHN
9:1–10:42

OUTLINE

DAY **1** ◆ John 9:1-12

READING: **JOHN 9:1-12**

Begin with prayer, asking God to give you insight, understanding, and an open heart to listen to and follow his word.

Jesus performs another healing on the Sabbath by healing a man who had been born blind. The whole of chapter 9 is ironic as the man who was blind gradually gains spiritual enlightenment and the religious leaders who are supposed to be spiritually enlightened move into greater and greater darkness. See study note on 9:1-41.

STUDY

The disciples raise an interesting question in 9:2. Is illness/disability always caused by sin? Is it ever caused by sin?

How could this man's blindness have "happened so the power of God could be seen in him"?

What is the significance of the name of the pool of Siloam, according to the note on 9:7?

FURTHER STUDY (Optional)

The saliva of a powerful person was sometimes considered in the ancient world to have healing benefit. Why else might Jesus have used this method of healing?

Read 2 Kgs 5 (especially v. 10). How might that episode provide light on this one?

REFLECTION

Can you identify some difficult time or situation in your life where God was glorified because you trusted in him to bring you through?

What do you think God is saying to you through your study of this passage?

Talk to God about what you have read, any questions or concerns you might have, and what you think he might be saying to you today. You can write your prayer here if you wish.

DAY 2 ◆ John 9:13-34

READING: JOHN 9:13-34

Begin with prayer, asking God to give you insight, understanding, and an open heart to listen to and follow his word.

The man who has been healed is taken to the Pharisees, to verify the healing and because of the possibility that the Sabbath has been violated.

STUDY

Read about the Pharisees in the study note on 9:13. In what way do they reveal their heart attitude?

Why do you think the Pharisees called in the man's parents? What were they hoping to achieve? See the study note on 9:18.

What is the significance of the statement that they threw the man out of the synagogue? Read the study note on 9:34.

FURTHER STUDY (Optional)

How does this passage show the healed blind man becoming more enlightened as the story progresses?

REFLECTION

In what ways can our petty jealousies, relationship problems, or cultural insensitivities blind us to what God is doing in the world? How can we change this?

What do you think God is saying to you through your study of this passage?

Talk to God about what you have read, any questions or concerns you might have, and what you think he might be saying to you today. You can write your prayer here if you wish.

DAY 3 ◆ John 9:35-41

READING: JOHN 9:35-41

Begin with prayer, asking God to give you insight, understanding, and an open heart to listen to and follow his word.

The opening situation has now been reversed: the blind man now sees, while the Pharisees are blind.

STUDY

Read the study note on 9:35. What does the title "Son of Man" mean? Why do you think Jesus used it with reference to himself?

Prior to this, the man came to believe Jesus was a prophet (9:17); now he expresses faith in him as the Son of Man. What is the difference between these two confessions?

FURTHER STUDY (Optional)

In what sense were the Pharisees blind?

Go back through the story and trace the increasing blindness of the Pharisees. What provokes this progression?

REFLECTION

What kinds of thing cause spiritual blindness in our world today? How can our own spiritual blindness become spiritual sight?

What do you think God is saying to you through your study of this passage?

Talk to God about what you have read, any questions or concerns you might have, and what you think he might be saying to you today. You can write your prayer here if you wish.

DAY 4 ◆ John 10:1-21

READING: JOHN 10:1-21
Begin with prayer, asking God to give you insight, understanding, and an open heart to listen to and follow his word.

This passage takes place during the Jewish Festival of Dedication (Hanukkah). Jesus describes himself as both the good shepherd, and the gate for the sheep into the sheepfold.

STUDY
What are the characteristics of the good shepherd, according to 10:3-4?

Jesus next describes himself as the good shepherd who sacrifices himself for the sheep. Contrast the character traits of the good shepherd with those of a mere hired hand.

Read about Middle Eastern shepherds in the study note on 10:1-21. Israel's leaders were considered to be the nation's shepherds (see Isa 56:9-12 and Jer 23:1-4). How does Jesus' description of himself as the "good shepherd" contrast with Israel's leaders?

FURTHER STUDY (Optional)
Jesus says he is the gate to the sheepfold. Read about a sheepfold in the study note on 10:1. What does it mean that Jesus is the gate?

Who are the "other sheep" Jesus mentions in 10:16? See the study note on 10:16.

REFLECTION

You can be a shepherd in your family, at church, at work and in your social relationships. What are some ways you can be a better shepherd to others?

What do you think God is saying to you through your study of this passage?

PRAYER

Talk to God about what you have read, any questions or concerns you might have, and what you think he might be saying to you today. You can write your prayer here if you wish.

DAY 5 ◆ John 10:22-42

READING: JOHN 10:22-42

Begin with prayer, asking God to give you insight, understanding, and an open heart to listen to and follow his word.

STUDY

Read 10:30, 38. What do these verses tell us about Jesus' identity with respect to his relationship with God the Father?

What question do the people ask Jesus and how does he respond (10:24-25)? What is the proof of his identity?

Why did the people try to stone Jesus in 10:31? What did he claim?

What does Jesus mean when he quotes Ps 82:6 in 10:34-36? Read the study note on 10:34-36. How is this a scriptural defense of his identity?

FURTHER STUDY (Optional)

What does Jesus mean when he says, "The Father and I are one" (10:30)? See also Matt 28:19; Mark 1:10-11; 2 Cor 13:14.

REFLECTION

What does it mean to hear the voice of the shepherd and to follow him? Can you give some examples of this in your own life?

What do you think God is saying to you through your study of this passage?

PRAYER

Talk to God about what you have read, any questions or concerns you might have, and what you think he might be saying to you today. You can write your prayer here if you wish.

GROUP SESSION

READING: JOHN 9:1–10:42

Read John 9:1–10:42 together as a group.

DISCUSSION

You can use the following questions to guide what you share in the discussion. Give each person at least one opportunity to share with the others.

What did you learn from John 9:1–10:42? What was one thing that stood out to you as you studied this passage? How did John 9:1–10:42 surprise you? Do you have questions about this passage or the study materials that haven't been answered? What does God seem to be saying to you through what you have studied?

TOPICS FOR DISCUSSION

You can choose from among these topics to generate a discussion among the members of your group, or you can write your thoughts about one or more of these topics if you're studying solo.

1. What does it means to be spiritually blind or to have spiritual sight? Can you give examples today of blindness to the truth?

2. The word "pastor" means "shepherd" and is drawn from the biblical image of a leader as a shepherd over God's flock. What are the key characteristics of a good shepherd of God's people? Which do you think is most important, and why?

3. Jesus identifies his relationship with the Father as one of unity (10:30, 38). Christians are also called to unity with one another. How is the unity of the Father and the Son similar to the unity Christians are called to? How is it different?

GROUP REFLECTION

What is God saying to us as a group through this passage?

ACTION

What are we going to do, individually or as a group, in response to what God is saying to us?

PRAYER

How should we pray for each other in response to God's message to us in this passage?

Take turns talking to God about this passage and about what he is saying.

NEXT: **JOHN 11:1–12:50 (Foreshadowing Jesus' Death and Resurrection)**

WEEK
SEVEN

*Foreshadowing
Jesus' Death
and Resurrection*

JOHN
11:1–12:50

OUTLINE

DAY 1 ◆ John 11:1-44

READING: **JOHN 11:1-44**

Begin with prayer, asking God to give you insight, understanding, and an open heart to listen to and follow his word.

The raising of Lazarus is a key turning point in John's Gospel. It was the greatest of Jesus' miraculous signs, and it provoked the religious leaders to plot against Jesus. It also signifies the whole purpose for Jesus' coming: to bring new life to those who believe.

STUDY

What did Jesus mean when he said that Lazarus's sickness would not end in death? For what reason did Lazarus get sick (11:4)? Why do you think Jesus stayed where he was for the next two days (see note on 11:6)?

Why did the disciples object when Jesus said, "Let's go back to Judea" (11:7)?

When Jesus tells Martha that her brother will rise from the dead, in what way did she misunderstand Jesus? See study note on 11:24.

What did Jesus mean when he said, "I am the resurrection and the life" (11:25)?

FURTHER STUDY (Optional)

In what ways is Lazarus's resurrection a preview to Jesus' resurrection? In what ways are the two events different?

See 1 Cor 15 for a description of the final resurrection of believers. In what way is our final resurrection like and unlike the resurrections of Lazarus and Jesus?

REFLECTION

Can you identify a time in your life when you thought God's timing was bad or that he was putting you through unnecessary difficulties? Did you later come to understand God's purpose in it?

What do you think God is saying to you through your study of this passage?

PRAYER
Talk to God about what you have read, any questions or concerns you might have, and what you think he might be saying to you today. You can write your prayer here if you wish.

DAY 2 ◆ John 11:45-57

READING: JOHN 11:45-57
Begin with prayer, asking God to give you insight, understanding, and an open heart to listen to and follow his word.

Jesus' raising of Lazarus so disturbed the religious leaders that they decided they must act against him.

STUDY
What were the two types of responses to the raising of Lazarus (11:45, 53)?

Why did the high council decide they must get rid of Jesus? What did they fear, according to 11:48?

Caiaphas, the high priest, makes an inadvertent prophecy about what Jesus will accomplish (11:48-52). What did Caiaphas originally mean by this prophecy? How did later Christians understand it? See study note on 11:50-51.

FURTHER STUDY (Optional)
How did Jesus respond to the plot against him (11:53-54)? Why do you think he did this?

REFLECTION
Sometimes the actions of evil people are used by God to accomplish something great. Can you identify an example of this from your own life? How did God work things out for good?

What do you think God is saying to you through your study of this passage?

Talk to God about what you have read, any questions or concerns you might have, and what you think he might be saying to you today. You can write your prayer here if you wish.

DAY 3 ◆ John 12:1-19

READING: JOHN 12:1-19

Begin with prayer, asking God to give you insight, understanding, and an open heart to listen to and follow his word.

Mary anoints Jesus with expensive perfume as a sign of love and devotion to him. Then, Jesus enters Jerusalem and for the first time publicly presents himself as the Messiah.

STUDY

What is the cultural significance of Mary loosening her hair and using it to wipe off the perfume? See study note on 12:3. What was Mary awareness of about Jesus' presence?

While Mary's actions were ones of love and devotion, how did Jesus interpret them after the objection by Judas (12:7)?

What did the crowds say about Jesus as he was entering Jerusalem the next day (12:13)? Why was this seen as a threat by the religious leaders? What do the palm branches symbolize, according to the note on 12:13-14?

FURTHER STUDY (Optional)

What is the significance that Jesus entered Jerusalem on a donkey (instead of a warhorse)? See the study note on 12:14.

Read the study notes on 12:13-14. Then read Ps 118:25-26 and Zech 9:9. In what ways did Jesus fulfill the expectations of those passages?

REFLECTION

Just as Mary demonstrated self-sacrificial love for Jesus, what could you do today to demonstrate your self-sacrificial love for God and for his people?

What do you think God is saying to you through your study of this passage?

PRAYER

Talk to God about what you have read, any questions or concerns you might have, and what you think he might be saying to you today. You can write your prayer here if you wish.

DAY 4 ◆ John 12:20-36

READING: JOHN 12:20-36

Begin with prayer, asking God to give you insight, understanding, and an open heart to listen to and follow his word.

Some Greeks who are in Jerusalem for Passover approach Philip about meeting Jesus. Jesus responds by discussing what was about to happen.

STUDY

John 12:23 is an important turning point because throughout the Gospel Jesus had often said his "time had not yet come." What does he say now? Read the study note on 12:23.

What does "entering his glory" mean, and how does Jesus' analogy of a kernel of wheat relate to it? Did Jesus forgo one kind of glory for another kind? Explain.

In 12:27 Jesus says his soul is deeply troubled. Why was this? What did Jesus wish for most?

What would soon happen to Satan? What would be the result of Jesus' being "lifted up"? See the study note on 12:31-33; see also the study notes on 3:14-15 and 8:28.

FURTHER STUDY (Optional)

The crowds wondered about Jesus' teaching that the Messiah must die, since they believed the Messiah would live forever (12:34). One of the key stumbling blocks for the Jews was Jesus' death, which for them disqualified him from being the Messiah. But read Isa 52:13–53:12. What do we learn about the Messiah and his suffering in this passage?

Once again, Philip brings people to meet Jesus (cp. 1:45). Identify someone in your life that needs to meet Jesus, and think about how you might be able to introduce them to him.

Jesus says that anyone who wants to be his disciple must "follow" him (12:26). What does it mean to follow Jesus?

What do you think God is saying to you through your study of this passage?

PRAYER

Talk to God about what you have read, any questions or concerns you might have, and what you think he might be saying to you today. You can write your prayer here if you wish.

DAY 5 ◆ John 12:37-50

READING: JOHN 12:37-50

Begin with prayer, asking God to give you insight, understanding, and an open heart to listen to and follow his word.

This last section of Jesus' public teaching summarizes some of the key themes of this Gospel.

STUDY

The people's rejection of Jesus was related to two prophecies of Isaiah, Isa 53:1 and 6:10. Read these two passages. What are they about in their original context? In light of that, how do they apply to Jesus and his ministry?

John makes it clear that many did believe in Jesus, but they were unwilling to say so publicly. Why was this (see 12:42)? How did Jesus warn them (12:47-48)? See also study note on 12:42-43.

What role does 12:44-50 have in John's Gospel? See the study note on 12:44-50. What does this summary of the Gospel say about light and darkness, eternal life and judgment?

FURTHER STUDY (Optional)

Read the following other places where Isa 6 is quoted. Identify who quotes it and what the purpose was in each case:

Matt 13:13-15

Acts 28:26-27

REFLECTION

Why do some Christians today keep quiet about their faith? What are some ways we can become bolder in our Christian witness?

What do you think God is saying to you through your study of this passage?

PRAYER

Talk to God about what you have read, any questions or concerns you might have, and what you think he might be saying to you today. You can write your prayer here if you wish.

GROUP SESSION

READING: JOHN 11:1–12:50

Read John 11:1–12:50 together as a group.

DISCUSSION

You can use the following questions to guide what you share in the discussion. Give each person at least one opportunity to share with the others.

What did you learn from John 11:1–12:50? What was one thing that stood out to you as you studied this passage? How did John 11:1–12:50 surprise you? Do you have questions about this passage or the study materials that haven't been answered? What does God seem to be saying to you through what you have studied?

TOPICS FOR DISCUSSION

You can choose from among these topics to generate a discussion among the members of your group, or you can write your thoughts about one or more of these topics if you're studying solo.

1. In 1 Cor 15:20, Jesus is called "the first of a great harvest of all who have died." If this is so, what happened to Lazarus and others who were raised from the dead? See Matt 27:52-53; Mark 5:21-43; Luke 7:11-17; John 11:1-44; 1 Cor 15:51-58; 1 Thes 4:13-18.

2. Why did the raising of Lazarus result in a plot against Jesus' life? Are there analogies in your experience or in our world today?

3. How did Jesus' anointing at Bethany and his messianic entry into Jerusalem prepare the way for his coming death?

GROUP REFLECTION

What is God saying to us as a group through this passage?

ACTION

What are we going to do, individually or as a group, in response to what God is saying to us?

PRAYER

How should we pray for each other in response to God's message to us in this passage?

Take turns talking to God about this passage and about what he is saying.

NEXT: **JOHN 13:1–14:31 (The Servant's Way)**

*The Servant's
Way*

JOHN
13:1–14:31

OUTLINE

DAY **1** ◆ John 13:1-20

READING: **JOHN 13:1-20**

Begin with prayer, asking God to give you insight, understanding, and an open heart to listen to and follow his word.

John 13–17 occurred during Jesus' last meal with his disciples. In 13:1-20, Jesus washes the disciples' feet. Read the study note on 13:1-38 for background.

STUDY

Why did Peter protest when Jesus tried to wash his feet? What was Jesus' response, and what did he mean?

Peter next says that he wants to be washed completely. How did Jesus respond and what did he mean? See the study notes on 13:9 and 13:10.

What does Jesus mean that since he, their Lord, has washed their feet, they ought to wash one another's feet (13:15)?

FURTHER STUDY (Optional)

In 13:18 Jesus says that the one who eats with him has turned against him. What did eating together mean in that culture according to the study note? What does this tell us about Jesus and about his betrayer, Judas Iscariot?

REFLECTION

What does Jesus' command to wash the feet of others mean in our cultural context? What are some culturally appropriate ways you could obey this command?

What do you think God is saying to you through your study of this passage?

PRAYER

Talk to God about what you have read, any questions or concerns you might have, and what you think he might be saying to you today. You can write your prayer here if you wish.

DAY 2 ◆ John 13:21-30

READING: **JOHN 13:21-30**

Begin with prayer, asking God to give you insight, understanding, and an open heart to listen to and follow his word.

After washing the disciples' feet, Jesus predicts the betrayal by Judas.

STUDY

How did the disciples respond when Jesus predicted that he would be betrayed?

This is the first reference to "the disciple Jesus loved," who appears several more times. Read 13:23-25 and the study note on 13:23. What do we learn about this disciple here?

How does Jesus identify his betrayer in 13:26? Read the study note on 13:26. Why do you think Jesus identified the betrayer in this way?

In what way is the text symbolic when it says that Judas went out into the night (13:30)?

FURTHER STUDY (Optional)

What do you think it means that Satan entered Judas (see also 13:2)? Was Judas still responsible for his actions?

Why do you think Jesus announced to his disciples that he would be betrayed?

Read the profile of "John the Apostle, Son of Zebedee" on p. 1801. What insights about the Gospel of John arise from knowing more about its probable human author?

REFLECTION

Have you ever been betrayed by someone close to you? If so, how did this make you feel? Have you experienced God's comfort in this situation? How so?

What do you think God is saying to you through your study of this passage?

PRAYER

Talk to God about what you have read, any questions or concerns you might have, and what you think he might be saying to you today. You can write your prayer here if you wish.

DAY 3 ◆ John 13:31-38

READING: JOHN 13:31-38

Begin with prayer, asking God to give you insight, understanding, and an open heart to listen to and follow his word.

The next four chapters are part of Jesus' farewell discourse to his disciples, where he prepares them for his departure and for the role that they will play in his church. In this passage he gives them a "new command"—to love one another.

STUDY

The time had come for Jesus to "enter into his glory" (13:31). What does this mean?

In what way is loving each other a "new commandment" (13:34)?

Jesus says he is going away and his disciples cannot follow him now (but they will follow him later). What did Jesus mean in saying these things?

FURTHER STUDY (Optional)

Both Judas and Peter failed Jesus. What was the difference between the two?

REFLECTION

What role does Satan play in the evil deeds people do? How much is failure our own doing, and how much can it be attributed to Satan or other forces outside our control?

What are some ways we can live out Jesus' new commandment to love one another?

A72

What do you think God is saying to you through your study of this passage?

PRAYER

Talk to God about what you have read, any questions or concerns you might have, and what you think he might be saying to you today. You can write your prayer here if you wish.

DAY 4 ◆ John 14:1-14

READING: **JOHN 14:1-14**

Begin with prayer, asking God to give you insight, understanding, and an open heart to listen to and follow his word.

Jesus promises that, though he is going away, he will come again for his disciples, because he is the true way to eternal life and to the Father. He reveals the Father so that "anyone who has seen me has seen the Father" (14:9).

STUDY

What does Jesus mean when he says "There is more than enough room in my Father's home"? Where is "my Father's home"?

Jesus promises to come and get his disciples (14:3). What might this mean?

What do Jesus' responses—when Thomas says they don't know the way (14:6) and when Philip asks him to show them the Father—tell you about Jesus?

What promise does Jesus give (14:12-14) to those who believe in him? What does this mean?

FURTHER STUDY (Optional)

Is Jesus' statement in John 14:6 completely exclusive—is he the only way to God?

Jesus says in 14:13 that he will give his disciples anything they ask in his name. Does this mean that Christians will always get what they ask for? What do you think it means to ask in the name of Jesus?

REFLECTION

Jesus promised that he would come again to bring his disciples into his Father's house and that they would be with him there forever. Do you find encouragement in this promise? Why or why not?

What do you think God is saying to you through your study of this passage?

PRAYER

Talk to God about what you have read, any questions or concerns you might have, and what you think he might be saying to you today. You can write your prayer here if you wish.

DAY 5 ◆ John 14:15-31

READING: JOHN 14:15-31

Begin with prayer, asking God to give you insight, understanding, and an open heart to listen to and follow his word.

Jesus explains the role the Holy Spirit will play in the lives of his disciples. He promises that the Holy Spirit will be another "Advocate" who will never leave them and who will lead them into all truth.

STUDY

What are the "commandments" that those who love Jesus will "obey"?

What fundamental role does the Holy Spirit play, according to 14:16-19?

The word translated "Advocate" is the Greek word *paraklētos*. What else can this word mean, according to the study note on 14:16? What did Jesus mean by calling the Holy Spirit "another Advocate"?

Read "Our Advocate," p. 1802. What does this article add to your understanding of the Holy Spirit and his role?

FURTHER STUDY (Optional)

How would you summarize Jesus' answer to the question that Judas (not Iscariot) asked in 14:22?

In 14:30, Jesus said that he didn't have much more time to talk to the disciples because the ruler of this world was approaching. What did Jesus mean?

REFLECTION

In what ways does the Holy Spirit guide you and reveal truth to you?

What do you think God is saying to you through your study of this passage?

PRAYER

Talk to God about what you have read, any questions or concerns you might have, and what you think he might be saying to you today. You can write your prayer here if you wish.

GROUP SESSION

READING: **JOHN 13:1–14:31**

Read John 13:1–14:31 together as a group.

DISCUSSION

You can use the following questions to guide what you share in the discussion. Give each person at least one opportunity to share with the others.

What did you learn from John 13:1–14:31? What was one thing that stood out to you as you studied this passage? How did John 13:1–14:31 surprise you? Do you have questions about this passage or the study materials that haven't been answered? What does God seem to be saying to you through what you have studied?

TOPICS FOR DISCUSSION

You can choose from among these topics to generate a discussion among the members of your group, or you can write your thoughts about one or more of these topics if you're studying solo.

1. There has been a great deal of scholarly debate about the identity of the author of the book, who is identified only as "the disciple Jesus loved." The best option remains the apostle John. What do we know about John? Does it make a difference to you in how you read the book whether "the disciple Jesus loved" was the apostle John or someone else? Why or why not?

2. Jesus says that whoever loves him will obey him. What is the relationship between love for God and obedience to him?

3. What are some of the things Jesus says about the Holy Spirit and his role in the life of the believer? How have you experienced the ministry of the Holy Spirit in your life and in your community?

GROUP REFLECTION

What is God saying to us as a group through this passage?

ACTION

What are we going to do, individually or as a group, in response to what God is saying to us?

PRAYER

How should we pray for each other in response to God's message to us in this passage?

Take turns talking to God about this passage and about what he is saying.

NEXT: **JOHN 15:1–17:26 (Staying Close to Jesus through the Holy Spirit)**

*Staying Close to
Jesus through the
Holy Spirit*

JOHN
15:1–17:26

OUTLINE

DAY **1** ◆ John 15:1-17

READING: **JOHN 15:1-17**

Begin with prayer, asking God to give you insight, understanding, and an open heart to listen to and follow his word.

Jesus' farewell discourse to his disciples continues as he identifies himself as the "true grapevine" to which the disciples, the "branches," must stay connected in order to survive and thrive spiritually.

STUDY

Jesus says, "I am the true grapevine" (15:1). What does Jesus mean by this?

What happens to those branches that don't bear fruit? What happens to those that do?

Why can those who "remain" ask for anything and receive it? See the study note on 15:7.

What is Christ's primary command, according to 15:12? What is the greatest act of love imaginable, according to 15:13?

FURTHER STUDY (Optional)

Read "Remaining in Christ" on p. 1803. What does it mean to remain in Christ, and how do we live it out?

REFLECTION

Jesus says we will only bear spiritual fruit if we stay connected to him, the true vine. What are some ways we stay connected to Jesus?

How can you fulfill Jesus' primary command?

What do you think God is saying to you through your study of this passage?

PRAYER

Talk to God about what you have read, any questions or concerns you might have, and what you think he might be saying to you today. You can write your prayer here if you wish.

DAY 2 ◆ John 15:18–16:15

READING: JOHN 15:18–16:15

Begin with prayer, asking God to give you insight, understanding, and an open heart to listen to and follow his word.

In this passage, Jesus tells the disciples that the world will hate and persecute them because of their allegiance to Jesus (15:18–16:4). Although he is going away, he will send the Holy Spirit to guide and protect them.

STUDY

Why would the world hate Jesus' followers?

Jesus says that those who hate him in fact hate the Father. Why is this the case?

Read through 16:8-15. What are the various roles of the Advocate, the Holy Spirit?

FURTHER STUDY (Optional)

In 16:1, Jesus predicts his disciples being expelled from the synagogue. See similar references in 9:22, 34; 12:42. Also read the study note on 9:34. What social impact do you think it would have for a Jewish Christian to be expelled from the synagogue?

What does it mean that the Advocate (the Holy Spirit) will "convict the world of its sin, and of God's righteousness, and of the coming judgment" (16:8)?

REFLECTION

Jesus says that the world will hate his followers. Have you ever experienced hatred or animosity because of your faith in Christ? How did you respond?

What do you think God is saying to you through your study of this passage?

PRAYER

Talk to God about what you have read, any questions or concerns you might have, and what you think he might be saying to you today. You can write your prayer here if you wish.

DAY 3 ◆ John 16:16-33

READING: JOHN 16:16-33

Begin with prayer, asking God to give you insight, understanding, and an open heart to listen to and follow his word.

Jesus ends the teaching section of his farewell discourse. He says that the disciples will experience sorrow at his departure and persecution from the world, but that he will give them peace and joy because he has overcome the world.

STUDY

Jesus says that the disciples will experience great sorrow, but then that sorrow will turn to wonderful joy. What does he mean? See the study note on 16:20.

Jesus compares the suffering and joy the disciples will have to the labor pains and birth experience of a pregnant woman. How does this analogy relate to the disciples' experience? See the study note on 16:21.

Jesus says in 16:23 that the Father will grant the disciples' requests because they ask using his name. What does it mean to ask using Jesus' name?

Jesus tells his disciples to take heart, because he has overcome the world (16:33). What does he mean by this?

FURTHER STUDY (Optional)

Jesus says that he has been speaking to them in figures of speech, such as the birth analogy. What other figures of speech have you come across in John's Gospel?

REFLECTION

Identify a time in your life when God brought you through deep sorrow into true joy. In what way did the sorrow or pain produce spiritual growth in your life?

What do you think God is saying to you through your study of this passage?

PRAYER

Talk to God about what you have read, any questions or concerns you might have, and what you think he might be saying to you today. You can write your prayer here if you wish.

DAY 4 ◆ John 17:1-12

READING: **JOHN 17:1-12**

Begin with prayer, asking God to give you insight, understanding, and an open heart to listen to and follow his word.

This chapter represents Jesus' longest prayer in the Gospels. Jesus prays as a mediator between the disciples and God the Father. Notice throughout the prayer how Jesus expresses his great love and devotion to his followers.

STUDY

Again Jesus says, "The hour has come" (17:1; see also 2:4; 7:30; 8:20; 12:23, 27; 13:1). What does this mean? See the study note on 17:1.

What does Jesus mean when he prays, "Glorify your Son"? See the study note on 17:1. What is Jesus' glorification in John's Gospel?

What is the way to eternal life, according to 17:3? How do people come to know God, according to 17:6? Read the study note on 17:6.

Why does Jesus pray for the protection of his followers? What dangers are coming?

Jesus says his followers bring glory to him in 17:10. In what ways do we bring Christ glory? See study note.

Read "The World," p. 1807. What is the nature of the "world" and its opposition to Jesus?

REFLECTION

Jesus prays for spiritual protection for his followers. What are some of the spiritual dangers we face as followers of Christ? How can we overcome them?

What do you think God is saying to you through your study of this passage?

PRAYER

Talk to God about what you have read, any questions or concerns you might have, and what you think he might be saying to you today. You can write your prayer here if you wish.

DAY 5 ◆ John 17:13-26

READING: JOHN 17:13-26

Begin with prayer, asking God to give you insight, understanding, and an open heart to listen to and follow his word.

Jesus concludes his prayer by asking God to make his followers holy, including not only his present disciples, but also all those who will follow him in future generations. In other words, this prayer is also for us!

STUDY

Jesus says that he is not praying for God to take the disciples out of the world. Why is it important to stay in the world?

Jesus prays that God will keep his disciples safe from the evil one. Who is the evil one?

What does it mean to be "holy" (17:17)? See the study note on 17:16-18.

Jesus prays that his disciples may be "one, just as you and I are one." Why is unity essential to accomplish God's purpose on earth?

FURTHER STUDY (Optional)

Jesus speaks about being "in" the Father and being "in" believers. What does this mean? See the study note on 17:21.

REFLECTION

What does it mean practically to remain in the world, but not be "of the world"? What is the balance between participating in the world and not becoming part of the evil world system?

What do you think God is saying to you through your study of this passage?

PRAYER

Talk to God about what you have read, any questions or concerns you might have, and what you think he might be saying to you today. You can write your prayer here if you wish.

GROUP SESSION

READING: JOHN 15:1–17:26

Read John 15:1–17:26 together as a group.

DISCUSSION

You can use the following questions to guide what you share in the discussion. Give each person at least one opportunity to share with the others.

What did you learn from John 15:1–17:26? What was one thing that stood out to you as you studied this passage? How did John 15:1–17:26 surprise you? Do you have questions about this passage or the study materials that haven't been answered? What does God seem to be saying to you through what you have studied?

TOPICS FOR DISCUSSION

You can choose from among these topics to generate a discussion among the members of your group, or you can write your thoughts about one or more of these topics if you're studying solo.

1. How do believers "remain" in Christ? How can you do so?

2. What is the nature of the "world" and its opposition to Jesus? What are some examples of this opposition that you have seen?

3. Jesus says in 17:9 that he is not praying for the world, but for those God has given him. There is a very strong dualism in John's Gospel between the world and the followers of Jesus. In what situations in our cultural context is this "us versus them" perspective important to stress? Are there times when it is inappropriate and another approach is better?

GROUP REFLECTION

What is God saying to us as a group through this passage?

ACTION

What are we going to do, individually or as a group, in response to what God is saying to us?

PRAYER

How should we pray for each other in response to God's message to us in this passage?

Take turns talking to God about this passage and about what he is saying.

NEXT: **JOHN 18:1–19:37 (Jesus' Suffering and Death)**

WEEK
TEN

*Jesus' Suffering
and Death*

JOHN
18:1–19:37

OUTLINE

DAY 1 ... John 18:1-12

DAY 2 ... John 18:13-27

DAY 3 ... John 18:28–19:16

DAY 4 ... John 19:17-27

DAY 5 ... John 19:28-37

Group Session

DAY **1** ◆ John 18:1-12

READING: **JOHN 18:1-12**

Begin with prayer, asking God to give you insight, understanding, and an open heart to listen to and follow his word.

The Gospel nears its climax as Jesus is arrested in the Garden of Gethsemane. Jesus makes it clear that everything is going according to God's perfect plan.

STUDY

Read the study note on 18:1-2 and find the Kidron Valley and Gethsemane on the map at the study note on 18:1–19:27 on p. 1809. The map shows the route Jesus took from Gethsemane to the house of Caiaphas.

In 18:4, 11, Jesus is aware of what will happen to him. What does this tell us about John's perspective on Jesus' suffering and death?

When Jesus identifies himself in 18:5, the soldiers fall back (18:6). What is the significance of this scene? Read the study notes on 18:5 and 18:6.

FURTHER STUDY (Optional)

Read the cross-references cited in the study note on 18:6 (Isa 6:5; Ezek 1:28; Dan 10:9; Acts 9:4; Rev 1:7). How do people respond when confronted with the presence of God?

How are Simon Peter's actions in 18:10 characteristic of his actions elsewhere?

Why does Jesus stop his disciples from fighting? What does he say in 18:11?

REFLECTION

Jesus knew all that was going to happen (18:4) and accepted the suffering God had given to him. Can you identify a situation in your life where it was important for you to know that God was going to bring you through your darkest hour?

What do you think God is saying to you through your study of this passage?

PRAYER

Talk to God about what you have read, any questions or concerns you might have, and what you think he might be saying to you today. You can write your prayer here if you wish.

DAY 2 ◆ John 18:13-27

READING: JOHN 18:13-27

Begin with prayer, asking God to give you insight, understanding, and an open heart to listen to and follow his word.

Jesus is taken first to Annas, who questions him. Outside in the courtyard Peter, the disciple who boldly tried to defend Jesus in the Garden, now denies he even knows him.

STUDY

Why was Jesus first taken to Annas, the father-in-law of the high priest, and then to Caiaphas, the official high priest? Read the study note on 18:12-14.

In what way was Caiaphas's earlier statement, repeated in 18:14, prophetic? See the study note on 18:14.

Contrast Peter's response in 18:17 with Jesus' response in 18:20-21. How are they different? See the study note on 18:16-17.

FURTHER STUDY (Optional)

Read the study note on 18:19. How was the high priest's questioning contrary to proper Jewish legal procedures?

REFLECTION

Peter's actions began with courage in following Jesus, but then he repeatedly denied he knew Jesus. Can you identify a situation in your life where you felt like you failed God because of your fear, lack of faith, or lack of boldness? What did God teach you through it?

What do you think God is saying to you through your study of this passage?

Talk to God about what you have read, any questions or concerns you might have, and what you think he might be saying to you today. You can write your prayer here if you wish.

DAY 3 ◆ John 18:28–19:16

READING: JOHN 18:28–19:16

Begin with prayer, asking God to give you insight, understanding, and an open heart to listen to and follow his word.

At his trial before the Roman governor Pilate, Jesus acknowledges that he is indeed a king, but that his Kingdom is not of this world. Jesus has come into the world for something far more significant than defeating the Romans.

STUDY

Read 18:28-32 and the accompanying study notes. Why did the Jewish authorities have to take Jesus to Pilate in order to get a death sentence?

In 18:37, how does Jesus' description of his mission on earth relate to the discussion of whether he is a king?

In their final rejection of Jesus, the Jewish leaders cry out "We have no king but Caesar!" Read the study note on 19:15. Why is their response heresy? Why is it ironic?

FURTHER STUDY (Optional)

Pilate he said mockingly, "What is truth?" in 18:38. In what ways does this characterize the perspective of many people in this world?

Why do you think Pilate eventually turned Jesus over to be crucified (despite repeatedly declaring him innocent)? What was his motivation?

REFLECTION

What does it mean for us that Jesus is our king? How should it determine the way that we act and the decisions that we make?

What do you think God is saying to you through your study of this passage?

PRAYER

PRAYER

Talk to God about what you have read, any questions or concerns you might have, and what you think he might be saying to you today. You can write your prayer here if you wish.

DAY 4 ◆ John 19:17-27

READING: JOHN 19:17-27

Begin with prayer, asking God to give you insight, understanding, and an open heart to listen to and follow his word.

All that is happening—even the soldiers' division of Jesus' clothing—is fulfilling prophecy. Despite the agony and horror of crucifixion, Jesus has the presence of mind to think of his mother and to entrust her care into the hands of the disciple he loved.

STUDY

Why did the religious leaders object to the sign Pilate placed on the cross? What was Pilate's response and why did he respond this way? See the study note on 19:19-22.

The solders divided Jesus' clothes except for his robe. What did they do with them, and why? What prophecy did this fulfill?

Read the study note on 19:27. What are the implications for the relationships that we have with the people in our churches and with Christians around the world?

FURTHER STUDY (Optional)

Read "The Cross and Passover," p. 1812. What parallels do you see between Jesus and the Passover lamb?

REFLECTION

Despite his agony, Jesus still was concerned about the welfare of his mother (cp. Phil 2:4). How could you follow Jesus' example and look out for someone else's needs?

What do you think God is saying to you through your study of this passage?

PRAYER

Talk to God about what you have read, any questions or concerns you might have, and what you think he might be saying to you today. You can write your prayer here if you wish.

DAY 5 ◆ John 19:28-37

READING: JOHN 19:28-37

Begin with prayer, asking God to give you insight, understanding, and an open heart to listen to and follow his word.

In perhaps the most profound and important sentence in human history, Jesus announces at his death, "It is finished!" Jesus has accomplished the task for which he came.

STUDY

What spiritual significance might the hyssop bush have? See the study note on 19:28-29.

In this Gospel, Jesus' last words from the cross are, "It is finished!" What was finished? What had Jesus accomplished? See 19:30 and study note.

Why did the Jewish leaders want the legs of the crucifixion victims broken? See the note on 19:31-33. What happened when they came to Jesus? What is the significance of this?

When Jesus' side was pierced with a spear, water and blood came out. What might be the physical and spiritual significance of this? See the study note on 19:34.

FURTHER STUDY (Optional)

The author notes in 19:35 that this is an eyewitness account. Why was this an important point to make?

In 19:37, the author quotes Zech 12:10. Read the study note on 19:37 and then go back and read this verse in its Old Testament context. What does it say about those who rejected Jesus?

REFLECTION

The religious leaders wanted to keep the law scrupulously by getting the crucified bodies down before the Sabbath, yet they lacked concern for justice the night before. In what ways do you see the same danger today of holding firmly to religious tradition while ignoring greater concerns of love and justice?

How should we respond to the fact that Jesus was willing to give up his life in order to complete our salvation?

What do you think God is saying to you through your study of this passage?

PRAYER

Talk to God about what you have read, any questions or concerns you might have, and what you think he might be saying to you today. You can write your prayer here if you wish.

GROUP SESSION

READING: JOHN 18:1–19:37

Read John 18:1–19:37 together as a group.

DISCUSSION

You can use the following questions to guide what you share in the discussion. Give each person at least one opportunity to share with the others.

What did you learn from John 18:1–19:37? What was one thing that stood out to you as you studied this passage? How did John 18:1–19:37 surprise you? Do you have questions about this passage or the study materials that haven't been answered? What does God seem to be saying to you through what you have studied?

TOPICS FOR DISCUSSION

You can choose from among these topics to generate a discussion among the members of your group, or you can write your thoughts about one or more of these topics if you're studying solo.

1. Discuss Jesus' role as the Passover lamb. What parallels do you see between Jesus and the Passover lamb?

2. Go back and read John 1:10-11. Why did Jesus have to suffer and die? Who bears the responsibility? Discuss the ramifications of this for us today.

3. Crucifixion was one of the most painful and cruel means of torture and execution ever devised. Yet it is often said that the physical pain Jesus suffered on the cross was exceeded by the spiritual pain that he suffered. What was this spiritual pain? What did Jesus mean when he said "It is finished!"?

GROUP REFLECTION

What is God saying to us as a group through this passage?

ACTION

What are we going to do, individually or as a group, in response to what God is saying to us?

PRAYER

How should we pray for each other in response to God's message to us in this passage?

Take turns talking to God about this passage and about what he is saying.

NEXT: **JOHN 19:38–20:29 (Jesus' Burial and Resurrection)**

Jesus' Burial and Resurrection

JOHN
19:38–20:29

OUTLINE

DAY **1** ◆ John 19:38-42

READING: **JOHN 19:38-42**

Begin with prayer, asking God to give you insight, understanding, and an open heart to listen to and follow his word.

Although most of the Jewish religious leaders opposed Jesus and plotted his death, here we learn that some of them became his followers. Joseph of Arimathea and Nicodemus request the body of Jesus and give him an honorable burial.

STUDY

Read the study note on 19:38. What do we learn elsewhere about Joseph of Arimathea? What personal danger might he have exposed himself to by asking for Jesus' body?

Nicodemus joins Joseph in the burial of Jesus. Read the study note on 19:39 for a reminder of where we have seen Nicodemus before. What do the facts about him suggest about his character? See the study note on 7:49-51.

Why did Joseph and Nicodemus have to hurry? See the study note on 19:42.

FURTHER STUDY (Optional)

Read the study note on 12:42-43. What was the danger of becoming a secret follower of Jesus?

What do we learn about Jewish burial customs in 19:39-42? See also the diagram on p. 1813 ("First-century Judean Tombs").

REFLECTION

The actions of Joseph and Nicodemus were a public demonstration of loyalty to Jesus that carried risk for their reputations and for their careers. What expressions of faith in your life might carry similar risks?

What do you think God is saying to you through your study of this passage?

Talk to God about what you have read, any questions or concerns you might have, and what you think he might be saying to you today. You can write your prayer here if you wish.

DAY 2 ◆ John 20:1-10

READING: JOHN 20:1-10

Begin with prayer, asking God to give you insight, understanding, and an open heart to listen to and follow his word.

Mary Magdalene, a devoted follower of Jesus, comes to the tomb on Sunday morning and finds the stone rolled away. She assumes Jesus' body has been stolen and runs to get Peter and another disciple. They, too, discover the empty tomb.

STUDY

Who was Mary Magdalene? Read about her in Luke 8:1-3 and Matt 27:55-56.

Why was Mary surprised to see the stone rolled away?

Who was the "other disciple" who came with Peter after Mary told them about the empty tomb? See the study note on 20:3-10.

In 20:8, the "other disciple" saw the empty tomb and "believed." What did he believe? What is the significance of the event?

FURTHER STUDY (Optional)

What was remarkable about the way the tomb was arranged when Peter and the other disciple found it? See the study note on 20:6-7.

REFLECTION

Has Jesus convinced you of the reality of his resurrection? If so, how has he? If not, what (if anything) would convince you?

What do you think God is saying to you through your study of this passage?

Talk to God about what you have read, any questions or concerns you might have, and what you think he might be saying to you today. You can write your prayer here if you wish.

DAY 3 ◆ John 20:11-18

READING: JOHN 20:11-18
Begin with prayer, asking God to give you insight, understanding, and an open heart to listen to and follow his word.

Mary Magdalene is the first to see the risen Jesus. Although she does not at first recognize him, he reveals himself to her when he says her name.

STUDY
What did Mary see when she looked in the tomb? What do you think she thought had happened?

Why do you think Mary did not recognize Jesus at first?

In 20:17 Jesus says, "Don't cling to me . . . for I haven't yet ascended to the Father." What does he mean by this? See the study note on 20:17.

FURTHER STUDY (Optional)
Why was this story about Jesus' appearance to Mary so astonishing in its first-century context? See the study note on 20:18.

How does this provide credibility to the resurrection narratives?

Mary Magdalene has often been misunderstood and misrepresented. Some readers wrongly assume that she is the immoral woman who anointed Jesus' feet in Luke 7:36-50, although there is no Scriptural evidence for this idea. What positive attributes do you see in her from this episode?

What does Mary's response to Jesus' resurrection suggest to you about your own response?

What do you think God is saying to you through your study of this passage?

PRAYER

Talk to God about what you have read, any questions or concerns you might have, and what you think he might be saying to you today. You can write your prayer here if you wish.

DAY 4 ◆ John 20:19-23

READING: **JOHN 20:19-23**

Begin with prayer, asking God to give you insight, understanding, and an open heart to listen to and follow his word.

After appearing to Mary Magdalene, Jesus appears to the rest of his disciples (except Thomas) that evening, convincing them that he is truly alive. He gives them their commission and the empowering presence of the Holy Spirit to carry it out.

STUDY

Why were the disciples meeting behind closed doors?

What evidence did Jesus give the disciples that he was truly alive?

What commission does Jesus give his disciples in 20:21?

Jesus gives his disciples the Holy Spirit by breathing on them (20:22). Yet in the book of Acts, the Holy Spirit does not come until 40 days later on the day of Pentecost. What is happening here? See the study note on 20:22.

FURTHER STUDY (Optional)

"Peace be with you" (20:19, 21) is a common Jewish greeting. But in this context it probably means more. What does it indicate according to the study note on 20:19? Look up the Old Testament passages cited there (Isa 9:6; 52:7).

See study note on 20:23. What does it mean that the disciples will have the authority to forgive sins?

REFLECTION

How do we as Christ's followers fulfill the role of offering God's forgiveness to sinners? How does the Holy Spirit help us?

What do you think God is saying to you through your study of this passage?

PRAYER

Talk to God about what you have read, any questions or concerns you might have, and what you think he might be saying to you today. You can write your prayer here if you wish.

DAY 5 ◆ John 20:24-29

READING: JOHN 20:24-29

Begin with prayer, asking God to give you insight, understanding, and an open heart to listen to and follow his word.

Since he was absent at the previous appearance to the disciples, Thomas doubts that Jesus is truly alive. Jesus appears once again and shows Thomas the wounds on his hands and side. Thomas responds with a profound statement of faith: "My Lord and my God!"

STUDY

Thomas refuses to believe in the resurrection without physical evidence. What does Thomas want?

Why does Thomas respond as he does when Jesus appears to him and shows him the wounds in his hands and his side?

According to 20:29, to whom did Jesus promise the greatest blessing? Why do you think it is so?

FURTHER STUDY (Optional)

Were Thomas's questions and doubts about the resurrected Jesus wrong? How did Jesus respond to them? What do you think is the purpose of this story in the context of John's Gospel?

REFLECTION

Do you ever have doubts about Jesus like Thomas did? When do doubts become destructive to our spiritual life? How should we deal with our doubts?

What do you think God is saying to you through your study of this passage?

PRAYER

Talk to God about what you have read, any questions or concerns you might have, and what you think he might be saying to you today. You can write your prayer here if you wish.

GROUP SESSION

READING: JOHN 19:38–20:29

Read John 19:38–20:29 together as a group.

DISCUSSION

You can use the following questions to guide what you share in the discussion. Give each person at least one opportunity to share with the others.

What did you learn from John 19:38–20:29? What was one thing that stood out to you as you studied this passage? How did John 19:38–20:29 surprise you? Do you have questions about this passage or the study materials that haven't been answered? What does God seem to be saying to you through what you have studied?

TOPICS FOR DISCUSSION

You can choose from among these topics to generate a discussion among the members of your group, or you can write your thoughts about one or more of these topics if you're studying solo.

1. The four Gospels recount a variety of resurrection appearances to different people on different occasions. Paul mentions even more in 1 Cor 15:3-9. Why is it important that Jesus rose from the dead? What did he accomplish by it? What did it prove about his death?

2. Discuss the actions of Peter, John, and Mary Magdalene in the resurrection accounts of John 20. What can we learn about true discipleship from the actions of each?

3. Discuss the issue of doubt in the Christian faith. Are doubts always wrong? When do doubts turn into unbelief? Despite his doubts, Thomas made one of the greatest confessions of faith in the whole New Testament (20:28). Why is this statement so significant?

GROUP REFLECTION

What is God saying to us as a group through this passage?

ACTION

What are we going to do, individually or as a group, in response to what God is saying to us?

PRAYER

How should we pray for each other in response to God's message to us in this passage?

Take turns talking to God about this passage and about what he is saying.

NEXT: JOHN 20:30–21:25 (The Epilogue)

OUTLINE

DAY **1** ◆ John 20:30-31

READING: **JOHN 20:30-31**
> Begin with prayer, asking God to give you insight, understanding, and an open heart to listen to and follow his word.

STUDY
> Why did John write this Gospel, according to 20:30-31?

> In what ways does John's Gospel support the purpose for which he wrote it?

> How does life come through believing in Jesus and by the power of his name?

REFLECTION
> What is your own response to the things that you have read in John's Gospel?

> What do you think God is saying to you through your study of this passage?

PRAYER
> Talk to God about what you have read, any questions or concerns you might have, and what you think he might be saying to you today. You can write your prayer here if you wish.

DAY 2 ◆ John 21:1-14

READING: **JOHN 21:1-14**

Begin with prayer, asking God to give you insight, understanding, and an open heart to listen to and follow his word.

This final chapter functions as an epilogue to the book. It includes another resurrection appearance, a conversation between Jesus and Peter that brings about Peter's restoration, and a closing comment about the author as an eyewitness to the events of the Gospel.

STUDY

Some have claimed that Peter and the others were demonstrating a lack of faith by going fishing. What is a better explanation, according to the study note on 21:2?

Jesus already has breakfast cooking when the men arrive on shore. What do the miraculous catch and the prepared breakfast teach us about Jesus' ability to provide for our needs?

Why do you think John tells us the exact number of fish? See the study note on 21:11.

FURTHER STUDY (Optional)

A similar miracle had occurred at the beginning of Jesus' ministry. Go back and read Luke 5:1-11. What are the similarities? What was the result of that event?

What do you think is the significance of Jesus' now doing a similar miracle as the one he had done at the beginning of his ministry?

REFLECTION

After the disciples had a long night of unsuccessful fishing, at dawn Jesus provided them with an abundant catch. Can you identify a time in your life when, after a long and unsuccessful time, God acted to provide for you?

What do you think God is saying to you through your study of this passage?

PRAYER

Talk to God about what you have read, any questions or concerns you might have, and what you think he might be saying to you today. You can write your prayer here if you wish.

DAY 3 ◆ John 21:15-17

READ: JOHN 21:15-17

Begin with prayer, asking God to give you insight, understanding, and an open heart to listen to and follow his word.

In this episode, Jesus restores Peter from his three-fold denial by asking him three times if he loves him. After each affirmation, Jesus encourages Peter to shepherd or take care of the people that Jesus is entrusting to him.

STUDY

Read the study note on 21:15-17, which responds to a common, but likely erroneous, interpretation of this passage. If the passage is not about two different kinds of love, what is it about?

Read again the study note on 21:15-17. What is Jesus' commission to Peter?

What does Jesus mean by "more than these" in 21:15? Does Jesus mean, "Do you love me more than you love the other disciples?" or does he mean, "Do you love me more than the other disciples love me?" See the study note on 21:15.

FURTHER STUDY (Optional)

Read 1 Pet 5:2-4. What reflections of the experiences of John 21:15-17 do you find there?

REFLECTION

Many of us have times in our lives when we have denied our relationship with Jesus and need to be restored and renewed in our relationship to him. Can you think of one of those times in your own life? How has Jesus brought you back to himself?

What do you think God is saying to you through your study of this passage?

PRAYER

Talk to God about what you have read, any questions or concerns you might have, and what you think he might be saying to you today. You can write your prayer here if you wish.

DAY 4 ◆ John 21:18-23

READING: JOHN 21:18-23

Begin with prayer, asking God to give you insight, understanding, and an open heart to listen to and follow his word.

Having restored Peter to a leadership role, Jesus foretells aspects of Peter's life in the future and encourages Peter to follow him faithfully.

STUDY

Read 21:18-19 and the accompanying study notes. What point is Jesus making about Peter's future?

What does Peter mean when he says, "What about him, Lord?" in 20:21? How does Jesus respond?

What misunderstanding did Jesus' response in 21:22 create in the church, according to 20:23? In what way does 21:22-23 refute this misunderstanding? What did Jesus actually say?

REFLECTION

If Jesus told you that you would suffer greatly in the future for him, would you continue to follow him?

What do you think God is saying to you through your study of this passage?

PRAYER

Talk to God about what you have read, any questions or concerns you might have, and what you think he might be saying to you today. You can write your prayer here if you wish.

DAY 5 ◆ John 21:24-25

READING: JOHN 21:24-25

Begin with prayer, asking God to give you insight, understanding, and an open heart to listen to and follow his word.

At the close of his book, the author is identified and the veracity of his testimony is affirmed.

STUDY

What does 21:24 teach us about the authority and accuracy of the events recorded in this Gospel? See the study note on 21:24.

What does 21:25 tell us about the selectivity of the Gospel writer? Why do you think he chose to include some stories but not others?

The statement in 21:25 about the whole world is obviously hyperbole. But what is the author's point concerning the ministry of Jesus? See the study note on 21:25.

FURTHER STUDY (Optional)

Why do you think the Gospel writer waited to the very last verse to use the personal "I"?

REFLECTION

In these verses the Gospel of John is described as a "testimony" about what Jesus has done. What is your testimony of what Jesus has done in your life?

What do you think God is saying to you through your study of this passage?

PRAYER

Talk to God about what you have read, any questions or concerns you might have, and what you think he might be saying to you today. You can write your prayer here if you wish.

GROUP SESSION

READING: JOHN 20:30–21:25

Read John 20:30–21:25 together as a group.

DISCUSSION

You can use the following questions to guide what you share in the discussion. Give each person at least one opportunity to share with the others.

What did you learn from John 20:30–21:25? What was one thing that stood out to you as you studied this passage? How did John 20:30–21:25 surprise you? Do you have questions about this passage or the study materials that haven't been answered? What does God seem to be saying to you through what you have studied?

TOPICS FOR DISCUSSION

You can choose from among these topics to generate a discussion among the members of your group, or you can write your thoughts about one or more of these topics if you're studying solo.

1. Why do you think this Epilogue was added to the end of John's Gospel? What purpose does it play?

2. Why was Peter's restoration important for Peter and for the church that Jesus was about to launch? What does reconciliation teach us about the nature of the gospel message?

3. Now that you have finished studying John's Gospel, what are some of the key passages or themes in John's Gospel that made an impression on you? How do these passages contribute to John's central theme?

GROUP REFLECTION

What is God saying to us as a group through this passage?

ACTION

What are we going to do, individually or as a group, in response to what God is saying to us?

PRAYER

How should we pray for each other in response to God's message to us in this passage?

Take turns talking to God about this passage and about what he is saying.

THE GOSPEL OF JOHN

THE GOSPEL ACCORDING TO
JOHN

John wrote his Gospel to inspire faith. John knew Jesus
intimately, and John's Gospel provides an intimate portrait
of the Lord. John referred to himself as "the disciple Jesus
loved." His Gospel has become the "beloved Gospel" of the
church. Here we meet Nicodemus, doubting Thomas, Lazarus, and the Samaritan woman at the well. John records for
us Jesus' most memorable sayings, his longest sermons, and
his most profound miracles. Here we meet God face to face.

SETTING

A small community of Christians lived in ancient Ephesus during the late
first century AD. They had learned the remarkable story of Jesus from the
apostles Paul and John. This early church became strong in faith under
the leadership of these men. While many stories circulated about Jesus,
the apostle John had his own recollections and insights. In the later years
of his life, John wrote these stories down, providing his followers—and
us—with the fourth Gospel.

As an evangelist, pastor, and theologian,
John's desire above all was for his followers to believe that Jesus Christ is the Son
of God (20:31). He realized that they had
not had the privilege of seeing Jesus' many
signs and miracles as he had (20:29).
John's authority and deep experience with
Jesus ring out from every story he told. As
a valued eyewitness to Jesus' life (19:35),
John was the source of many stories from
faraway Galilee and Judea. John had heard,
seen, and touched the Word of life (see
1 Jn 1:1-4). He told about Nicodemus and
rebirth, described Jesus' miracle at Cana,
and recorded many other episodes.

As the Christians of Ephesus told their
fellow citizens about Jesus, they quickly
found themselves debating about Jesus
with rabbis in the local synagogues. Was
Jesus truly the Son of God? How could he

◄ **Key Places in the Gospel of John.** The book of John
describes Jesus' ministry in GALILEE (2:1-12; 4:43-54;
6:1–7:9), JERUSALEM (2:13–3:21; 5:1-47; 7:10-10:42;
12:12-50), JUDEA (3:22; 11:1-44; 12:1-11), and SAMARIA
(4:4-42). The book includes a full account Jesus' death
and resurrection in JERUSALEM (13:1–20:31) and his post-
resurrection appearance to his disciples beside the SEA OF
GALILEE (21:1-23).

be the Messiah? Can Christians legitimately claim to be "children of Abraham"? Could anyone prove that Jesus' claim of being sent from God was true? Guided by the Holy Spirit in his teaching and writing, John brilliantly led his Christian readers through these debates.

Tensions grew. As more Jews converted, small churches grew up alongside synagogues and began converting their members. Opposition to the Christian believers was inevitable. However, John stood by the church during terrible persecution and conflict. When it seemed that the fledgling church's struggle with the prestigious synagogue community would overwhelm them, John courageously gave witness to the ministry of Jesus Christ. When false teachers later brought internal controversy and conflict to the church, John again gave the community strength. Writing letters to encourage and exhort (see 1, 2, and 3 John), John became the heroic pastor–theologian of Asia Minor.

John's writing is as beloved today as it was in the earliest years of the church. Few books of the Bible have influenced Christian life and thought like John's profound and dynamic Gospel. By combining intimacy of expression with penetrating insight, John provides a deeply satisfying portrait of Christ.

OUTLINE

1:1-18
*Prologue: Christ,
the Eternal Word*

1:19–12:50
*The Book of Signs:
The Word Displays His Glory*

13:1–20:31
*The Book of Glory:
The Word Is Glorified*

21:1-25
*Epilogue: The Word
Commissions His Followers*

SUMMARY

John divided his Gospel into two main sections: chs 1–12 and chs 13–21. The first section, which has been called "The Book of Signs," tells about Jesus' public ministry of revealing himself to the Jewish world. The second section, sometimes called "The Book of Glory," records Jesus' private words to his disciples and tells of his death and resurrection.

Chapters 1–12. The Gospel prologue (1:1-18) artfully summarizes the entrance of God's Word into the world. Jesus was baptized and called his earliest followers (1:19-51). Then a series of remarkable events (chs 2–4) highlights Jesus' revelation of himself to the Jews. At a wedding in Cana, Jesus turned water into wine. In Jerusalem, he used a whip to drive corruption and money-dealing out of the Temple. He debated the meaning of spiritual rebirth with a rabbi named Nicodemus. At a well in Samaria, he met a woman with a checkered marital history and offered her "living water," which no well can ever duplicate. In each of these events, Jesus unveiled his identity.

In the following section (chs 5–10), Jesus appears at a number of Jewish festivals, using ancient OT symbols and practices to reveal himself to God's people. On the Sabbath, Jesus worked by healing a lame man. On Passover, Jesus provided bread for 5,000. In the symbolic light of the Festival of Shelters, Jesus healed a blind man, reinforcing his own identity as the light of the world. John's clear message is that Jesus came to fulfill what Judaism had promised since OT times.

Then Jesus began to prepare for his death and resurrection. John describes Jesus' arrival in Bethany, a town just east of Jerusalem (ch 11). His friend Lazarus had died, and Jesus raised him to life. Following this event (ch 12), Jesus made his final public appeal to the world to believe in him and his mission.

Chapters 13–21. John turns to Jesus' death and resurrection, reminding readers that the cross is not a sign of despair but a picture of glory and wonder. Jesus was returning to the Father and needed to prepare his disciples for his departure. At his final Passover meal (chs 13–17), Jesus disclosed to his disciples the things nearest to his heart. He told them candidly about his death and departure to the Father. He reassured them that he would not abandon them, but that he would return and turn their sorrow into joy. He promised them the gift of the Holy Spirit. Finally, Jesus prayed for them.

Following this Passover meal, Jesus led his followers east of the city and across a valley to an olive grove called Gethsemane (ch 18). Judas soon appeared with a large contingent of Roman soldiers and Temple guards. Following his arrest, Jesus stood before the Jewish high council to be interrogated, first by Annas and then by Caiaphas, the reigning high priest. By morning, the Jewish leaders took Jesus to the Roman governor, Pontius Pilate, who asked probing questions about Jesus' identity. Pilate, coaxed by the Jewish leaders, decided to crucify Jesus (ch 19).

The climax of John's Gospel is Jesus' resurrection from the dead (ch 20). This event begins a series of dramatic stories in which Jesus appeared to his followers and encouraged them. He gave them the Holy Spirit and commissioned them to represent him to the world. Jesus then gave his disciples their marching orders (ch 21). He reminded them of his power (21:1-14), reinstated Peter (21:15-17), and instructed him to follow him in his mission (21:18-23).

AUTHOR AND DATE

As with the other Gospels, John provides no explicit evidence as to its author, although the enigmatic figure of the "beloved disciple" provides clear clues (see 13:23; 19:26-27; 20:2-10; 21:7, 20-24). The Gospel of John must be connected with this person, for he is identified as the eyewitness source of this record of Jesus' life (19:35; 21:24).

Who was this beloved disciple? Leaders in the early church, beginning in AD 125, wrote that it was the apostle John, the son of Zebedee (see, e.g., Eusebius, *Church History* 3.23). This traditional view is sound and fully defensible. John was one of the Twelve and, along with James (his brother) and Peter, formed an inner circle around Jesus (Mark 3:17; Acts 1:13). The Gospel reflects this close perspective as it highlights Peter and John. Most scholars believe that John completed writing his Gospel by AD 90.

RECIPIENTS

John most likely wrote his Gospel for Jewish Christians living abroad in the Mediterranean world; with their grasp of Hebrew slipping, these believers were caught between the Jewish and Greek cultures.

The truth which this Gospel enshrines— the truth that Jesus Christ is the very Word Incarnate— [is] the one study which alone can fitly prepare us for a joyful immortality hereafter.

J. B. LIGHTFOOT,
Biblical Essays

John's knowledge of Palestine and Judaism is reflected throughout his Gospel.

John assumed that his audience was unfamiliar with some particulars of Jesus' world. For example, he explained that *rabbi* is a Hebrew word meaning "teacher" (1:38), and he gave an alternate name for the Sea of Galilee (6:1). At the same time, John assumed that his readers were familiar with Jewish traditions, concepts, and festivals. They probably were also familiar with the basic story presented in Mark's Gospel. For example, John refers to John the Baptist's imprisonment (3:24) without ever telling the complete story.

MEANING AND MESSAGE

Revelation and Redemption. "The light shines in the darkness, and the darkness can never extinguish it" (1:5). The light of God has inhabited the world: Christ reveals the Father (14:9). In Christ we see the glory of God in a human being. Even though Jesus was persecuted, tried, and crucified, the light cannot be extinguished. Jesus' purpose in revealing God is to redeem people: "The Word gave life to everything that was created, and his life brought light to everyone" (1:4). Those who embrace Christ's revelation and redemption with faith will gain eternal life.

Worship and the Spirit. Worship must take place "in spirit and in truth" (4:24), energized and formed by the Spirit of God. Nicodemus had to be born of "water and Spirit" to enter the Kingdom of God (3:5). In Galilee, after feeding the 5,000, Jesus told the crowd that living bread is available in his body, which was to be sacrificed. He instructed them to consume his body and blood, symbolic of the Lord's Supper (6:51-59). Yet worship focusing only on the individual elements and not accompanied by the Spirit of God is worth nothing (6:63).

Jesus Christ. John recorded Jesus' descriptions about his nature, origin, and relationship to the Father. Jesus affirmed his oneness with the Father (10:30; 14:9-10) and their unity of purpose (5:17; 8:42), as well as their personal distinctiveness (14:28; 17:1-5). Jesus even used the very title ("I Am") that God used for himself in the OT, thus affirming his own deity (8:58; 18:5; Exod 3:14).

The Holy Spirit. John's Gospel underscores the Holy Spirit as a central feature of Jesus' human experience (chs 4, 7) and of our lives (ch 3). The transforming power of God's Spirit is a hallmark of true discipleship.

The Mission of the Church. God sent Jesus into the world (8:18) to proclaim his glory and to testify to the Good News of redemption. In his departure, the Son passed this mission on to the Spirit (16:5-11), who in turn would fill the church and empower believers to fulfill the mission of Jesus in the world (20:20-23; Matt 28:18-20; Acts 1:7-8).

The End Times. Early Christians anticipated the return of Christ, and John affirms this anticipation. Yet in the meantime, believers can experience Jesus' longed-for presence in the Holy Spirit. Jesus' announcement of the Spirit's coming echoes the language of his own second coming (see 14:15-23). In a vital way, Jesus is already with us in the Spirit as we continue to look forward to Christ's personal return at the end of history.

I like the comparison of John's Gospel to a pool in which a child may wade and an elephant can swim. It is both simple and profound. It is for the beginner in the faith and for the mature Christian. Its appeal is immediate and never failing.

LEON MORRIS,
The Gospel according to John

FURTHER READING

CRAIG L. BLOMBERG
The Historical Reliability of John's Gospel: Issues and Commentary (2001)

F. F. BRUCE
The Gospel of John: Introduction, Exposition and Notes (1983)

GARY M. BURGE
John (2000)

PHILIP W. COMFORT
I Am the Way: A Spiritual Journey through the Gospel of John (2001)

GRANT OSBORNE
John in *Cornerstone Biblical Commentary*, vol. 13 (2007)

RODNEY A. WHITACRE
John (1999)

1. PROLOGUE: CHRIST, THE ETERNAL WORD (1:1-18)

1 ¹In the beginning the ªWord already existed.
The ªWord was with God,
and the ªWord was God.
² He existed in the beginning with God.
³ God created everything through him,
and nothing was created except through him.
⁴ The Word gave life to everything that was created,
and his life brought light to everyone.
⁵ The light shines in the darkness,
and the darkness can never extinguish it.

⁶God sent a man, John the Baptist, ⁷to tell about the light so that everyone might believe because of his testimony. ⁸John himself was not the light; he was simply a witness to tell about the light. ⁹The one who is the true light, who gives light to everyone, was coming into the world.

¹⁰He came into the very world he created, but the world didn't recognize him. ¹¹He came to his own people, and even they rejected him. ¹²But to all who believed him and accepted him, he gave the right to become children of God. ¹³They are reborn—not with a physical birth resulting from human passion or plan, but a birth that comes from God.

¹⁴So the ᵇWord became ᶜhuman and made his home among us. He was full of unfailing love and faithfulness. And we have seen his ᵈglory, the ᵈglory of the Father's ᵉone and only Son.

¹⁵John testified about him when he shouted to the crowds, "This is the one I was talking about when I said, 'Someone is coming after me who is far greater than I am, for he existed long before me.'"

¹⁶From his abundance we have all received one gracious blessing after another.

1:1
Gen 1:1
Col 1:15
ªlogos (3056)
› John 1:14

1:3
1 Cor 8:6
Col 1:16-17
Heb 1:2

1:4
John 8:12; 11:25; 14:6
1 Jn 5:12, 20

1:5
John 3:19; 9:5

1:9
1 Jn 2:8

1:12
Rom 8:15-16, 29

1:14
Rom 8:3
Gal 4:4-7
Phil 2:6-8
1 Tim 3:16
1 Jn 1:1; 4:2-3
ᵇlogos (3056)
› Acts 6:2
ᶜsarx (4561)
› John 3:6
ᵈdoxa (1391)
› Rom 3:23
ᵉmonogenēs (3439)
› John 1:18

1:1-18 The beginning of this prologue (1:1-5) might be a poem or hymn sung by the earliest Christians. The prologue's themes—the coming of the light into the world, the rejection of the light, and its gift of new life to believers—prepares readers for the story that follows.

1:1 Echoing Gen 1:1, John's Gospel introduces Jesus Christ, through whom God created everything (1:3); Jesus also creates new life in those who believe (1:12-13). The Gospel opens with its central affirmation, that Jesus Christ, *the Word* (Greek *logos*), not only revealed God but *was God*. In Greek thought, the *logos* was the rational principle guiding the universe and making life coherent. For Jewish people, the *logos* was the word of the Lord, an expression of God's wisdom and creative power. By Jesus' time, the *logos* was viewed as coming from God and having his personality (see Ps 33:6, 9; Prov 8:22-31); John affirmed this understanding (1:14).

1:3-4 *and nothing was created except through him. The Word gave life to everything that was created:* Or *and nothing that was created was created except through him. The Word gave life to everything.* The Greek grammar allows either possibility.

1:3 God is the *logos* (1:1-2); all that God does, the *logos* likewise does. Throughout his Gospel, John rightly viewed Jesus' actions as divine activity.

1:4-5 God created *light* and dispelled the *darkness* (Gen 1:2-5). The darkness resists God (3:19-21; 12:35; Matt 6:23; Acts 26:17-18; Eph 4:17-19; 5:7-14; 2 Pet 1:19; 1 Jn 1:5-7; 2:9-11).

1:4 *The Word gave life:* Life was God's original gift to his creatures (Gen 1:20-28; 2:7). Now the *logos* would give these creatures the possibility of new life through rebirth (1:13). • As one of his first creative acts, God *brought light* (Gen 1:3). Now, in the re-creation of humanity through Jesus Christ, God offered light and life anew. Light is a key theme in John's Gospel.

1:5 *the darkness can never extinguish it:* Or *the darkness has not understood it;* literally *the darkness cannot grasp it.* The Greek word *katalambanō* ("grasp") can mean either "understand" or "be hostile"; in John's Gospel, it means hostility. The darkness would try to destroy Jesus (the light), but it would fail. The light would successfully bring salvation to the world.

1:6-9 *God sent a man, John the Baptist* (literally *a man named John*) to herald Jesus' coming and to prepare God's people to receive Jesus as God's Son and Messiah (see 1:19-37; Luke 1:5-25, 57-80; 3:1-22; see also Isa 40:3; Mal 4:5-6).

1:8 Some Jews speculated that John the Baptist was the Messiah; some of his followers were even reluctant to follow Jesus (3:22-30). However, John the Baptist *was not the light;* his role was to announce Jesus (1:19-34).

1:10 *The world* cannot *recognize* the true light even when it encounters its Creator. The world lives in rebellion, loving darkness more than light (3:19; see "The World" at 17:5-26, p. 1807).

1:12 Only through divine renewal can people follow the light and enter God's family (3:1-17). • Individuals must believe in Christ *to become children of God* (12:35-36).

1:13 *a birth that comes from God:* People can escape the darkness only by God's grace (8:12; 12:35-36, 44-46).

1:14 The idea that *the Word became human* (literally *became flesh*) stunned both Greeks and Jews. Greeks separated the sphere of God from the mundane world of humanity, which they called *flesh* (Greek *sarx*). John wrote that God himself became *flesh* in Christ (cp. 1:1). Jesus' humanity and divinity were complete, not partial. The two ideas—Jesus as 100-percent divine and 100-percent human—form the bedrock of a Christian understanding of Christ. • *the Word . . . made his home* (Greek *skēnoō*, "pitched his tent") *among us:* This Greek word is related to the word used for the OT Tabernacle (Greek *skēnē*, "tent, tabernacle"), the tent in the wilderness where the Lord's glory resided and where Israel came to worship (Exod 25:8-9). The Father's glory in the Tabernacle (Exod 40:34-38) was now present in Jesus Christ (2:11; 12:23-28, 41; 17:1-5). • Jesus offered God's *unfailing love and faithfulness* (or *grace and truth*). Despite the world's hostile darkness, Jesus entered the world to save it (3:15-17).

1:15 *he existed long before me:* In a society where age was respected and honored (Lev 19:32; contrast Isa 3:5), John the Baptist emphasized Jesus' honor by pointing to his existence even before creation (1:1-3).

1:16 *received one gracious blessing after another:* Or *received the grace of Christ rather than the grace of the law;* a literal translation is *received grace upon grace.*

1:17
Exod 31:18; 34:28
'*christos* (5547)
▸ John 1:41

1:18
Col 1:15
ᵍmonogenēs (3439)
▸ John 3:16

1:19-28
Matt 3:1-12
Mark 1:2-8
Luke 3:1-16

1:20
Luke 3:15
John 3:28

1:21
Deut 18:15
Mal 4:5
Matt 11:14

1:23
*Isa 40:3
Mal 3:1

1:26
Matt 3:11
Mark 1:8
Luke 3:16

¹⁷For the law was given through Moses, but God's unfailing love and faithfulness came through Jesus ᶠChrist. ¹⁸No one has ever seen God. But the ᵍunique One, who is himself God, is near to the Father's heart. He has revealed God to us.

2. THE BOOK OF SIGNS: THE WORD DISPLAYS HIS GLORY (1:19–12:50)

Jesus and John the Baptist (1:19-51)

The Testimony of John the Baptist

John 1:23 // Matt 3:1-3 // Mark 1:2-3 // Luke 3:2b-6
John 1:24-28 // Matt 3:11-12 // Mark 1:7-8 //
Luke 3:15-18

¹⁹This was John's testimony when the Jewish leaders sent priests and Temple assistants from Jerusalem to ask John, "Who are you?" ²⁰He came right out and said, "I am not the Messiah."

²¹"Well then, who are you?" they asked. "Are you Elijah?"

"No," he replied.

"Are you the Prophet we are expecting?"

"No."

²²"Then who are you? We need an answer for those who sent us. What do you have to say about yourself?"

²³John replied in the words of the prophet Isaiah:

"I am a voice shouting in the wilderness,
  'Clear the way for the LORD's coming!' "

²⁴Then the Pharisees who had been sent ²⁵asked him, "If you aren't the Messiah or Elijah or the Prophet, what right do you have to baptize?"

²⁶John told them, "I baptize with water, but right here in the crowd is someone you

. . . .

The Word (1:1-18)

Gen 1:3-28
Ps 33:6, 9
Prov 8:22-31
Isa 40:8
1 Jn 1:1
Rev 19:13

John raises the curtain on his Gospel with a stunning description of Jesus Christ as "the Word" (Greek *logos,* 1:1). Both Greek and Jewish listeners in the first century would immediately recognize the profound meaning of this title. Greeks would have thought of the seminal forces that sustain the universe. Jewish minds would have thought back to God creating the world with his word (Gen 1:3-28). In Jesus' day, the word of God took on creative personal attributes (Ps 33:6, 9). Jews viewed God's word as personifying divine wisdom. Through Wisdom, God extended himself into the cosmos, creating the world (Prov 8:22-31).

In John's drama, Jesus shares the same essence as God; the Son existed before time, and he was the agent of all creation. John anchors the divinity of Jesus in this ancient Jewish concept of Wisdom. The divine Wisdom that has existed from before time with God can now be known in Jesus Christ. In perhaps the most outrageous verse penned by an apostle, John writes that this Logos, this Wisdom, became flesh and lived among us as a human (1:14). What God is, the Logos is. The Logos is Jesus Christ.

. . . .

1:17 *the law:* That is, the Torah, the first five books of the Bible (Genesis through Deuteronomy). • Although *God's unfailing love and faithfulness* (or *grace and truth*) are in the Torah, these qualities are fully revealed in Christ (3:16; 13:1).

1:18 Moses was denied his desire to see God directly (Exod 33:18-20). Only Jesus has seen the Father, so he alone completely knows him and can tell us about him (3:32-35; 14:9-10). • *But the unique One, who is himself God* (some manuscripts read *But the one and only Son*): The Son, who sees the Father, *is himself God*—not simply a messenger who knows something about God. John explicitly affirms Christ's deity. Jesus shares the substance of God's being.

1:19–12:50 Jesus reveals himself to the world through his miraculous signs and sermons. Audiences were divided: Some wanted to believe in him; others opposed him. This division intensifies as the book unfolds. Jesus ended his public ministry with a final appeal for

people to believe in him (12:44-50).

1:19-51 John's Gospel gives limited attention to John the Baptist compared to the synoptic Gospels (Matt 3:1-6; Mark 1:2-6; Luke 1:1-24, 57-80; 3:1-13). Yet the apostle John wants us to see that John the Baptist correctly identified and exalted Jesus. John the Baptist's disciples leave him and follow Jesus; Jesus took over the ministry John began, increasing as John decreased (3:30).

1:19 *Jewish leaders:* See "The Jewish Leaders" at 5:9-18, p. 1779. • *and Temple assistants:* Literally *and Levites.*

1:20 The Jews expected the *Messiah* (the Hebrew form of the Greek word *Christ*) to bring spiritual leadership and political redemption to Israel (see Deut 18:15; see also the Jewish intertestamental book *Psalms of Solomon*).

1:21 *Elijah* was to be the Messiah's forerunner (Mal 4:5). John the Baptist fulfilled the forerunner's role, though he denied being the prophet Elijah (see Matt 11:14; Luke 1:17). • *Are you the*

Prophet we are expecting? Literally *Are you the Prophet?* See Deut 18:15, 18; Mal 4:5-6; see also John 6:14; 7:40-41.

1:22-23 *Then who are you?* John the Baptist simply wanted to be known as *a voice shouting in the wilderness* (see Isa 40:3).

1:24 The *Pharisees* were deeply devoted to the Scriptures and earnestly desired a righteous life (see "Pharisees" at Matt 3:7, p. 1581). They also believed in the coming Messiah, which explains their inquiries here. Some Pharisees became believers in Jesus (Acts 15:5), including the apostle Paul (Acts 26:5; Phil 3:5).

1:25-26 Jewish baptisms were ritual washings for becoming ceremonially pure following contact with impurity (Lev 8:6; Num 19:7). • John's announcement of the Messiah's arrival required that participants confess their sins and be baptized (Matt 3:6). Baptism later became the symbol of membership in Jesus' kingdom (Acts 2:38; see also John 4:1-2). • *with:* Or *in;* also in 1:31, 33.

do not recognize. ²⁷Though his ministry follows mine, I'm not even worthy to be his slave and untie the straps of his sandal."

²⁸This encounter took place in Bethany, an area east of the Jordan River, where John was baptizing.

Jesus, the Lamb of God
John 1:29-34 // Matt 3:13-17 // Mark 1:9-11 // Luke 3:21-22

²⁹The next day John saw Jesus coming toward him and said, "Look! The ʰLamb of God who takes away the sin of the world! ³⁰He is the one I was talking about when I said, 'A man is coming after me who is far greater than I am, for he existed long before me.' ³¹I did not recognize him as the Messiah, but I have been baptizing with water so that he might be revealed to Israel."

³²Then John testified, "I saw the Holy Spirit descending like a dove from heaven and resting upon him. ³³I didn't know he was the one, but when God sent me to baptize with water, he told me, 'The one on whom you see the Spirit descend and rest is the one who will baptize with the Holy Spirit.' ³⁴I saw this happen to Jesus, so I testify that he is the Chosen One of God."

The First Disciples
³⁵The following day John was again standing with two of his disciples. ³⁶As Jesus walked by, John looked at him and declared, "Look! There is the ⁱLamb of God!" ³⁷When John's two disciples heard this, they followed Jesus.

³⁸Jesus looked around and saw them following. "What do you want?" he asked them.

They replied, "ʲRabbi" (which means "Teacher"), "where are you staying?"

³⁹"Come and see," he said. It was about four o'clock in the afternoon when they went with him to the place where he was staying, and they remained with him the rest of the day.

⁴⁰Andrew, Simon Peter's brother, was one of these men who heard what John said and then followed Jesus. ⁴¹Andrew went to find his brother, Simon, and told him, "We have found the ᵏMessiah" (which means "Christ").

⁴²Then Andrew brought Simon to meet Jesus. Looking intently at Simon, Jesus said, "Your name is Simon, son of John—but you will be called Cephas" (which means "ᵃPeter").

⁴³The next day Jesus decided to go to Galilee. He found Philip and said to him, "Come, follow me." ⁴⁴Philip was from Bethsaida, Andrew and Peter's hometown.

⁴⁵Philip went to look for Nathanael and told him, "We have found the very person Moses and the prophets wrote about! His name is Jesus, the son of Joseph from Nazareth."

⁴⁶"Nazareth!" exclaimed Nathanael. "Can anything good come from Nazareth?"

"Come and see for yourself," Philip replied.

⁴⁷As they approached, Jesus said, "Now here is a genuine son of Israel—a man of complete integrity."

⁴⁸"How do you know about me?" Nathanael asked.

Jesus replied, "I could see you under the fig tree before Philip found you."

1:27
Mark 1:7
John 1:15
Acts 13:25

1:28
John 3:26; 10:40

1:29
Isa 53:7
1 Cor 5:7
1 Pet 1:19
ʰamnos (0286)
▸John 1:36

1:30
John 1:15, 27

1:32
Matt 3:16
Mark 1:10
Luke 3:22

1:33
Luke 3:16
Acts 1:5

1:34
John 1:49; 10:36;
11:27; 20:30-31

1:36
ⁱamnos (0286)
▸Acts 8:32

1:38
ʲrhabbi (4461)
▸John 1:49

1:40
Matt 4:18-22
Mark 1:16
Luke 5:2-11

1:41
Ps 2:2
John 4:25
ᵏmessias (3323)
▸John 4:25

1:42
Matt 16:18
1 Cor 15:5
1 Pet 2:5
ᵃpetros (4074)
▸1 Cor 10:4

1:43
John 6:5-6; 12:20-22

1:45
Luke 24:25-27

. . . .

1:27 A menial task such as removing a *sandal* was reserved for a *slave;* these tasks were never performed by a disciple.

1:29 The phrase *Lamb of God* might refer to the Passover sacrifice of a lamb (see "The Cross and Passover" at 19:17-36, p. 1812) or to the daily sacrifice in the Temple (Exod 29:38-46; Heb 10). See also Rev 5.

1:32 John the Baptist's second testimony (see 1:19-23) told what happened when Jesus was baptized. • In the OT, kings and prophets were anointed with *the Holy Spirit,* but these anointings were temporary and tied to a particular office or occasion. By contrast, with the Spirit's *resting* on him, Jesus' anointing was permanent (see 3:34).

1:34 *the Chosen One of God:* Some manuscripts read *the Son of God.* See also Isa 42:1.

1:35-51 This section introduces the template for discipleship in John's Gospel. Disciples desired to *come and*

see Jesus (1:39), and when they encountered him, they *remained* with him (see "Disciples of Jesus" at 9:1-41, p. 1789).

1:40-42 Simon is well known in the Gospels, not for his courage and faith, but for his failings (see 18:15-18, 25-27). Jesus named him *Cephas* ("the rock"; see 1:42 and note), referring to the great church leader he would later become (see Acts 1–5, 8–12, 15).

1:41 *Messiah* (a Hebrew term) and *Christ* (a Greek term) both mean "the Anointed One."

1:42 The names *Cephas* (from Aramaic) and *Peter* (from Greek) both mean "rock."

1:43-44 *Galilee* was the region of northern Israel around the Sea of Galilee. • *Bethsaida* ("house of fishing") was a village on Galilee's north shore and the home of Peter, Andrew, Nathanael, and Philip. Later, Peter and Andrew moved to Capernaum, a village west of Bethsaida (Mark 1:21, 29).

1:45 *Philip,* a Greek name, and

Nathanael, a Hebrew name, represent the mix of cultures in Galilee. Jesus' message there addressed both audiences. When Greeks wanted to see Jesus in Jerusalem, they approached Philip (12:20-22). • *Moses:* Literally *Moses in the law.* • Jesus grew up in *Nazareth,* a mountain village southwest of the Sea of Galilee.

1:46 *Can anything good come from Nazareth?* This village was not considered famous enough to be the hometown for a great leader (cp. Matt 13:53-58).

1:47 Jesus referred to Nathanael as *a man of complete integrity,* contrasting with Jacob, the scheming, deceitful patriarch whom God renamed *Israel* (see Gen 25:27-34; 27:1-36; 32:22-32). It is as though Nathanael embodied God's ideal for Israel.

1:48-49 Jesus captured Nathanael's attention by knowing his character (1:47), then he captured his worship by supernaturally knowing his previous actions. Nathanael witnessed a miracle and took a remarkable step of faith.

1:49
2 Sam 7:14
Ps 2:2
John 1:34; 20:31
ᵇ*rhabbi* (4461)
 ᐧ John 3:2

1:51
Gen 28:12

⁴⁹Then Nathanael exclaimed, "ᵇRabbi, you are the Son of God—the King of Israel!"

⁵⁰Jesus asked him, "Do you believe this just because I told you I had seen you under the fig tree? You will see greater things than this." ⁵¹Then he said, "I tell you the truth, you will all see heaven open and the angels of God going up and down on the Son of Man, the one who is the stairway between heaven and earth."

Jesus and Jewish Institutions (2:1–4:54)
The Wedding at Cana: Purification Water Turned to Wine

2 The next day there was a wedding celebration in the village of Cana in Galilee. Jesus' mother was there, ²and Jesus and his disciples were also invited to the celebration. ³The wine supply ran out during the festivities, so Jesus' mother told him, "They have no more wine."

JOHN THE BAPTIST (1:19-37)

John 3:23-36; 4:1-3;
10:40-42
Matt 3:1-15; 4:12;
9:14; 11:2-19; 14:1-
12; 16:14; 17:10-13;
21:24-27, 31-32
Mark 1:1-9, 14;
2:18; 6:14-29; 8:28;
9:11-13; 11:29-33
Luke 1:13-17, 36,
39-43, 57-66, 76-80;
3:1-21; 5:33; 7:18-
35; 9:7-9, 19; 11:1;
16:16; 20:3-8
Acts 1:5; 10:37;
11:16; 18:25-26;
19:1-7

John the Baptist was a fiery open-air preacher who called people to repent and be baptized, to prepare for the coming of the Messiah. John acted in the role of Elijah, to prepare people for "the great and dreadful day of the LORD" (Mal 4:4-5; see Matt 11:14; 17:12; Mark 9:13).

John's birth, like that of Jesus, was miraculous. His parents had been unable to have children and were elderly (Luke 1:5-25). His mother, Elizabeth, was a relative of Mary, the mother of Jesus (Luke 1:36), so John was related to Jesus. The two miraculous births near the same time signaled the beginning of God's redeeming work.

John was filled with the Holy Spirit from birth and devoted his life to preparing people for the coming of the Lord (Luke 1:15-17). Living in the desert (Luke 1:80), he began preaching when he was about thirty years old. Dressed like a prophet and subsisting on desert food (locusts and wild honey, Matt 3:4; Mark 1:6), he called everyone to repent and be baptized (Matt 3:1-2; Mark 1:4; Luke 3:1-3). He even castigated the religious leaders who came to hear him (Matt 3:7).

Though John reluctantly baptized Jesus (Matt 3:13-17; Luke 3:21), he considered Jesus his superior, the one who would "baptize with the Holy Spirit and with fire" (1:33; Matt 3:11; Mark 1:7-8; Luke 3:16; cp. 3:23-30). He encouraged his followers to become Jesus' disciples—and many did, including Andrew and possibly John (1:35-40), as well as Apollos (Acts 18:24-26) and the twelve disciples at Ephesus (Acts 19:1-7).

Herod Antipas received harsh judgment from John because of Herod's unlawful marriage to Herodias, his brother Philip's wife. To please Herodias, Herod imprisoned John and then beheaded him (Matt 14:3-12; Mark 6:17-29; Luke 3:19-20). John's imprisonment marked the beginning of Jesus' public preaching (Matt 4:12; Mark 1:14).

Shortly before his death, John seemed to be confused about Jesus and sent messengers from prison to ask him if he really was the Messiah. Jesus did not do what most people anticipated the Messiah to do. Rather than bringing judgment and a visible kingdom, he brought forgiveness, healing, and a spiritual kingdom. To reassure John, Jesus spoke of the miraculous things God was doing through him (Luke 7:18-23).

John remained faithful to his calling throughout his life, consistently preaching repentance and the judgment of God, even to people who had no desire to hear it. Jesus referred to John as one of the greatest servants of God who had ever lived (Matt 11:2-19; Luke 7:18-35), the end of a long line of prophets anticipating the coming of the Kingdom of God (Luke 16:16). John stood on the threshold of the new age, proclaiming its coming to all who would hear.

1:51 *I tell you the truth* (Greek *amēn amēn*): Jesus often used this expression to emphasize what he was about to say. In John's Gospel, the Greek word *amēn* is always doubled. • *you will all see heaven open:* Jesus made the comparison with Jacob explicit (see note on 1:47; see Gen 28:10-22). Like Jacob, Nathanael would see God at work. Jesus himself is the new Bethel ("house of God," Gen 28:19), the place where God lives. • *going up and down on the Son of Man, the one who is the stairway between heaven and earth:* Literally *going up and down on the Son of Man;*

see Gen 28:10-17. "Son of Man" is a title Jesus used for himself (see note on 9:35; see also Dan 7:13-14; Mark 8:31). • John the apostle used several names for Jesus (Son of God, Son of Man, Messiah). Knowing Jesus' true identity is necessary to fully understanding and following him.

2:1–10:42 Jesus illustrated his identity and work through the institutions and festivals of Judaism (see 2:1; 5:1).

2:1-25 Jesus appeared at two symbolic Jewish ceremonies. At a wedding in Cana (2:1-12), he replaced the ritual cleansing

water with his own superior wine. Later he cleansed the Temple (2:13-25).

2:1 *The next day:* Literally *On the third day;* see 1:35, 43. • The ceremonies surrounding *a wedding celebration* could last as long as a week; weddings often included dramatic processions in which the groom would bring the bride to his home for the festivities (Matt 25:1-13).

2:3 When *the wine supply ran out,* the host's family would face embarrassment for failure to plan properly. Perhaps Jesus arrived unexpectedly (cp. Matt 25:1-13), bringing his circle of

4"Dear woman, that's not our problem," Jesus replied. "My time has not yet come."

5But his mother told the servants, "Do whatever he tells you."

6Standing nearby were six stone water jars, used for Jewish ceremonial washing. Each could hold twenty to thirty gallons. 7Jesus told the servants, "Fill the jars with water." When the jars had been filled, 8he said, "Now dip some out, and take it to the master of ceremonies." So the servants followed his instructions.

9When the master of ceremonies tasted the water that was now wine, not knowing where it had come from (though, of course, the servants knew), he called the bridegroom over. 10"A host always serves the best wine first," he said. "Then, when everyone has had a lot to drink, he brings out the less expensive wine. But you have kept the best until now!"

11This miraculous sign at Cana in Galilee was the first time Jesus revealed his glory. And his disciples believed in him.

12After the wedding he went to Capernaum for a few days with his mother, his brothers, and his disciples.

The Jerusalem Temple Is Cleansed
John 2:13-16; cp. Matt 21:12-13 // Mark 11:15-17 // Luke 19:45-46

13It was nearly time for the Jewish Passover celebration, so Jesus went to Jerusalem. 14In the Temple area he saw merchants selling cattle, sheep, and doves for sacrifices; he also saw dealers at tables exchanging foreign money. 15Jesus made a whip from some ropes and chased them all out of the Temple. He drove out the sheep and cattle,

2:4
John 7:30; 8:20

2:6
Mark 7:3-4
John 3:25

2:9
John 4:46

2:11
John 2:23; 3:2; 4:54;
6:14; 11:47; 12:37

2:12
Matt 12:46-50

2:13-22
//Matt 21:12-17
//Mark 11:15-19
//Luke 19:45-48

2:13
Deut 16:1-6
John 6:4; 11:55

Miraculous Signs (2:1-11)

John 2:18, 23; 3:2;
4:48, 54; 6:2, 14,
26, 30; 7:31; 9:16;
10:41; 11:47; 12:18,
37; 15:24; 20:30
Exod 4:8-31; 7:3
Num 14:11, 22
Deut 4:34
Ps 74:9; 78:43
Matt 12:38-39
Acts 2:43; 4:16, 22,
30; 5:12; 8:6; 14:3;
15:12
Rom 15:19

The Gospels use three words to describe Jesus' miraculous works. In Matthew, Mark, and Luke, the Greek word *dunamis* ("power") describes an act of raw force that amazes observers and leads to the inevitable conclusion that God must be at work in Jesus (see Mark 6:2).

In John, however, this response of amazement is absent. John does not use the popular term *dunamis*. Instead, he labels each of Jesus' miracles as a "sign" (Greek *sēmeion*), an event that has a deeper meaning. John also describes Jesus' miracles as "works" (Greek *erga*, see 10:25; see 7:3, "miracles"; 9:3, "power"). Christ's miracles were part of the work that God gave him to do (17:4), revealing the Father to the world.

John selectively records seven miraculous signs that occurred during Jesus' ministry: (1) changing water to wine (2:1-11); (2) healing the official's son (4:46-54); (3) healing a paralyzed man (5:1-17); (4) feeding 5,000 (6:1-15); (5) walking on water (6:16-21); (6) healing a blind man (9:1-41); and (7) raising Lazarus from the dead (11:38-44). John also records the miraculous catch of fish after Jesus' resurrection (21:4-14). Most of the seven signs were met with belief (2:11; 4:48, 53; 11:45-48). However, the sign itself was not Jesus' purpose. Instead, the message behind the sign is always in view, so the signs are usually matched to a discourse by Jesus. Jesus fed the 5,000, for example, not just to meet their needs, but so that people would see him as the bread of life (6:35), given for them when he died on the cross (6:51).

disciples, which might explain why his *mother* brought the problem to him.
• A wedding banquet was a primary celebration in Jewish village life, and this episode also symbolized the joy of the Messiah's arrival.

2:4 Jesus initially distanced himself from the *problem*. His mission and its timing could not be set by a human agenda. • Jesus' *time* (literally *hour*) would come in the future when he was glorified as he was lifted up on the cross (12:23; 17:1).

2:6 Carved from solid rock, the *stone water jars* were used for religious washing ceremonies (see Mark 7:1-4). Jesus was about to fill Jewish ceremony with new content. • *twenty to thirty gallons:* Greek *2 or 3 measures* [75 to 113 liters].

2:9-10 The *master of ceremonies* cited

a proverb. The *best wine* was always served *first* when palates were most sensitive; yet this miraculous wine, served last, was the very best imaginable. Good wine symbolized God's blessing (Amos 9:13-14). The Messiah, God's greatest blessing, had arrived at last.

2:11 Jesus had offered his first *miraculous sign* (see "Miraculous Signs" at 2:1-11, above). In it, he revealed the glory of God (see also 1:14; 11:4, 40).

2:13 *Passover*, an annual spring festival, commemorated Israel's rescue from slavery in Egypt (Exod 12). Jews traveled to *Jerusalem* to participate in the festival (Deut 16:1-16). Because John refers to three Passover Festivals (2:13; 6:4; 11:55), many experts conclude that Jesus had a three-year public ministry.

2:14-17 Those who came for Passover needed to have approved sacrifices for worship. From this need grew a considerable industry for selling animals and exchanging money, but this business was being conducted in the Temple. Jesus, like a prophet, demanded that God's house be returned to its intended uses—worship, prayer, instruction, and sacrifice. This put Jesus at odds with the Temple leadership. • The synoptic Gospels place the clearing of the Temple near the end of Jesus' ministry (Matt 21:12-13; Mark 11:15-17; Luke 19:45-46). John might have placed his account of the event here to emphasize a connection with the miracle that transformed the water in purification jars into wine (2:1-11). The Temple and the stone jars were both instruments of purification in Judaism. Stone jars filled with water for ritual washing

2:16
Luke 2:49

2:17
*Ps 69:9

2:19
Matt 26:61; 27:40
Mark 14:58
Acts 6:14

2:21
John 10:38; 14:2, 10;
17:21
1 Cor 3:16; 6:19

2:22
Luke 24:6-8
John 12:16; 14:26

2:23
John 7:31; 11:47-48

3:1-2
John 7:50; 19:39

3:2
Matt 22:16
Acts 2:22; 10:38
ᶜrhabbi (4461)
▸ John 11:8

3:3
John 1:13
ᵈanōthen gennaō
(0509, 1080)
▸ John 3:7

scattered the money changers' coins over the floor, and turned over their tables. ¹⁶Then, going over to the people who sold doves, he told them, "Get these things out of here. Stop turning my Father's house into a marketplace!"

¹⁷Then his disciples remembered this prophecy from the Scriptures: "Passion for God's house will consume me."

¹⁸But the Jewish leaders demanded, "What are you doing? If God gave you authority to do this, show us a miraculous sign to prove it."

¹⁹"All right," Jesus replied. "Destroy this temple, and in three days I will raise it up."

²⁰"What!" they exclaimed. "It has taken forty-six years to build this Temple, and you can rebuild it in three days?" ²¹But when Jesus said "this temple," he meant his own body. ²²After he was raised from the dead, his disciples remembered he had said this,

and they believed both the Scriptures and what Jesus had said.

Nicodemus: A Religious Leader Visits Jesus

²³Because of the miraculous signs Jesus did in Jerusalem at the Passover celebration, many began to trust in him. ²⁴But Jesus didn't trust them, because he knew human nature. ²⁵No one needed to tell him what mankind is really like.

3 There was a man named Nicodemus, a Jewish religious leader who was a Pharisee. ²After dark one evening, he came to speak with Jesus. "ᶜRabbi," he said, "we all know that God has sent you to teach us. Your miraculous signs are evidence that God is with you."

³Jesus replied, "I tell you the truth, unless you are ᵈborn again, you cannot see the Kingdom of God."

NICODEMUS (3:1-9)

John 7:50; 19:39-42

Nicodemus was a highly respected Jewish Pharisee (3:1), one of the prominent members of the high council, who appears to have become a convert of Jesus. He is mentioned only in the Gospel of John.

Intrigued by the authority of Jesus and the miracles he was doing, Nicodemus went to see him secretly, at night, in a serious attempt to discover who he really was. Jesus challenged him with the need to be born again, if he wished to be in the Kingdom of God (3:1-8). The Gospel does not give us Nicodemus's response.

Later, however, in opposition to his colleagues on the Jewish high council, he strongly argued that Jesus should be given a fair trial (7:50). After Jesus was crucified, he bought seventy-five pounds of expensive perfumed ointment for his burial, took it to the tomb, and assisted Joseph of Arimathea in burying him (19:39-42). Thus, Nicodemus appears to be an example of a Jewish Pharisee who came to believe in Jesus and was willing to express that commitment publicly after his death.

now contained Jesus' wine, and a stone Temple dedicated to sacrificial purification would be replaced by Christ himself (2:19-21). Another view is that Jesus cleared the Temple at the beginning and again at the end of his ministry.

2:17 *Passion for God's house will consume me:* Or *"Concern for God's house will be my undoing."* See Ps 69:9.

2:19 *Destroy this temple:* Herod the Great began reconstructing the Temple's magnificent structure in 20 BC, and work on it continued until AD 64. This explains why Jesus' audience was amazed when he claimed he could destroy and rebuild it in a few days. However, Jesus spoke figuratively of his body as the temple where God was present (see 1:14; 1:51)—his body was destroyed and restored in three days through the resurrection, rendering the Jerusalem Temple and its services obsolete. Later, at his trial, Jesus' symbolic

reference to destroying the Temple was used as evidence of blasphemy (Mark 14:58).

2:22 *they believed:* Witnessing a miracle from God can inspire belief, but it is not the deepest faith possible (20:29).

2:24 *Jesus didn't trust them:* John uses a play on words here. Because of his signs, many people trusted in Jesus (2:23), but Jesus *didn't trust them.* This did not refer to specific people Jesus met in Jerusalem, but to his knowledge of all humanity.

3:1 John links 2:25 and 3:1 by referring to humanity as a whole ("mankind," 2:25) and then to one specific *man* using the same Greek word (*anthrōpos*) in both verses.• *Nicodemus* was saturated in religious knowledge and had witnessed Jesus' work (2:13-24), but he had not experienced spiritual rebirth. • *a Pharisee:* See note on 1:24. He was elite, proud of his

spiritual purity, and well educated in Jewish law.

3:2 *After dark:* Nicodemus might have feared public association with Jesus. Night also symbolizes the realm of evil, untruth, and unbelief (9:4; 11:10; 13:30).

3:3 *born again:* Or *born from above;* also in 3:7. John's expression "from above" (3:31; 19:11) means "from God." To experience spiritual rebirth, a person must be completely renewed through God's power. • Nicodemus interpreted Jesus' words physically; he demonstrated that those in darkness, who do not have spiritual rebirth, cannot understand Jesus or other "heavenly things" (3:12). Jesus sometimes used ironic misunderstanding as a teaching strategy (see "Misunderstanding" at 7:32-36, p. 1785).

⁴"What do you mean?" exclaimed Nicodemus. "How can an old man go back into his mother's womb and be born again?"

⁵Jesus replied, "I assure you, no one can enter the Kingdom of God without being born of water and the Spirit. ⁶ᵉHumans can reproduce only ᵉhuman life, but the Holy Spirit gives birth to spiritual life. ⁷So don't be surprised when I say, 'You must be ᶠborn again.' ⁸The wind blows wherever it wants. Just as you can hear the wind but can't tell where it comes from or where it is going, so you can't explain how people are born of the Spirit."

⁹"How are these things possible?" Nicodemus asked.

¹⁰Jesus replied, "You are a respected Jewish teacher, and yet you don't understand these things? ¹¹I assure you, we tell you what we know and have seen, and yet you won't believe our testimony. ¹²But if you don't believe me when I tell you about earthly things, how can you possibly believe if I tell you about heavenly things? ¹³No one has ever gone to heaven and returned. But the Son of Man has come down from heaven. ¹⁴And as Moses lifted up the bronze snake on a pole in the wilderness, so the Son of Man must be lifted up, ¹⁵so that everyone who believes in him will have eternal life.

¹⁶"For God loved the world so much that he gave his ᵍone and only Son, so that everyone who believes in him will not perish but have eternal life. ¹⁷God sent his Son into the world not to judge the world, but to save the world through him.

¹⁸"There is no judgment against anyone who believes in him. But anyone who does not believe in him has already been judged for not believing in God's ʰone and only Son. ¹⁹And the judgment is based on this fact: God's light came into the world, but people loved the darkness more than the light, for their actions were evil. ²⁰All who do evil hate the light and refuse to go near it for fear their sins will be exposed. ²¹But those who do what is right come to the light so others can see that they are doing what God wants."

John the Baptist Exalts Jesus

²²Then Jesus and his disciples left Jerusalem and went into the Judean countryside. Jesus spent some time with them there, baptizing people. ²³At this time John the Baptist was baptizing at Aenon, near Salim, because there was plenty of water there; and people kept coming to him for baptism. ²⁴(This was before John was thrown into prison.) ²⁵A debate broke out between John's disciples and a certain Jew over ceremonial cleansing. ²⁶So John's disciples came to him and said, "Rabbi, the man you met on the other side of the Jordan River, the one you identified as the

Cross-references

3:5 Ezek 36:26-27; Titus 3:5; 2 Pet 1:11
3:6 John 1:13; Rom 8:15-16; 1 Cor 15:50; Gal 4:6; ᵉsarx (4561) ▸Rom 8:4
3:7 ᶠanōthen gennaō (0509, 1080) ▸John 3:31
3:8 Eccl 11:5
3:13 John 6:38, 42; Eph 4:8-10
3:14 Num 21:8-9; John 8:28; 12:34
3:15 John 20:31; 1 Jn 5:11-12
3:16 Rom 5:8; 8:32; 1 Jn 4:9-10; 5:13; ᵍmonogenēs (3439) ▸John 3:18
3:17 John 12:47
3:18 John 5:24; ʰmonogenēs (3439) ▸Heb 11:17
3:19 John 1:5, 9; 8:12; 9:5; 12:46
3:20 Eph 5:11-13
3:21 1 Jn 1:6
3:22 John 3:26; 4:1-2

. . . .

3:5 *water and the Spirit* (or *and spirit;* the Greek word *Spirit* can also be translated *wind;* see note on 3:8): John the Baptist baptized with water; Jesus baptizes with the Spirit (1:33).

3:6 *the Holy Spirit gives birth to spiritual life:* Literally *what is born of the Spirit is spirit.*

3:7 The Greek word translated *You* is plural; also in 3:12.

3:8 *Wind* translates the same word in Greek as *spirit* (Greek *pneuma*). The wind is an apt image for *the Spirit,* who is sent from heaven and cannot be contained or controlled.

3:13 There is great distance between this world and *heaven* (see 1:51; 3:31; 6:38, 42). Jesus bridged that distance, validating his divine status by defeating death and returning to heaven (16:5-11). • *Son of Man:* Some manuscripts add *who lives in heaven.* "Son of Man" is a title Jesus used for himself.

3:14-15 Jesus was *lifted up* on the cross so that all people could understand the way of salvation, look to him in faith, and *have eternal life.*

3:15 *everyone who believes in him will have eternal life:* Or *everyone*

who believes will have eternal life in him. The Greek syntax allows for either interpretation.

3:16-21 Because there are no quotation marks around Jesus' speech in Greek, translators debate where Jesus' speech ends and John's commentary begins; 3:16-21 might be John's commentary.

3:16 The truth that *God loved the world* is basic to Christian understanding (1 Jn 4:9-10). God's love extends beyond the limits of race and nation, even to those who oppose him (see "The World" at 17:5-26, p. 1807). • The *Son* came to save—not condemn (3:17)—men and women who habitually embrace the darkness (3:19-21).

3:18 As light penetrates and exposes the world's darkness, God's *judgment* on the world *has already* begun. Those who see this light and recognize the tragedy of their own situation have the responsibility of *believing in God's . . . Son* (3:16-17).

3:19-20 When *people* live in spiritual *darkness,* they do not desire to be enlightened by Jesus, "the light of the world" (8:12; 9:5). Evil and darkness do not ignore the light; they wage war

against it, trying to bring it down. But the darkness cannot extinguish the light (1:5). Those who refuse to believe live in darkness (cp. 13:30) and stumble because they cannot see (11:10). In the end, however, *their sins will be exposed* (5:28-30; Rev 20:11-15).

3:21 *can see that they are doing what God wants:* Or *can see God at work in what he is doing.* The Greek syntax allows for either interpretation.

3:22-36 John the Baptist identifies Jesus as the one who is truly from above (3:31); this requires John's followers to shift their allegiance to Jesus.

3:22 *Jesus spent some time . . . baptizing:* See 4:2, which clarifies that Jesus' disciples did the baptizing.

3:24 *Before John was thrown into prison* (see Matt 14:1-12; Mark 1:14; 6:14-29; Luke 3:19-20), he and Jesus worked together at the Jordan River. Once John was arrested, Jesus moved north into Galilee (Mark 1:14).

3:25 *a certain Jew:* Some manuscripts read *some Jews.*

3:26 *everybody is going to him:* Jesus' popularity made some of John's followers envious.

Cross references (left margin):

3:24 — Matt 4:12
3:26 — John 1:7, 34
3:27 — John 19:11; 1 Cor 4:7; Heb 5:4
3:28 — Mal 3:1; John 1:20, 23
3:29 — Matt 9:15; 2 Cor 11:2; Rev 21:9
3:31 — 1 Jn 4:5; *anōthen* (0509) ▸ 1 Pet 1:3
3:33 — 1 Jn 5:10
3:34 — Luke 4:18
3:35 — Matt 28:18
3:36 — 1 Jn 5:12-13; *orgē* (3709) ▸ Rom 1:18
4:5-6 — Gen 33:19; Josh 24:32

Messiah, is also baptizing people. And everybody is going to him instead of coming to us." ²⁷John replied, "No one can receive anything unless God gives it from heaven. ²⁸You yourselves know how plainly I told you, 'I am not the Messiah. I am only here to prepare the way for him.' ²⁹It is the bridegroom who marries the bride, and the best man is simply glad to stand with him and hear his vows. Therefore, I am filled with joy at his success. ³⁰He must become greater and greater, and I must become less and less.

³¹"He has come from ʰabove and is greater than anyone else. We are of the earth, and we speak of earthly things, but he has come from heaven and is greater than anyone else. ³²He testifies about what he has seen and heard, but how few believe what he tells them! ³³Anyone who accepts his testimony can affirm that God is true. ³⁴For he is sent by God. He speaks God's words, for God gives him the Spirit without limit. ³⁵The Father loves his Son and has put everything into his hands. ³⁶And anyone who believes in God's Son has eternal life. Anyone who doesn't obey the Son will never experience eternal life but remains under God's ʲangry judgment."

The Samaritan Woman at the Well

4 Jesus knew the Pharisees had heard that he was baptizing and making more disciples than John ²(though Jesus himself didn't baptize them—his disciples did). ³So he left Judea and returned to Galilee.

⁴He had to go through Samaria on the way. ⁵Eventually he came to the Samaritan village of Sychar, near the field that Jacob gave to his son Joseph. ⁶Jacob's well was there; and Jesus, tired from the long walk, sat wearily beside the well about noontime. ⁷Soon a Samaritan woman came to draw water, and Jesus said to her, "Please give me a drink." ⁸He was alone at the time because his disciples had gone into the village to buy some food.

. . . .

Believing (3:10-18)

Cross references:
John 1:12-13; 3:36; 4:39, 42; 5:24; 6:35-36; 7:38-39; 9:35-38; 11:25-27; 12:37; 20:25-31; Gen 15:6; 2 Kgs 17:14; Isa 28:16; Mark 1:15; 9:23-24; Acts 10:43; 13:39; Rom 1:5, 16-17; 3:25; 10:9-10; Gal 3:5-7; Heb 4:3; 1 Jn 3:23; 5:10, 13

Believing occupies a central place in John's Gospel. John does not use the noun *faith* that appears frequently elsewhere in the NT (e.g., see Matt 8:8-10; Mark 11:22-24; Acts 20:21; Rom 1:17; 3:27-31; 4:3-5; Heb 11:1-39; Jas 2:14-24; 1 Pet 1:5-7). John prefers the verb *believe* to underscore that faith is not static like a doctrine or a dogma, but dynamic, requiring action. In John's Gospel, "believing" in Jesus is the trait of all true disciples.

In the Gospel of John, the verb translated "believe" is often followed by the Greek preposition *eis* ("into"). No parallel exists for this in ancient Greek usage. For John, faith is not a status, but an investment in the person of Jesus. Faith means accepting who Jesus is and what he claims to be. Faith constitutes a commitment to let his call change the way we live. Faith is the work God wants from us (6:29) as we abide in Jesus' word, as we love him, and as we obey his commands (8:31; 15:1-17; see 1 Jn 5:10).

. . . .

3:27-35 John the Baptist's speech was inspired by two issues: (1) Some had questioned the legitimacy of his baptism (see 1:26); and (2) his disciples were concerned that people were beginning to follow Jesus instead of John (3:26).

3:29 John the Baptist saw Jesus as the *bridegroom* and himself as *the best man*. His response deflected glory from himself and elevated Jesus' stature.

3:31 Jesus had *come from above*, so he was uniquely able to reveal the Father (1:18; 3:13). • Some manuscripts do not include *and is greater than anyone else*.

3:34-35 The Father *gives* the Son *the Spirit without limit* as a sign of his profound love (3:35). It also illustrates Jesus' divinity. John presents the one God as three persons (cp. 1 Jn 5:12).

3:36 God gave the gift of *eternal life*, promising new life and intimacy in a present experience with God. • Those who reject the Son will not see life. The world in its darkness stands under *God's angry judgment* (Rom 1–3).

4:1-42 At a historic well in Samaria, Jesus offered himself as living water. Jesus engaged and confronted people with the revelation of God, and they either followed or fell away. • The *Samaritan woman* contrasted with Nicodemus at every turn: a woman (not a man), a Samaritan (not a Jew), a sinner (not righteous), and an outcast (not one of Israel's rabbis). While Nicodemus fell silent and never responded to Jesus' challenges (3:1-21), this woman acknowledged Jesus as Lord, remained in the light, and exhibited signs of discipleship (see 1:35-51).

4:1 *Jesus:* Some manuscripts read *The Lord.*

4:2 *Jesus himself didn't baptize* anyone, but left water baptism to *his disciples.* After his glorification on the cross (7:37-

39), Jesus baptized in the Holy Spirit (1:33; Acts 2:4).

4:3 After John the Baptist had been imprisoned (see Mark 6:14-29), Jesus *left Judea* (cp. Mark 1:14).

4:4-6 In going north to Galilee, Jesus took the less-preferred route through *Samaria*. Samaria had a long history of tension with Judea (see 2 Kgs 17:24-41; Ezra 4:1-5; Neh 4:1-23; 6:1-19). In Jesus' day, harsh racial and cultural conflict existed between Jews and Samaritans. Jews normally avoided Samaria by first going east to Jericho, then following the Jordan Valley north. • *Sychar* was probably in the region of Shechem. Jesus had come to *Jacob's well*; Jacob had owned land near Shechem (Gen 33:18-19).

4:7 Due to the heat, it was customary for the women to *draw water* in early morning or evening. However, this woman lived in isolation, separated from her community. Jesus was compassionate toward outcasts.

9The woman was surprised, for Jews refuse to have anything to do with Samaritans. She said to Jesus, "You are a Jew, and I am a Samaritan woman. Why are you asking me for a drink?"

10Jesus replied, "If you only knew the gift God has for you and who you are speaking to, you would ask me, and I would give you living water."

11"But sir, you don't have a rope or a bucket," she said, "and this well is very deep. Where would you get this living water? 12And besides, do you think you're greater than our ancestor Jacob, who gave us this well? How can you offer better water than he and his sons and his animals enjoyed?"

13Jesus replied, "Anyone who drinks this water will soon become thirsty again. 14But those who drink the water I give will never be thirsty again. It becomes a fresh, bubbling spring within them, giving them eternal life."

15"Please, sir," the woman said, "give me this water! Then I'll never be thirsty again, and I won't have to come here to get water."

16"Go and get your husband," Jesus told her.

17"I don't have a husband," the woman replied.

Jesus said, "You're right! You don't have a husband—18for you have had five husbands, and you aren't even married to the man you're living with now. You certainly spoke the truth!"

19"Sir," the woman said, "you must be a prophet. 20So tell me, why is it that you Jews insist that Jerusalem is the only place of worship, while we Samaritans claim it is here at Mount Gerizim, where our ancestors worshiped?"

21Jesus replied, "Believe me, dear woman, the time is coming when it will no longer matter whether you worship the Father on this mountain or in Jerusalem. 22You Samaritans know very little about the one you worship, while we Jews know all about him, for salvation comes through the Jews. 23But the time is coming—indeed it's here now—when true worshipers will worship the Father in spirit and in truth. The Father is looking for those who will worship him that way. 24For God is Spirit, so those who worship him must worship in spirit and in truth."

25The woman said, "I know the kMessiah is coming—the one who is called Christ. When he comes, he will explain everything to us."

26Then Jesus told her, "I AM the Messiah!"

27Just then his disciples came back. They were shocked to find him talking to a woman, but none of them had the nerve to ask, "What do you want with her?" or "Why are you talking to her?" 28The woman left

4:9
Ezra 4:1-3; 9–10
Matt 10:5
Luke 9:52-53
John 8:48
Acts 10:45
1 Cor 12:13

4:10
Isa 12:3; 44:3
Jer 2:13; 17:13
John 7:37-39
Rev 7:17; 21:6; 22:17

4:14
John 6:35; 7:38

4:15
John 6:34

4:19
Matt 21:46
John 7:40; 9:17

4:20
Deut 11:29; 12:5-14
Josh 8:33

4:21
Mal 1:11
1 Tim 2:8

4:22
2 Kgs 17:28-41
Isa 2:3
Rom 3:1-2; 9:4-5

4:23-24
2 Cor 3:17-18
Phil 3:3

4:25
Deut 18:15
kmessias (3323)
› Acts 2:31

4:26
Mark 14:61-62
John 9:37

. . . .

4:9 *The woman was surprised* because social taboos would keep a Jewish teacher like Jesus from speaking to her (4:18). However, Jesus did not let social taboos constrain him from giving her what she truly needed. • Some manuscripts do not include the first sentence of this verse.

4:10 Shechem had no rivers and thus no *living water* (see "Living Water," facing page). However, Jesus was speaking symbolically: This gift from God was the Holy Spirit (7:37-39).

4:11 Jacob's *well* was more than 100 feet (30 meters) deep, and required a long *rope* for drawing water. The woman misunderstood Jesus' words because she was still in darkness (see "Misunderstanding" at 7:32-36, p. 1785).

4:12 *our ancestor Jacob:* The Samaritan woman appealed with reverence to the sacred traditions attached to the well rather than to the presence of God before her.

4:14 The notion of *a fresh, bubbling spring* was a powerful image in the dry climate of Israel. Those who come to God will neither hunger nor thirst (see Isa 49:10; 55:1-3; Jer 2:13).

4:15 The woman asked Jesus for *this water,* but she did not grasp the spiritual implications of his words. To overcome the spiritual barrier, Jesus addressed her sin (4:16-18).

4:16-18 Immorality blocked the woman's understanding. Her marital affairs, including having *five husbands,* underscored her sinful life.

4:19-20 The woman dodged Jesus' moral probing and brought up the historical ethnic division between Jews and Samaritans.

4:19 *a prophet:* Jesus revealed knowledge about the woman (4:16-18) that was inaccessible to the average person (cp. 1:48). • As the woman's understanding of Jesus unfolded, her names for him became increasingly well informed. Earlier she recognized him as *a Jew* (4:9) and called him *sir* (4:11, 15, 19). Later she thought he might be *the Messiah* (4:29). Finally, the people of the village recognized him as *Savior of the world* (4:42). Her growing understanding of Jesus' identity is a testimony to John's readers (see 20:31).

4:20 The Samaritans worshiped *at Mount Gerizim* (literally *on this moun-*

tain), which towered above Shechem. Both were important OT locations (see Gen 12:6-7; 33:19; Deut 11:29; Josh 8:33; 24:1, 25, 32).

4:21-22 Jesus affirmed that the *Jews* had preserved the right understanding of *the one you worship.* • *salvation comes through the Jews:* God gave the Jews a special relationship with him, and the Messiah was to be a Jew (see also Rom 9:4-5).

4:24 *in spirit and in truth:* One Greek preposition governs both words (literally *in spirit and truth*) and makes them a single concept. True worship occurs as God's Spirit reveals God's truth and reality to the worshiper. Jesus Christ is the Truth (14:6; cp. 14:17; 15:26).

4:26 *I AM the Messiah* (or *"The 'I AM' is here"*; or *"I am the LORD"*; Greek reads *"I am, the one speaking to you"*; see Exod 3:14): Jesus' phrase was unusual and emphatic, and it suggests identity with God (see 8:58; Exod 3:14).

4:27-30 *The woman* was tentative about Jesus' identity (4:29), yet she ran to *the village* and told *everyone* to *come and see.* Testifying to others is a mark of discipleship (see 1:39, 46).

4:29
John 7:26

4:34
John 5:30, 36; 6:38;
17:4

4:35
Matt 9:37
Luke 10:2

4:37
Job 31:8
Mic 6:15
1 Cor 3:6

4:42
Luke 2:11
1 Jn 4:14
ᵃsōtēr (4990)
  ▸ Acts 5:31

4:43-54
//Matt 8:5-13
//Luke 7:1-10

4:44
Matt 13:57
Luke 4:24

4:45
John 2:23

4:46
John 2:1-11

her water jar beside the well and ran back to the village, telling everyone, 29"Come and see a man who told me everything I ever did! Could he possibly be the Messiah?" 30So the people came streaming from the village to see him.

31Meanwhile, the disciples were urging Jesus, "Rabbi, eat something."

32But Jesus replied, "I have a kind of food you know nothing about."

33"Did someone bring him food while we were gone?" the disciples asked each other. 34Then Jesus explained: "My nourishment comes from doing the will of God, who sent me, and from finishing his work. 35You know the saying, 'Four months between planting and harvest.' But I say, wake up and look around. The fields are already ripe for harvest. 36The harvesters are paid good wages, and the fruit they harvest is people brought to eternal life. What joy awaits both the planter and the harvester alike! 37You know the saying, 'One plants and another harvests.' And it's true. 38I sent you to harvest where you didn't plant; others had already done the work, and now you will get to gather the harvest."

Many Samaritans Believe

39Many Samaritans from the village believed in Jesus because the woman had said, "He told me everything I ever did!" 40When they came out to see him, they begged him to stay in their village. So he stayed for two days, 41long enough for many more to hear his message and believe. 42Then they said to the woman, "Now we believe, not just because of what you told us, but because we have heard him ourselves. Now we know that he is indeed the ªSavior of the world."

Jesus Heals a Government Official's Son

43At the end of the two days, Jesus went on to Galilee. 44He himself had said that a prophet is not honored in his own hometown. 45Yet the Galileans welcomed him, for they had been in Jerusalem at the Passover celebration and had seen everything he did there.

46As he traveled through Galilee, he came to Cana, where he had turned the water into wine. There was a government official in nearby Capernaum whose son was very sick. 47When he heard that Jesus had come from Judea to Galilee, he went and begged

. . . .

Living Water (4:10-14)

John 7:38-39
Lev 14:5-6, 50-51;
15:13
Num 19:17-19
Song 4:15
Jer 2:13; 17:13
Jas 3:11-12

In Israel, a land that frequently experienced drought, people were keenly aware of water sources and water quality. Springs and rivers that ran all year were few, so the land relied on cisterns to catch and store the winter rains and wells to tap underground water tables. In Jewish culture, "dead water" referred to standing and stored water. "Living water" referred to moving water, as in rivers, springs, and rainfall. Such water was precious because it was fresh. Because it came directly from God, it was used for ritual washings (see Lev 14:5-6, 50-51; 15:13; Num 19:17-19).

The distinction between "dead" and "living" water explains why the woman of Samaria was so perplexed when Jesus offered her living water (4:12). Samaria has no river. If Jacob had to dig a well there, how could Jesus offer superior water?

Jesus mentioned living water again in Jerusalem at the autumn Festival of Shelters (7:37-39). The festival, which fell during a dry time of year, included an emphasis on water. In this setting, Jesus stepped forward and made an extravagant claim: Anyone looking for living water should come to him and drink. Jesus is the source of living water; he came directly from God and brought divine renewal.

. . . .

4:32-34 While Jesus spoke to the Samaritan woman, the disciples were gone buying food (4:8); now they urged Jesus to eat. Jesus continued to speak symbolically, but they did not understand him (4:33). Later, when the disciples received the Spirit, they understood (2:22). Jesus received his nourishment from doing what his Father told him to do (see 5:30; 6:38; 7:18; 8:50; 9:4; 10:37-38; 12:49-50).

4:35 *Four months between planting and harvest:* Jesus cited a local parable to contrast the natural harvest with his

own. It was harvest time in Samaria, and the fields were *ripe* (literally *white*). Jesus, however, had planted seed at the well and now was *already* reaping the *harvest* of belief among the Samaritans (4:39-42).

4:38 *others:* Jesus might have meant John the Baptist, or he might have been referring to the work he had just done with the Samaritan woman.

4:39-40 *Many Samaritans:* The religiously sophisticated "chosen people" in Jerusalem did not respond to Jesus with faith (ch 3). By contrast, many *believed*

in Jesus because of the testimony of this outcast woman.

4:42 The Samaritans had experienced for themselves that Jesus was true. Their name for Jesus, *Savior of the world* (also used in 1 Jn 4:14), demonstrated that the Samaritans were keenly aware of their distance from Judaism. Jesus' ministry was not simply for Jews, but for all people (1:4-12; cp. 12:20-26).

4:44-45 Unlike Jesus' fellow Jews, *the Galileans welcomed him*, but their welcome was based on awe of Jesus' miracles (cp. 2:23-25), not true faith.

Jesus to come to Capernaum to heal his son, who was about to die.

⁴⁸Jesus asked, "Will you never believe in me unless you see miraculous signs and wonders?"

⁴⁹The official pleaded, "Lord, please come now before my little boy dies."

⁵⁰Then Jesus told him, "Go back home. Your son will live!" And the man believed what Jesus said and started home.

⁵¹While the man was on his way, some of his servants met him with the news that his son was alive and well. ⁵²He asked them when the boy had begun to get better, and they replied, "Yesterday afternoon at one o'clock his fever suddenly disappeared!" ⁵³Then the father realized that that was the very time Jesus had told him, "Your son will live." And he and his entire household believed in Jesus. ⁵⁴This was the second miraculous sign Jesus did in Galilee after coming from Judea.

Jesus and the Sabbath (5:1-47)
Jesus Heals a Man on the Sabbath

5 Afterward Jesus returned to Jerusalem for one of the Jewish holy days. ²Inside the city, near the Sheep Gate, was the pool of Bethesda, with five covered porches. ³Crowds of sick people—blind, lame, or paralyzed—lay on the porches. ⁵One of the men lying there had been sick for thirty- eight years. ⁶When Jesus saw him and knew he had been ill for a long time, he asked him, "Would you like to get well?"

⁷"I can't, sir," the sick man said, "for I have no one to put me into the pool when the water bubbles up. Someone else always gets there ahead of me."

⁸Jesus told him, "Stand up, pick up your mat, and walk!"

⁹Instantly, the man was healed! He rolled up his sleeping mat and began walking! But this miracle happened on the Sabbath, ¹⁰so the Jewish leaders objected. They said to the man who was cured, "You can't work on the Sabbath! The law doesn't allow you to carry that sleeping mat!"

¹¹But he replied, "The man who healed me told me, 'Pick up your mat and walk.' "

¹²"Who said such a thing as that?" they demanded.

¹³The man didn't know, for Jesus had disappeared into the crowd. ¹⁴But afterward Jesus found him in the Temple and told him, "Now you are well; so stop sinning, or something even worse may happen to you." ¹⁵Then the man went and told the Jewish leaders that it was Jesus who had healed him.

Jesus Claims to Be the Son of God
¹⁶So the Jewish leaders began harassing Jesus for breaking the Sabbath rules. ¹⁷But

4:48 1 Cor 1:22
4:50 Matt 8:13; Mark 7:29
4:53 Acts 11:14; 16:14-15
4:54 John 2:11
5:1 Lev 23:1-2; Deut 16:1; John 2:13
5:2 Neh 3:1; 12:39
5:8 Matt 9:6; Mark 2:11; Luke 5:24
5:10 Neh 13:15-20; Jer 17:21; Matt 12:2
5:14 John 8:11
5:17 John 9:4; 14:10
5:18 John 1:1, 18; 10:30, 33; 20:28; Phil 2:6; Titus 2:13; 2 Pet 1:1; 1 Jn 5:21

4:48 Jesus sharply criticized the Galileans who desired *miraculous signs and wonders* before they would believe (see "Miraculous Signs" at 2:1-11, p. 1772; see also 6:30).

4:50 *Your son will live!* Jesus also healed the centurion's slave (Matt 8:5-13) and the Phoenician woman's daughter (Matt 15:21-28) from a distance.

4:53 Just like many others (2:23; 4:39), the official and his *household believed in Jesus* because of the miracle.

4:54 *second miraculous sign . . . in Galilee:* Two miracles at Cana (2:11; 4:46) frame this section of John's Gospel.

5:1–10:42 In this section Jesus appears at a series of Jewish festivals and uses their imagery to reveal more profound truths about himself. He appears at Sabbath (ch 5), Passover (ch 6), the Festival of Shelters (chs 7–9), and Hanukkah (ch 10). In each case, Jesus himself replaces some vital element in the ceremonies of the festival.

5:1-40 This chapter reads like a courtroom drama, with a description of the crime (5:1-15), followed by a decision to prosecute (5:16), a description of the charges (5:18), and Jesus' defense (5:17, 19-40).

5:1 *one of the Jewish holy days:* Because Jesus *returned to Jerusalem* for the celebration, it was probably one of the three pilgrimage festivals of Judaism (see Exod 23:14-17; Deut 16:16). These festivals lasted one week.

5:2 Greek copyists who had never been to Jerusalem had difficulty interpreting and spelling the name *Bethesda:* Other manuscripts read *Beth-zatha;* still others read *Bethsaida.* The best choice is *Beth-esda* ("house of flowing").

5:3 The pool of Bethesda had become a healing sanctuary for *crowds of sick people* who believed miraculous cures were possible. • Some manuscripts add an expanded conclusion to verse 3 and all of verse 4: *waiting for a certain movement of the water, ⁴for an angel of the Lord came from time to time and stirred up the water. And the first person to step in after the water was stirred was healed of whatever disease he had.* Most scholars believe this was not part of John's original text, but it represents an ancient tradition that provided helpful background information.

5:5 No social program helped this man,

who had been ill for *thirty-eight years.* Hygiene and mobility were impossible, and he likely begged for a living from people who came to use the pool (see 5:7). His situation seemed hopeless.

5:8-9 Jesus healed the sick man *instantly,* only asking for his obedience. As proof of healing, Jesus told him to *pick up* his *mat and walk.* • Jesus worked this miracle *on the Sabbath,* a weekly day of rest on which all work was prohibited (based on Gen 2:2; Exod 20:8). Jewish tradition outlined thirty-nine categories of work that were not allowed (*Mishnah Shabbat* 7:2). Carrying something such as a *sleeping mat* from one place to another was banned (5:10). Therefore, the healed man broke the tradition by obeying Jesus' command.

5:12 *Who said such a thing?* The story ominously turns from a miraculous wonder to a Sabbath crime requiring the identity of the healer who breached tradition.

5:14 *stop sinning:* Though the man had been healed physically, he still needed to learn obedience to the Lord. The man's next action (5:15) might indicate that he didn't listen.

5:16 *harassing:* Or *persecuting.*

5:19
John 8:28; 12:49;
14:10

5:21
John 11:25
ᵇzōopoieō (2227)
‣ John 6:63

5:22
John 3:17; 5:27

5:23
1 Jn 2:23

5:24
John 3:15; 20:30-31
1 Jn 3:14; 5:13

5:25
John 4:21; 6:63, 68

5:26
John 1:4; 6:57
1 Jn 5:11-12

5:27
John 9:39
Acts 10:42; 17:31

5:29
Dan 12:2
Matt 25:46
Acts 24:15
ᶜanastasis (0386)
‣ John 11:24

5:30
John 5:19; 6:38

5:31
John 8:13-14

5:32
John 8:18

Jesus replied, "My Father is always working, and so am I." ¹⁸So the Jewish leaders tried all the harder to find a way to kill him. For he not only broke the Sabbath, he called God his Father, thereby making himself equal with God.

¹⁹So Jesus explained, "I tell you the truth, the Son can do nothing by himself. He does only what he sees the Father doing. Whatever the Father does, the Son also does. ²⁰For the Father loves the Son and shows him everything he is doing. In fact, the Father will show him how to do even greater works than healing this man. Then you will truly be astonished. ²¹For just as the Father ᵇgives life to those he raises from the dead, so the Son ᵇgives life to anyone he wants. ²²In addition, the Father judges no one. Instead, he has given the Son absolute authority to judge, ²³so that everyone will honor the Son, just as they honor the Father. Anyone who does not honor the Son is certainly not honoring the Father who sent him.

²⁴"I tell you the truth, those who listen to my message and believe in God who sent me have eternal life. They will never be con-

demned for their sins, but they have already passed from death into life.

²⁵"And I assure you that the time is coming, indeed it's here now, when the dead will hear my voice—the voice of the Son of God. And those who listen will live. ²⁶The Father has life in himself, and he has granted that same life-giving power to his Son. ²⁷And he has given him authority to judge everyone because he is the Son of Man. ²⁸Don't be so surprised! Indeed, the time is coming when all the dead in their graves will hear the voice of God's Son, ²⁹and they will rise again. Those who have done good will ᶜrise to experience eternal life, and those who have continued in evil will ᶜrise to experience judgment. ³⁰I can do nothing on my own. I judge as God tells me. Therefore, my judgment is just, because I carry out the will of the one who sent me, not my own will.

Witnesses to Jesus
³¹"If I were to testify on my own behalf, my testimony would not be valid. ³²But someone else is also testifying about me, and I assure you that everything he says about me is true. ³³In fact, you sent investigators

. . . .

The Jewish Leaders (5:9-18)

John 1:19-24;
2:18-20; 7:1, 10-13,
35-36; 9:13-34;
11:45-54; 12:41-43;
18:28-36; 19:6-8, 12-
16, 31, 38; 20:19
Acts 6:10-12; 7:54-
58; 12:11; 21:11;
25:1-3, 7; 26:1-11;
28:17-24
2 Cor 11:24

Jesus experienced numerous conflicts with Jewish leaders throughout his public ministry. These opponents viewed themselves as defending the Temple and its sacrifices or the synagogue and its teachings. In Jesus' final week in Jerusalem, these debates intensified (Matt 23) and contributed to the case against him.

When John wrote his Gospel, Christians were being persecuted by local Jewish synagogues, and the language of their debate spilled over into John's Gospel (see Acts 14:19; 1 Thes 2:14; cp. Gal 1:13-14). The Greek term translated "the Jewish leaders" could be literally translated "the Jews." This word took on a technical meaning: It refers to the Temple leadership who confronted Jesus, judged him, and orchestrated his crucifixion (see 1:19; 2:18; 5:9-18; 9:18-22).

This is important because the NT—and particularly John's Gospel—has often been seen as anti-Semitic. But the truth is that Jesus, who was himself a Jew, did not wrestle with "Jews" in general. His antagonists were the "Jewish leaders"—the brokers of religious power in first-century Jerusalem.

. . . .

5:17 *My Father is always working, and so am I:* Although work was prohibited on the Sabbath, even rabbis agreed that God worked on the Sabbath in giving life (births) and in taking life (deaths). The heart of Jesus' defense was to compare himself to God; the Jewish leaders objected to this claim of divine privilege.

5:19-30 Jesus claimed that his work on the Sabbath was the same as God's work on the Sabbath. Jesus claimed to be equal with God, doing the things God does. Yet he submitted to God's will, doing *only what . . . the Father* willed.

5:21 Most Jews firmly believed in resurrection but viewed it as something God

alone could accomplish. Jesus claimed that he *gives life.*

5:22 In addition to giving life, Jesus claimed the *absolute authority to judge,* which belongs to God alone.

5:23 *the Father . . . sent him:* In the ancient world, a person could send an authorized representative to seal a contract or make an authoritative decision. Jesus claimed to be God's representative, so obeying him is the same as obeying God, and dishonoring Jesus is dishonoring God.

5:24 Jesus is the giver of *life* as well as the judge (see 5:21-22), but he never works independently of the Father.

5:27 *Son of Man* is a title Jesus used for himself.

5:31-40 God's law requires more than one witness in a trial (Deut 17:6), so Jesus acknowledged that his own testimony was admissible only when confirmed by other witnesses. Thus, he introduced a series of witnesses for his defense.

5:32 The first witness for Jesus' defense was God himself. Jesus might have had in mind God's voice at his baptism (Mark 1:11) or the presence of God that enabled Jesus to perform miracles.

to listen to John the Baptist, and his testimony about me was true. 34Of course, I have no need of human witnesses, but I say these things so you might be saved. 35John was like a burning and shining lamp, and you were excited for a while about his message. 36But I have a greater witness than John—my teachings and my miracles. The Father gave me these works to accomplish, and they prove that he sent me. 37And the Father who sent me has testified about me himself. You have never heard his voice or seen him face to face, 38and you do not have his message in your hearts, because you do not believe me—the one he sent to you.

39"You search the Scriptures because you think they give you eternal life. But the Scriptures point to me! 40Yet you refuse to come to me to receive this life.

41"Your approval means nothing to me, 42because I know you don't have God's dlove within you. 43For I have come to you in my Father's name, and you have rejected me. Yet if others come in their own name, you gladly welcome them. 44No wonder you can't believe! For you gladly honor each other, but you don't care about the honor that comes from the one who alone is God.

45"Yet it isn't I who will accuse you before the Father. Moses will accuse you! Yes, Moses, in whom you put your hopes. 46If you really believed Moses, you would believe me, because he wrote about me. 47But since you don't believe what he wrote, how will you believe what I say?"

Jesus and Passover (6:1-71)
Jesus Feeds Five Thousand
John 6:1-15 // Matt 14:13-21 // Mark 6:32-44 // Luke 9:10b-17

6 After this, Jesus crossed over to the far side of the Sea of Galilee, also known as the Sea of Tiberias. 2A huge crowd kept following him wherever he went, because they saw his miraculous signs as he healed the sick. 3Then Jesus climbed a hill and sat down with his disciples around him. 4(It was nearly time for the Jewish Passover celebration.) 5Jesus soon saw a huge crowd of people coming to look for him. Turning to Philip, he asked, "Where can we buy bread to feed all these people?" 6He was testing Philip, for he already knew what he was going to do.

7Philip replied, "Even if we worked for months, we wouldn't have enough money to feed them!"

8Then Andrew, Simon Peter's brother, spoke up. 9"There's a young boy here with five barley loaves and two fish. But what good is that with this huge crowd?"

10"Tell everyone to sit down," Jesus said. So they all sat down on the grassy slopes. (The men alone numbered about 5,000.) 11Then Jesus took the loaves, gave thanks to God, and distributed them to the people. Afterward he did the same with the fish. And they all ate as much as they wanted. 12After everyone was full, Jesus told his disciples, "Now gather the leftovers, so that nothing is wasted." 13So they picked up the pieces and filled twelve baskets with scraps left by the

5:36
John 10:25, 38; 14:11; 15:24
1 Jn 5:9

5:37
Deut 4:12
John 1:18; 8:18
1 Tim 1:17

5:38
1 Jn 2:14

5:39
Luke 24:27, 44
Acts 13:27
Rom 2:17-20

5:41
John 12:43

5:42
dagapē (0026)
John 15:9

5:45
John 9:28
Rom 2:17

5:46
Gen 3:15
Deut 18:15, 18
Luke 24:27, 44
Acts 26:22-23

5:47
Luke 16:31

6:1-13
//Matt 14:13-21
//Mark 6:32-44
//Luke 9:10-17

6:4
John 11:55

6:5
John 1:43

6:8
John 1:40

6:9
2 Kgs 4:43
John 21:9, 13

. . . .

5:33-35 Jesus' second witness was *John the Baptist*, who pointed to Jesus as Messiah (1:29-34).

5:36 Jesus' third witness, his *teachings* and *miracles*, were signs that unveiled his true identity and pointed to the Father who sent him.

5:39-40 Jesus' fourth witness was *the Scriptures*. The OT pointed to the Messiah, and Jesus fulfilled its prophecies (see Luke 24:25-27).

5:41-47 Jewish trials sought to discover the truth. Falsely accused defendants could not only prove their innocence but also prosecute their accusers, which Jesus did here.

5:42 Jesus charged that the Jewish leaders did not *have God's love within* them. Without God's love, it was impossible for them to understand the things he was doing.

5:44 The Jewish leaders pursued *honor* and prestige from *each other*. They loved religious life, but they had forgotten to love God. This hypocrisy

made them liable to judgment (5:45-46). • *from the one who alone is God:* Some manuscripts read *from the only One.*

5:45-46 Jesus' fifth and final witness was *Moses*, the founding father of Judaism. John had already compared Jesus with Moses (1:17; see also 6:14-15). The Jewish leaders were ignoring Moses' clear words about the Messiah (e.g., Deut 18:15).

6:1-71 Each story in this chapter uses the setting of the Passover Festival (6:4) to communicate a deeper meaning.

6:1-15 Jesus' feeding the 5,000 recalls the great OT miracle of bread when Israel was in the wilderness (Exod 16:1-36). The rabbis of Jesus' day expected the coming Messiah to "rain down food from heaven" once again (Exod 16:4), and he did.

6:5 *Where can we buy bread:* When the Israelites left Egypt following the first Passover and entered the desert,

finding food and water was also their first concern (Exod 15:22–16:3).

6:7 *Even if we worked for months, we wouldn't have enough money:* Literally *200 denarii would not be enough.* A denarius was equivalent to a laborer's full day's wage.

6:9 *Barley* was the grain of the poor. The *loaves* were similar to pita bread. The *two fish* would have been salted, and with the *five* loaves of bread would make one meal.

6:10 The headcount of *about 5,000* reflected the *men alone* (Matt 14:21), as social custom dictated. With women and children included, the total number was far greater.

6:11 The modest meal provided the crowd with *as much as they wanted,* echoing the miraculous provision of manna in the wilderness (Exod 16:35). Moses had first supplied Israel with heavenly bread; Jesus was the new supplier (see note on 6:1-15).

6:14
Deut 18:15, 18
Acts 3:22; 7:37

6:16-23
//Matt 14:23-33
//Mark 6:47-51

6:19
Job 9:8

6:20
Matt 14:27

6:23
John 6:11

6:27
Matt 3:17; 17:5
Mark 1:11; 9:7
Luke 3:22
John 1:33; 4:14; 6:50-
51, 54, 58
Acts 2:22
Rom 6:23

6:29
1 Jn 3:23

6:31
Exod 16:15
Num 11:7-9
Neh 9:15
*Ps 78:24; 105:40

6:33
John 6:41, 50

6:35
John 4:14; 6:48;
7:37-38

people who had eaten from the five barley loaves.

14When the people saw him do this miraculous sign, they exclaimed, "Surely, he is the Prophet we have been expecting!" 15When Jesus saw that they were ready to force him to be their king, he slipped away into the hills by himself.

Jesus Walks on Water
John 6:16-21 // Matt 14:22-33 // Mark 6:45-52

16That evening Jesus' disciples went down to the shore to wait for him. 17But as darkness fell and Jesus still hadn't come back, they got into the boat and headed across the lake toward Capernaum. 18Soon a gale swept down upon them, and the sea grew very rough. 19They had rowed three or four miles when suddenly they saw Jesus walking on the water toward the boat. They were terrified, 20but he called out to them, "Don't be afraid. I am here!" 21Then they were eager to let him in the boat, and immediately they arrived at their destination!

Jesus, the Bread of Life
22The next day the crowd that had stayed on the far shore saw that the disciples had taken the only boat, and they realized Jesus had not gone with them. 23Several boats from Tiberias landed near the place where the Lord had blessed the bread and the people had eaten. 24So when the crowd saw that neither Jesus nor his disciples were there, they got into the boats and went across to

Capernaum to look for him. 25They found him on the other side of the lake and asked, "Rabbi, when did you get here?"

26Jesus replied, "I tell you the truth, you want to be with me because I fed you, not because you understood the miraculous signs. 27But don't be so concerned about perishable things like food. Spend your energy seeking the eternal life that the Son of Man can give you. For God the Father has given me the seal of his approval."

28They replied, "We want to perform God's works, too. What should we do?"

29Jesus told them, "This is the only work God wants from you: Believe in the one he has sent."

30They answered, "Show us a miraculous sign if you want us to believe in you. What can you do? 31After all, our ancestors ate manna while they journeyed through the wilderness! The Scriptures say, 'Moses gave them bread from heaven to eat.' "

32Jesus said, "I tell you the truth, Moses didn't give you bread from heaven. My Father did. And now he offers you the true bread from heaven. 33The true bread of God is the one who comes down from heaven and gives life to the world."

34"Sir," they said, "give us that bread every day."

35Jesus replied, "I am the bread of life. Whoever comes to me will never be hungry again. Whoever believes in me will never be thirsty. 36But you haven't believed in me

. . . .

6:14 *him:* Some manuscripts read *Jesus.*
• *he is the Prophet we have been expecting!* The crowd understood the miracle as a fulfillment of OT promises (see Deut 18:15, 18; Mal 4:5-6).

6:15 The people *were ready to force* Jesus to become *their king.* To avoid this role, Jesus fled the crowd and commanded his disciples to go back across the lake (Mark 6:45-46).

6:18 East-west winds blowing down over the eastern cliffs of the Sea of Galilee late in the day commonly caused *very rough* waters and turbulent storms.

6:19 *three or four miles:* Greek *25 or 30 stadia* [4.6 or 5.5 kilometers]. • The disciples' fear of the storm was now surpassed by their fear of *Jesus,* who came *walking on the water* to help them. This act recalled Moses, who led Israel through the water (Exod 14; see Ps 77:19-20).

6:20 *I am here* (or *The 'I AM' is here;* Greek reads *I am;* see Exod 3:14): Jesus identified himself by the name God had revealed to Moses on Mount Sinai (see also 4:26; 6:35).

6:21 *immediately they arrived at their destination:* The immediacy was yet another of Jesus' miracles.

6:24 The *crowd* sailed north to *Capernaum* to search for Jesus because he had made Capernaum his home in Galilee (Mark 2:1).

6:26-59 This dialogue took place in the synagogue at Capernaum (6:59) shortly before Passover (6:4), when Jews read the account of the exodus from Egypt (see Exod 1–15).

6:26 The crowd, which had concluded that Jesus was a prophet and wanted to take advantage of him politically (see note on 6:15), failed to see the meaning of the miracle, which Jesus then explained (6:27-59).

6:27 Jesus' most profound gift was not physical bread, but eternal life, which the Father authorized him to give. Physical bread is *perishable;* the gift of Jesus, who is himself the bread of life (6:35), will last forever. • *Son of Man* is a title Jesus used for himself.

6:30 The crowd demanded *a miraculous sign* to demonstrate Jesus' status as

Messiah. Jews believed that when the Messiah appeared, he would duplicate the great miracle of Moses. Manna would once again fall, and everyone would consider it a second exodus.

6:31 *Moses gave them bread from heaven to eat:* Exod 16:4; Ps 78:24.

6:32-33 Jesus corrected the people's argument: God, not Moses, fed Israel in the wilderness. The most important quest is to find and consume *the true bread of God,* who gives eternal life.

6:34 *Sir, . . . give us that bread:* This request parallels the request of the Samaritan woman (4:15). Spiritual awakening begins with a request for God's gift.

6:35 Jesus' *I am* statements in John depict Jesus' identity and ministry (see also 4:26; 8:12; 9:5; 10:7-9, 11-14; 11:25; 14:6; 15:1-5). Jesus purposefully used a phrase that would make his listeners think of the OT name for God (Exod 3:14). • *I am the bread of life:* Jesus is the true manna that descended from God (6:38). He satisfies the spiritual hunger of those who believe in him (cp. 4:10-13).

even though you have seen me. ³⁷However, those the Father has given me will come to me, and I will never reject them. ³⁸For I have come down from heaven to do the will of God who sent me, not to do my own will. ³⁹And this is the will of God, that I should not lose even one of all those he has given me, but that I should raise them up at the last day. ⁴⁰For it is my Father's will that all who see his Son and believe in him should have eternal life. I will raise them up at the last day."

⁴¹Then the people began to murmur in disagreement because he had said, "I am the bread that came down from heaven." ⁴²They said, "Isn't this Jesus, the son of Joseph? We know his father and mother. How can he say, 'I came down from heaven'?"

⁴³But Jesus replied, "Stop complaining about what I said. ⁴⁴For no one can come to me unless the Father who sent me draws them to me, and at the last day I will raise them up. ⁴⁵As it is written in the Scriptures, 'They will all be taught by God.' Everyone who listens to the Father and learns from him comes to me. ⁴⁶(Not that anyone has ever seen the Father; only I, who was sent from God, have seen him.)

⁴⁷"I tell you the truth, anyone who believes has eternal life. ⁴⁸Yes, I am the bread of life! ⁴⁹Your ancestors ate manna in the wilderness, but they all died. ⁵⁰Anyone who eats the bread from heaven, however, will never die. ⁵¹I am the living bread that came down from heaven. Anyone who eats this bread will live forever; and this bread, which I will offer so the world may live, is my flesh."

⁵²Then the people began arguing with each other about what he meant. "How can this man give us his flesh to eat?" they asked.

⁵³So Jesus said again, "I tell you the truth, unless you eat the flesh of the Son of Man and drink his blood, you cannot have eternal life within you. ⁵⁴But anyone who eats my flesh and drinks my blood has eternal life, and I will raise that person at the last day. ⁵⁵For my flesh is true food, and my blood is true drink. ⁵⁶Anyone who eats my flesh and drinks my blood remains in me, and I in him. ⁵⁷I live because of the living Father who sent me; in the same way, anyone who feeds on me will live because of me. ⁵⁸I am the true bread that came down from heaven. Anyone who eats this bread will not die as your ancestors did (even though they ate the manna) but will live forever."

⁵⁹He said these things while he was teaching in the synagogue in Capernaum.

Many Disciples Desert Jesus

⁶⁰Many of his disciples said, "This is very hard to understand. How can anyone accept it?"

⁶¹Jesus was aware that his disciples were complaining, so he said to them, "Does this offend you? ⁶²Then what will you think if you see the Son of Man ascend to heaven again? ⁶³The Spirit alone ᵉgives eternal life. Human effort accomplishes nothing. And the very words I have spoken to you are spirit and life. ⁶⁴But some of you do not believe me." (For Jesus knew from the beginning which ones didn't believe, and he knew who would betray him.) ⁶⁵Then he said, "That is why I said that people can't come to me unless the Father gives them to me."

Cross-references

6:37 John 10:28-29; 17:2, 24
6:38 John 4:34; 5:30
6:39 John 10:28-29; 17:12; 18:9
6:40 John 12:45
6:41 John 6:33, 35, 51, 58
6:42 Luke 4:22; John 7:27-28
6:44 Jer 31:3; John 6:65; 12:32
6:45 *Isa 54:13; Jer 31:33-34; 1 Thes 4:9; Heb 8:10-11
6:46 John 1:18; 5:37; 7:29
6:47 John 3:15-16, 36
6:48 John 6:35, 41, 51, 58
6:51 John 10:10-11; Heb 10:10
6:54 John 6:39-40, 44
6:56 John 14:20; 15:4-7; 17:21-23; 1 Jn 2:24; 3:24
6:57 John 5:26
6:58 John 6:31
6:62 John 3:13; 17:5; Acts 1:9-11; Eph 4:8
6:63 John 3:34; Rom 8:2; 1 Cor 15:45; 2 Cor 3:6; 1 Pet 3:18; ᵉzōopoieō (2227) ▸ Rom 4:17
6:64 Matt 26:23; John 13:11

. . . .

6:37-40 Jesus' mission in the world is sure to succeed. God sent Jesus (6:38) and calls people to follow him (6:37, 44). Those who come to him are secure in Jesus' promise that he will not reject them or lose them (6:39).

6:37 *those the Father has given:* God moves in people's hearts, bringing them to Jesus.

6:41-42 When Jesus identified himself as the true *bread . . . from heaven,* the crowd faced a decision. • *people:* Literally *Jewish people;* also in 6:52. • *Isn't this . . . the son of Joseph?* They stumbled over their familiarity with Jesus made his claims seem outlandish.

6:43-51 *Stop complaining:* Rather than defending himself against their complaint (6:42), Jesus turns to the problem of their spiritual receptivity. Those who love the Father and listen to him will believe in Jesus.

6:45 *in the Scriptures:* Literally *in the prophets.* Isa 54:13.

6:49-50 Jesus connected the *manna* of the Exodus with himself, then pointed out a major difference: The Israelites remained mortal and *they all died,* whereas *the bread from heaven* (Jesus himself) provides eternal life (6:47, 51, 58).

6:51 *this bread . . . is my flesh:* The gift that brings life is now unveiled. On the cross, Jesus offered his flesh for the life of the world.

6:53-58 *eat the flesh . . . drink his blood:* Jesus answered the question the people asked (6:52). His words hinted at the Lord's Supper yet to come (see Luke 22:19). Since "flesh and blood" was a Jewish idiom for the whole person, Jesus might have been calling people to consume him fully by completely believing in him. Some Christian traditions see the bread as Christ's literal

flesh broken for us and the wine as his literal blood poured out for us. Receiving communion means no less than embracing Jesus' life-giving sacrifice.

6:60-61 Jesus' language (6:53-58) was shocking, offensive (see Gen 9:4-5), and *hard to understand* for his disciples, just as it was to the crowd. Were they to take him literally? How would they eat his flesh? Jesus' answer is in 6:63.

6:63 The essence of Jesus' gift is found in the Holy *Spirit alone,* not in *human effort* (literally *the flesh*). Life and understanding come through the gift of the Spirit (see 14:15-20; 20:21-22). True life can be found only when the Holy Spirit infuses human life. To "eat the flesh of the Son of Man and drink his blood" (6:53) involves a spiritual rather than a physical act (see note on 6:53-58).

6:65 *people can't come to me unless the Father gives them to me* (see 6:44): Only

6:65
John 6:44

6:68
John 6:63

6:69
Matt 16:16
Mark 1:24; 8:29
Luke 9:20
1 Jn 2:20

6:70-71
Matt 10:4; 26:14
John 13:27

7:1
John 5:18; 7:19;
8:37, 40

7:2
Lev 23:34
Deut 16:16

7:3
Matt 12:46

7:6
John 2:4; 7:30; 8:20

7:7
John 15:18

7:11
John 11:56

7:12
John 7:40-43

7:13
John 9:22-23

7:15
Matt 13:54
Luke 2:47
Acts 4:13

7:16
John 8:28; 12:49;
14:10

7:18
John 5:41, 44;
8:50, 54

7:19
John 1:17; 7:1, 25;
8:37-40

7:20
John 8:48, 52; 10:20

7:21-22
Gen 17:10-13
Lev 12:3

7:23
John 5:8-10, 16
Acts 7:8

66At this point many of his disciples turned away and deserted him. 67Then Jesus turned to the Twelve and asked, "Are you also going to leave?"

68Simon Peter replied, "Lord, to whom would we go? You have the words that give eternal life. 69We believe, and we know you are the Holy One of God."

70Then Jesus said, "I chose the twelve of you, but one is a devil." 71He was speaking of Judas, son of Simon Iscariot, one of the Twelve, who would later betray him.

Jesus and the Festival of Shelters (7:1–8:59)
Jesus and His Brothers

7 After this, Jesus traveled around Galilee. He wanted to stay out of Judea, where the Jewish leaders were plotting his death. 2But soon it was time for the Jewish Festival of Shelters, 3and Jesus' brothers said to him, "Leave here and go to Judea, where your followers can see your miracles! 4You can't become famous if you hide like this! If you can do such wonderful things, show yourself to the world!" 5For even his brothers didn't believe in him.

6Jesus replied, "Now is not the right time for me to go, but you can go anytime. 7The world can't hate you, but it does hate me because I accuse it of doing evil. 8You go on. I'm not going to this festival, because my time has not yet come." 9After saying these things, Jesus remained in Galilee.

Jesus Teaches Openly at the Temple

10But after his brothers left for the festival, Jesus also went, though secretly, staying out of public view. 11The Jewish leaders tried to find him at the festival and kept asking if anyone had seen him. 12There was a lot of grumbling about him among the crowds. Some argued, "He's a good man," but others said, "He's nothing but a fraud who deceives the people." 13But no one had the courage to speak favorably about him in public, for they were afraid of getting in trouble with the Jewish leaders.

14Then, midway through the festival, Jesus went up to the Temple and began to teach. 15The people were surprised when they heard him. "How does he know so much when he hasn't been trained?" they asked.

16So Jesus told them, "My message is not my own; it comes from God who sent me. 17Anyone who wants to do the will of God will know whether my teaching is from God or is merely my own. 18Those who speak for themselves want glory only for themselves, but a person who seeks to honor the one who sent him speaks truth, not lies. 19Moses gave you the law, but none of you obeys it! In fact, you are trying to kill me."

20The crowd replied, "You're demon possessed! Who's trying to kill you?"

21Jesus replied, "I did one miracle on the Sabbath, and you were amazed. 22But you work on the Sabbath, too, when you obey Moses' law of circumcision. (Actually, this tradition of circumcision began with the patriarchs, long before the law of Moses.) 23For if the correct time for circumcising your son falls on the Sabbath, you go ahead and do it so as not to break the law of Moses. So why should you be angry with me for healing

. . . .

God's light can penetrate the profound darkness of the world.

6:68-69 *Simon Peter* often served as spokesman for the Twelve (see also Matt 14:28-29; 16:16; 17:4; 18:21; 19:27; 26:33-35). • *you are the Holy One of God:* Other manuscripts read *you are the Christ, the Holy One of God;* still others read *you are the Christ, the Son of God;* and still others read *you are the Christ, the Son of the living God.* See Mark 1:24.

6:70-71 Once again Jesus demonstrated supernatural knowledge (see 1:47-49; 4:16-19). *Judas* would work for evil and *betray* Jesus to the authorities (12:4; 13:2; Matt 26:14-16). • *Iscariot* means "man from Kerioth," the home village of Judas's family.

7:1-52 This chapter is another account of Jesus during a Jewish festival, the Festival of Shelters. Jesus used elements of the festival to reveal his true identity to his Jewish compatriots and to show that he had fulfilled the festival's

essential meaning (see 7:37-39; 8:12).

7:2 Jewish men were required to come to the Temple for the *Festival of Shelters* (Exod 23:14-17; Deut 16:16), an annual seven-day autumn harvest festival in Jerusalem six months after Passover (6:4). People lived in temporary shelters for the seven days as a reminder of the tents Israel used for forty years in the wilderness.

7:3-5 *Jesus' brothers* (see also Mark 3:31) reminded him of his religious obligation to celebrate the festival. Their words were cynical because at this time they didn't *believe in him* (7:5).

7:6-8 Jesus said that it was *not the right time* for him to go publicly to Jerusalem, although he later went secretly (12:1-19; see note on 12:23).

7:8 *not going:* Some manuscripts read *not yet going.*

7:15 *people:* Literally *Jewish people.*
• The leaders wanted Jesus to show his

credentials. Jesus had not *been trained* under a rabbi but was taught by his heavenly Father (cp. Peter and John, Acts 4:13; contrast Paul, Acts 22:3).

7:17 Those who truly want *to do the will of God* receive and accept Jesus and his *teaching* (see also 5:42-47). Those who focus on the world, by contrast, are not receptive to Christ.

7:19 *Moses gave you the law, but none of you obeys it!* The Jewish leaders were proud of the law of Moses, but ironically, in *trying to kill* Jesus, they were breaking the law (Exod 20:13).

7:20 *You're demon possessed!* See also 8:48-52; 10:20-21.

7:22 The law required *circumcision* on the eighth day (Lev 12:3) and permitted a boy to be circumcised even if that day fell on *the Sabbath.* Jesus argued as a rabbi would, from "the lesser to the greater," using circumcision as a precedent for healing, both of which are religious works.

a man on the Sabbath? 24Look beneath the surface so you can judge correctly."

Is Jesus the Messiah?

25Some of the people who lived in Jerusalem started to ask each other, "Isn't this the man they are trying to kill? 26But here he is, speaking in public, and they say nothing to him. Could our leaders possibly believe that he is the Messiah? 27But how could he be? For we know where this man comes from. When the Messiah comes, he will simply appear; no one will know where he comes from."

28While Jesus was teaching in the Temple, he called out, "Yes, you know me, and you know where I come from. But I'm not here on my own. The one who sent me is true, and you don't know him. 29But I know him because I come from him, and he sent me to you." 30Then the leaders tried to arrest him; but no one laid a hand on him, because his time had not yet come.

31Many among the crowds at the Temple believed in him. "After all," they said, "would you expect the Messiah to do more miraculous signs than this man has done?"

32When the Pharisees heard that the crowds were whispering such things, they and the leading priests sent Temple guards to arrest Jesus. 33But Jesus told them, "I will be with you only a little longer. Then I will return to the one who sent me. 34You will search for me but not find me. And you cannot go where I am going."

35The Jewish leaders were puzzled by this statement. "Where is he planning to go?" they asked. "Is he thinking of leaving the country and going to the Jews in other lands? Maybe he will even teach the Greeks! 36What does he mean when he says, 'You will search for me but not find me,' and 'You cannot go where I am going'?"

Jesus Promises Living Water

37On the last day, the climax of the festival, Jesus stood and shouted to the crowds, "Anyone who is thirsty may come to me! 38Anyone who believes in me may come and drink! For the Scriptures declare, 'Rivers of living water will flow from his heart.'" 39(When he said "living water," he was speaking of the Spirit, who would be given to everyone believing in him. But the Spirit had not yet been given, because Jesus had not yet entered into his glory.)

40When the crowds heard him say this, some of them declared, "Surely this man is the Prophet we've been expecting." 41Others said, "He is the Messiah." Still others said, "But he can't be! Will the Messiah come from Galilee? 42For the Scriptures clearly state that the Messiah will be born of the royal line of David, in Bethlehem, the village where King David was born." 43So the crowd was divided about him. 44Some even wanted him arrested, but no one laid a hand on him.

45When the Temple guards returned without having arrested Jesus, the leading

7:24 Isa 11:3-4; John 8:15
7:27 John 9:29
7:28-29 John 8:26, 55; 17:25
7:30 John 8:20
7:31 John 2:23; 8:30; 10:42; 11:45; 12:11, 42
7:33 John 13:33; 16:5, 10, 16-18
7:34 John 8:21; 13:33
7:37 Isa 55:1; John 4:10, 14; 6:35; Rev 22:17
7:38 Prov 18:4; Isa 58:11; Ezek 47:1-10; Joel 3:18
7:39 John 14:17-18; 16:7; 20:22; Rom 8:9; 1 Cor 15:45; 2 Cor 3:17
7:40 Deut 18:15; John 6:14
7:41 John 1:46
7:42 2 Sam 7:12; Ps 89:3-4; Mic 5:2; Matt 1:1; 2:5-10; Luke 2:4; John 7:52
7:43 John 9:16; 10:19
7:44 John 7:30

7:27 Some of the crowd thought that since they could trace Jesus' earthly origins, he could not be the Messiah. They believed that the Messiah would *simply appear.*

7:29 *I come from him:* Jesus sidestepped the speculation (7:27, 40-44) about his earthly origins and focused on his heavenly origins. His astounding claim provoked the religious leaders to try to arrest him for blasphemy (7:30; cp. 10:30-33).

7:30 Jesus' opponents failed to arrest him because in God's sovereign plan, *his time* (literally *his hour*), when he would be glorified on the cross, *had not yet come* (see note on 12:23; see also 10:17-18; 18:6-8). All four arrest scenes in chs 7–8 stress that Jesus was in control, not the Jewish leaders.

7:32-36 Jesus announced his *return to the one who sent* him, the Father in heaven (17:1-7). However, the Pharisees misunderstood, thinking he was leaving Judea to go among Gentiles (whom Pharisees would never visit). • The leaders would *not find* Jesus after his

ascension. • *you cannot go where I am going:* These Pharisees, still in darkness, could not enter heaven, so Jesus would be beyond their reach there.

7:35 *the Jews in other lands?* Or the *Jews who live among the Greeks?*

7:37-38 *living water:* See "Living Water" at 4:10-14, p. 1777. A water ceremony was held each day during the Festival of Shelters, with prayer for God to send rain in the late autumn. The final day, called "the great day," was *the climax of the festival,* when the ceremony was repeated seven times. Water was poured over the altar as Levites sang Isa 12:3 (see Zech 14:8; see also *Mishnah Sukkah* ch 4). • *Anyone who is thirsty may come to me!* Jesus fulfilled an essential element in the Festival of Shelters. He himself is the source of living water, available to *anyone who believes.* • *Anyone who is thirsty may come to me!* 38Anyone who believes in me may come and drink! For the Scriptures declare, 'Rivers of living water will flow from his heart':* Or "Let anyone who is thirsty come to me and drink. 38For

the Scriptures declare, 'Rivers of living water will flow from the heart of anyone who believes in me.'" The syntax of the Greek allows for either interpretation.

7:39 In Jesus' crucifixion and resurrection, his life and *the Spirit* were poured out (see 19:34; 20:22). • *But the Spirit had not yet been given:* Some manuscripts read *But as yet there was no Spirit.* Still others read *But as yet there was no Holy Spirit.*

7:40 *Surely this man is the Prophet we've been expecting:* See Deut 18:15, 18; Mal 4:5-6.

7:41-42 These Jews, different from the crowd (7:25-27) who thought *the Messiah* would appear mysteriously, believed the prophecy that the Messiah would be from *Bethlehem* of Judea (see Mic 5:2). However, they stumbled over the fact that Jesus seemed to be from *Galilee,* where he grew up.

7:45-52 The story concludes with the Jewish leaders frustrated and the world divided over Jesus (cp. 7:25-27, 31-32). • *guards returned:* See 7:32.

priests and Pharisees demanded, "Why didn't you bring him in?"

⁴⁶"We have never heard anyone speak like this!" the guards responded.

⁴⁷"Have you been led astray, too?" the Pharisees mocked. ⁴⁸"Is there a single one of us rulers or Pharisees who believes in him? ⁴⁹This foolish crowd follows him, but they are ignorant of the law. God's curse is on them!"

⁵⁰Then Nicodemus, the leader who had met with Jesus earlier, spoke up. ⁵¹"Is it legal to convict a man before he is given a hearing?" he asked.

⁵²They replied, "Are you from Galilee, too? Search the Scriptures and see for yourself—no prophet ever comes from Galilee!"

[*The most ancient Greek manuscripts do not include John 7:53–8:11.*]

⁵³Then the meeting broke up, and everybody went home.

A Woman Caught in Adultery

8 Jesus returned to the Mount of Olives, ²but early the next morning he was back again at the Temple. A crowd soon gathered, and he sat down and taught them. ³As he was speaking, the teachers of religious law and the Pharisees brought a woman who had been caught in the act of adultery. They put her in front of the crowd.

⁴"Teacher," they said to Jesus, "this woman was caught in the act of adultery. ⁵The law of Moses says to stone her. What do you say?"

⁶They were trying to trap him into saying something they could use against him, but Jesus stooped down and wrote in the dust with his finger. ⁷They kept demanding an answer, so he stood up again and said, "All right, but let the one who has never sinned throw the first stone!" ⁸Then he stooped down again and wrote in the dust.

⁹When the accusers heard this, they slipped away one by one, beginning with the oldest, until only Jesus was left in the middle of the crowd with the woman. ¹⁰Then Jesus stood up again and said to the woman, "Where are your accusers? Didn't even one of them condemn you?"

¹¹"No, Lord," she said.

And Jesus said, "Neither do I. Go and sin no more."

Cross references (margin)

7:46 Matt 7:28
7:48 John 12:42
7:50 John 3:1-2; 19:39
7:51 Deut 1:16
7:52 Isa 9:1-2; Matt 4:14-16; John 1:46
8:2 Matt 26:55
8:5 Lev 20:10; Deut 22:22-24; Job 31:11
8:6 Matt 22:15
8:7 Deut 17:7
8:11 John 5:14

Misunderstanding (7:32-36)

John 1:10-11; 3:19-20; 9:40-41; 12:40
Isa 6:8-13; 56:10-11
Matt 13:11-17
Acts 26:18; 28:26-27
Rom 1:21
2 Cor 3:13-18; 4:3-4
Eph 4:17-19
Heb 5:2
2 Pet 2:12
1 Jn 2:9-11
Jude 1:10
Rev 3:17

Throughout John's Gospel, people encountering Jesus misunderstood him (see 3:4; 4:11, 33; 7:35; 11:12, 50). Jesus' hearers were divided over the question of Jesus' identity. When they perceived what he was really saying, some wanted to arrest him while others wanted to become his followers (7:43-44). Only later, when Jesus' disciples had received the Spirit (16:12-13), did they really understand its significance.

The world still lives in darkness and it cannot understand the realities of life or of God (1:5). Divine revelation is inaccessible to the world. In fact, when the light of God penetrates the darkness, exposing the ugliness of the world's life, many people flee deeper into the darkness because they prefer it to the light (3:19-20). Only the transforming power of God's Spirit can provide understanding and help people see clearly as children of God (3:21; 8:12; 12:35-36, 46).

7:49-51 *Nicodemus* (ch 3) was probably in the process of coming to faith (see 19:39). Contrary to the implication of 7:48, some of the Pharisees—not just the *ignorant* crowd—believed in Jesus.

7:52 *no prophet ever comes* (some manuscripts read *the prophet does not come*) *from Galilee!* The Jewish leaders were apparently unaware that Jesus had been born in Bethlehem of Judea, not in Galilee (see Matt 2:1; Luke 2:1-7).

7:53–8:11 This story, a later addition to the Gospel of John, does not appear in the earliest Greek manuscripts. However, it is likely an authentic story from Jesus' life.

8:3 The *teachers of religious law* were Jewish scholars who specialized in knowing the OT law and the oral

traditions that interpreted the law.

8:4 The form of the Greek sentence emphasizes the legal claim against the woman. She had been caught while committing the sin *of adultery*. The law required two witnesses and carefully outlined what evidence was needed.

8:5 The requirement of the *law . . . to stone her* indicates that the woman was engaged or married (Lev 20:10; Deut 22:23-24). The law also stated that her lover should be killed with her, but these religious leaders apparently ignored their obligation to that part of the statute. • These men could have dealt with the woman privately and kept her from public shame, but Jesus was their real target as they demanded, *What do you say?* Would he neglect the law since he had a reputation for mercy? Or

would he ignore the woman's tragedy?

8:6 It is impossible to know what *Jesus . . . wrote in the dust.* It has been suggested that he wrote the sins of the accusers.

8:7 Jesus' answer did not mean that an accuser had to be morally perfect to make legal accusations. His reference to *the one who has never sinned* points to the motives of the accusers.

8:9 The jury crumbled as *they slipped away.* One accuser departed, followed by another, and then a succession of bystanders.

8:11 *Neither do I:* Jesus' words of assurance did not suggest that the woman was innocent. Jesus views sin and judgment seriously, yet he looks graciously and forgivingly on those caught in sin's grip.

Jesus, the Light of the World

¹²Jesus spoke to the people once more and said, "I am the light of the world. If you follow me, you won't have to walk in darkness, because you will have the light that leads to life."

¹³The Pharisees replied, "You are making those claims about yourself! Such testimony is not valid."

¹⁴Jesus told them, "These claims are valid even though I make them about myself. For I know where I came from and where I am going, but you don't know this about me. ¹⁵You judge me by human standards, but I do not judge anyone. ¹⁶And if I did, my judgment would be correct in every respect because I am not alone. The Father who sent me is with me. ¹⁷Your own law says that if two people agree about something, their witness is accepted as fact. ¹⁸I am one witness, and my Father who sent me is the other."

¹⁹"Where is your father?" they asked.

Jesus answered, "Since you don't know who I am, you don't know who my Father is. If you knew me, you would also know my Father." ²⁰Jesus made these statements while he was teaching in the section of the Temple known as the Treasury. But he was not arrested, because his time had not yet come.

The Unbelieving People Warned

²¹Later Jesus said to them again, "I am going away. You will search for me but will die in your sin. You cannot come where I am going."

²²The people asked, "Is he planning to commit suicide? What does he mean, 'You cannot come where I am going'?"

²³Jesus continued, "You are from below; I am from above. You belong to this world; I do not. ²⁴That is why I said that you will die in your sins; for unless you believe that I Am who I claim to be, you will die in your sins."

²⁵"Who are you?" they demanded.

Jesus replied, "The one I have always claimed to be. ²⁶I have much to say about you and much to condemn, but I won't. For I say only what I have heard from the one who sent me, and he is completely truthful." ²⁷But they still didn't understand that he was talking about his Father.

²⁸So Jesus said, "When you have lifted up the Son of Man on the cross, then you will understand that I Am he. I do nothing on my

8:12
Isa 9:1-2
John 1:4-5, 9; 3:19;
9:5; 12:35-36, 46
2 Cor 4:6

8:14
John 7:28; 9:29

8:16
John 5:30

8:17-18
Deut 17:6; 19:15
John 5:37
1 Jn 5:7-9

8:19
John 14:7, 9

8:20
Mark 12:41
John 7:30

8:21
John 7:34, 36; 13:33

8:22
John 7:35

8:23
John 3:31; 17:14

8:24
Exod 3:14-15
John 4:26; 8:28, 58;
13:19

8:26
John 3:32-34; 12:49

8:28
John 3:14; 5:19; 8:24;
12:32

8:12-59 The debate about whether or not Jesus is the Messiah continues from 7:52. Jesus was still at the Festival of Shelters in Jerusalem. During the festival, the conflicts Jesus had endured in ch 7 continued and intensified.

8:12 During the Festival of Shelters, sixteen gold bowls in the inner courts of the Temple were filled with oil and lighted. Jesus stood beneath these lights in the Temple (8:20) and said that he was now the source of *the light*. Jesus' light brings salvation not only to Israel but to *the world*, regardless of race or locale.

8:13 The Pharisees charged that Jesus' *claims* were *not valid* because Jewish law (Deut 19:15) requires more than one witness (cp. 5:31-32; see 8:17).

8:14-15 Jesus answered the Pharisees' charges, saying that he could make such *claims* about himself because he knew both his origin (heaven) and his destination (heaven). He then pointed to the most vital witness for his case, his Father who sent him (8:16).

8:16 *The Father:* Some manuscripts read *The One*.

8:17 *if two people agree about something, their witness is accepted as fact:* See Deut 19:15.

8:19 Throughout the festival, Jesus' audience proved they were in the darkness as they misunderstood him (see "Misunderstanding" at 7:32-36, p. 1785). They wanted to meet Jesus' *father*, who is God. Since they did not truly know God, they were unable to understand Jesus.

8:20 The *Treasury* was located in the section of the Temple called the Court of the Women. Jesus often taught there so that both men and women could hear him (Mark 12:41). • *his time:* Literally *his hour*. See notes on 2:4; 12:23.

8:21 In the earlier debate at the festival, Jesus' origins were at issue (7:27). Here, Jesus mentioned *going away* to the place he came from, meaning heaven. However, once again, his words were misunderstood.

8:22 *people:* Literally *Jewish people;* also in 8:31, 48, 52, 57.

8:23 Jesus' listeners were *from below;* they could not comprehend Jesus' meaning because he was *from above* (3:31; see note on 3:3).

8:24 *unless you believe that I Am who I claim to be:* Literally *unless you believe that I am.* Jesus used God's divine name (see 4:26; Exod 3:14), but the listeners missed the nuance (8:25). • *die in your sins:* Jesus' presence in the world, as the light penetrating the darkness, is the world's only chance for salvation.

8:25 *Who are you?* Later they understood and tried to stone Jesus for blasphemy (8:59). • *The one I have always claimed to be:* Or *Why do I speak to you at all?* The Greek text can be interpreted either way.

8:28 *When you have lifted up the Son of Man on the cross, then you will understand that I Am he:* Literally *When you have lifted up the Son of Man, then you will know that I am.* "Son of Man" is a title Jesus used for himself. See note

▶ **Herod's Temple (John 8:20).** Herod the Great, king of Judea at the time of Jesus' birth (37–4 BC), rebuilt the Temple in Jerusalem. The new structure replaced and expanded on the Second Temple that had been built during the time of Haggai, after the Jews returned from exile in Babylon (see Ezra 1–6). Herod's massive project began in 20 BC, and the core of the new structure was finished in a decade, but the work was not fully completed until AD 64. This Temple was destroyed in AD 70, just six years after its completion. Many events of Jesus' life and ministry took place within the Temple compound (see also 1:19; 2:14-15, 19-21; 5:14; 7:14, 28-32; 8:2, 59; 10:23; 11:56; Matt 4:5; 21:12-15, 23; 24:1-2; 27:5-6, 51; Mark 11:11, 15-17, 27; 12:35, 41; 13:1-2; 15:38; Luke 1:8, 23; 2:27, 36-37, 46; 4:9; 10:32; 19:45-47; 20:1; 21:1, 5, 37-38; 23:45; 24:53; Acts 2:46; 3:1-8; 4:1; 5:12, 20-26; 21:23-30).

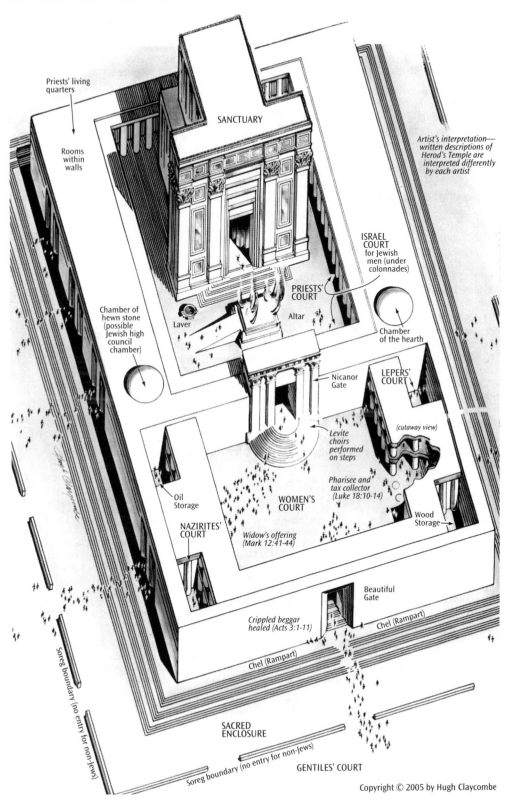

Priests' living quarters

Rooms within walls

SANCTUARY

Artist's interpretation—written descriptions of Herod's Temple are interpreted differently by each artist

ISRAEL COURT for Jewish men (under colonnades)

PRIESTS' COURT

Chamber of hewn stone (possible Jewish high council chamber)

Laver

Altar

Chamber of the hearth

Nicanor Gate

LEPERS' COURT

(cutaway view)

Levite choirs performed on steps

Pharisee and tax collector (Luke 18:10-14)

Oil Storage

WOMEN'S COURT

Wood Storage

NAZIRITES' COURT

Widow's offering (Mark 12:41-44)

Beautiful Gate

Crippled beggar healed (Acts 3:1-11)

Chel (Rampart)

Chel (Rampart)

Soreg boundary (no entry for non-Jews)

SACRED ENCLOSURE

Soreg boundary (no entry for non-Jews)

GENTILES' COURT

Copyright © 2005 by Hugh Claycombe

own but say only what the Father taught me. ²⁹And the one who sent me is with me—he has not deserted me. For I always do what pleases him." ³⁰Then many who heard him say these things ᶠbelieved in him.

Jesus and Abraham: True Freedom

³¹Jesus said to the people who believed in him, "You are truly my disciples if you remain faithful to my teachings. ³²And you will know the truth, and the truth will set you free."

³³"But we are descendants of Abraham," they said. "We have never been slaves to anyone. What do you mean, 'You will be set free'?"

³⁴Jesus replied, "I tell you the truth, everyone who sins is a slave of sin. ³⁵A slave is not a permanent member of the family, but a son is part of the family forever. ³⁶So if the Son sets you free, you are truly free. ³⁷Yes, I realize that you are descendants of Abraham. And yet some of you are trying to kill me because there's no room in your hearts for my message. ³⁸I am telling you what I saw when I was with my Father. But you are following the advice of your father."

³⁹"Our father is Abraham!" they declared.

"No," Jesus replied, "for if you were really the children of Abraham, you would follow his example. ⁴⁰Instead, you are trying to kill me because I told you the truth, which I heard from God. Abraham never did such a thing. ⁴¹No, you are imitating your real father."

They replied, "We aren't illegitimate children! God himself is our true Father."

⁴²Jesus told them, "If God were your Father, you would love me, because I have come to you from God. I am not here on my own, but he sent me. ⁴³Why can't you understand what I am saying? It's because you can't even hear me! ⁴⁴For you are the children of your father the ᵍdevil, and you love to do the evil things he does. He was a murderer from the beginning. He has always hated the truth, because there is no truth in him. When he lies, it is consistent with his character; for he is a liar and the father of lies. ⁴⁵So when I tell the truth, you just naturally don't believe me! ⁴⁶Which of you can truthfully accuse me of sin? And since I am telling you the truth, why don't you believe me? ⁴⁷Anyone who belongs to God listens gladly to the words of God. But you don't listen because you don't belong to God."

⁴⁸The people retorted, "You Samaritan devil! Didn't we say all along that you were possessed by a demon?"

⁴⁹"No," Jesus said, "I have no demon in me. For I honor my Father—and you dishonor me. ⁵⁰And though I have no wish to glorify myself, God is going to glorify me. He is the true judge. ⁵¹I tell you the truth, anyone who obeys my teaching will never die!"

⁵²The people said, "Now we know you are possessed by a demon. Even Abraham and the prophets died, but you say, 'Anyone who obeys my teaching will never die!' ⁵³Are you greater than our father Abraham? He died,

8:29
John 4:34; 6:38; 8:16;
14:10; 16:32

8:30
John 7:31
ᶠ*pisteuō* (4100)
▸ John 12:11

8:31
John 15:7
2 Jn 1:9

8:32
Rom 8:2
2 Cor 3:17
Gal 5:1, 13

8:33
Matt 3:9
Luke 3:8

8:34
Rom 6:16, 20
2 Pet 2:19

8:35
Gen 21:10
Gal 4:30

8:39
Matt 3:9
John 8:33
Gal 3:7, 14, 29

8:41
Deut 32:6
Isa 63:16; 64:8
Mal 1:6

8:42
1 Jn 5:1

8:44
Gen 3:4; 4:9
1 Jn 3:8
ᵍ*diabolos* (1228)
▸ Eph 4:27

8:45
John 18:37

8:47
1 Jn 4:6

8:50
John 5:41

8:51
John 5:24; 11:25-26

8:53
John 4:12

---

on 1:51. • The synoptic Gospels describe Jesus as predicting his death three times (e.g., Mark 8:31; 9:31; 10:33-34). John parallels this (3:14; 8:28; 12:33-34), showing that *the Father* governs his Son's fate.

8:30 Once again, the festival audience was divided. Earlier, the debate concluded with plans to arrest Jesus (8:20). Now *many . . . believed in him*, convinced that he was telling the truth. However, once Jesus' full identity was disclosed their faith was sorely challenged (8:31-59).

8:31-32 Discipleship is more than knowing who Jesus is. It is also about obeying his *teachings* (3:36; 14:15, 21, 23; 15:10). • Because Jesus is *the truth* (14:6), knowing him brings discernment of what is true and what is false. • *set you free:* The truth brings freedom from darkness, falsehood, and sin.

8:33 Jesus challenged a widely held assumption about Israel's status as God's chosen people. Their heritage as *descendants of Abraham* had inspired feelings of privilege and immunity rather than obligation and responsibility (cp. Amos

3:1-15). • The people misunderstood what it meant to be *set free*. Jesus was not referring to freedom from human slavery; he meant spiritual bondage to sin (8:34). Truth, not their religious heritage, would free them (8:32; Rom 6:17; 8:2; 1 Jn 3:4, 8, 9).

8:35 Jesus unfolded the logic of his argument: If Israel is a spiritual *slave*, it has the same insecurity as any slave in a household. Members of a *family* are secure, slaves are not. Only Jesus can change the status of slaves and make them free and secure.

8:37-41 The leaders' plot to kill Jesus (5:18) unmasked their true identity. They belonged to a different household, and their *father* was not Jesus' *Father*. They were relying on the fact that their ancestral father was Abraham, but Jesus challenged their spiritual pedigree. The climax of his challenge comes in 8:44.

8:39 *if you were really the children of Abraham, you would follow his example:* Some manuscripts read *if you are really the children of Abraham, follow his example.*

8:41 *your real father:* Jesus knew who controlled them. • *We aren't illegitimate children!* This was both a defense and an attack. In Greek, the pronoun *we* is emphatic: "*We* [in contrast to *you*] are not illegitimate," implying that Jesus was illegitimate (see Matt 1:18-25).

8:44 Since the unbelieving people did not love Jesus (8:42; 1 Jn 5:1), they were not *children* of the Father in heaven who sent his beloved Son (8:47). Their true spiritual ancestry was revealed in their desire to kill God's Son. This was the work of *the devil*, who brought death to the world (see Gen 3:1-20; Rom 5:12-14).

8:48-49 By calling Jesus a *Samaritan devil*, his opponents turned his charges back on him with a racial slur (see note on 4:4-6). Their statement that Jesus was demon possessed (also 7:20; 8:52; 10:20) countered his claim that they were linked to Satan (8:44). Jesus rightly replied that these words were a profound *dishonor*. In fact, it was a serious and unforgivable offense (Mark 3:22-29).

8:54
John 16:14; 17:5
8:55
John 7:28-29; 15:10
8:56
Gen 18:18; 22:17-18
Matt 13:17
Heb 11:13
8:58
Exod 3:14
Isa 43:10, 13
John 1:1; 8:24, 28
9:2
Exod 20:5
Ezek 18:20
Luke 13:2
John 9:34
9:3
John 11:4
9:4
John 5:17; 11:9; 12:35
9:5
Isa 49:6
John 1:4-5, 9; 8:12;
12:46
9:6
Mark 8:23
9:7
2 Kgs 5:10
Isa 35:5
9:8
Acts 3:10

and so did the prophets. Who do you think you are?"

⁵⁴Jesus answered, "If I want glory for myself, it doesn't count. But it is my Father who will glorify me. You say, 'He is our God,' ⁵⁵but you don't even know him. I know him. If I said otherwise, I would be as great a liar as you! But I do know him and obey him. ⁵⁶Your father Abraham rejoiced as he looked forward to my coming. He saw it and was glad."

⁵⁷The people said, "You aren't even fifty years old. How can you say you have seen Abraham?"

⁵⁸Jesus answered, "I tell you the truth, before Abraham was even born, I Aᴍ!" ⁵⁹At that point they picked up stones to throw at him. But Jesus was hidden from them and left the Temple.

Jesus Brings Light to the Blind

9 As Jesus was walking along, he saw a man who had been blind from birth. ²"Rabbi," his disciples asked him, "why was this man born blind? Was it because of his own sins or his parents' sins?"

³"It was not because of his sins or his parents' sins," Jesus answered. "This happened so the power of God could be seen in him. ⁴We must quickly carry out the tasks assigned us by the one who sent us. The night is coming, and then no one can work. ⁵But while I am here in the world, I am the light of the world."

⁶Then he spit on the ground, made mud with the saliva, and spread the mud over the blind man's eyes. ⁷He told him, "Go wash yourself in the pool of Siloam" (Siloam means "sent"). So the man went and washed and came back seeing!

⁸His neighbors and others who knew him as a blind beggar asked each other, "Isn't this the man who used to sit and beg?" ⁹Some said he was, and others said, "No, he just looks like him!"

Disciples of Jesus (9:1-41)

John 8:31-32; 12:25-26; 13:35; 18:36
Matt 5:11; 9:9-10;
10:16-22; 13:52;
16:24-28; 24:9;
27:57-58
Mark 15:40-41
Luke 14:26-33
Acts 9:2
Rom 15:5
1 Cor 3:4-11
Eph 1:1

In the first half of John's Gospel, he introduces a variety of people who model true discipleship (see 1:19-51; 4:1-42; 9:1-41). Taken together, John provides a profile of the mature follower, or "disciple," of Christ.

What is this profile of a disciple? (1) *Disciples know who Jesus is.* In each story, titles for Jesus identify him correctly (see, e.g., 1:25, 34, 36, 38, 41; 4:19, 25, 31; 9:2, 17, 22). (2) *Disciples believe in Jesus.* They see Jesus' mighty works, listen to his profound words, and believe (see 1:50; 4:39-41; 9:35-38; see also 20:8, 25-31). (3) *Jesus' disciples understand that they must follow him if their discipleship is to be successful* (1:37-43; 8:12; 10:4-5, 27; 12:26; 21:19-22). Following implies genuine devotion, leaving what we have to embrace the journey with Jesus.

8:53 *Who do you think you are?* This question was antagonistic and aggressive. However, if Jesus is immortal, ruling over life and death, then he is greater than *Abraham, the prophets,* or any of the greatest people in Israel's history (8:58).

8:54 *our God:* Some manuscripts read *your God.*

8:56 Like his opponents, Jesus appealed to *Abraham.* Rabbis taught that God had given Abraham prophetic insight, teaching him about the coming age of the Messiah.

8:57 *How can you say you have seen Abraham?* (Some manuscripts read *How can you say Abraham has seen you?*): The Jewish leaders misunderstood Jesus: He was talking about his divine pre-existence, not his physical age.

8:58 *before Abraham was even born, I Aᴍ!* (Or *before Abraham was even born, I have always been alive;* Greek reads *before Abraham was, I am.*) Jesus' life spans the past from before creation (1:1-2) and sweeps beyond the present into eternity. • *I Aᴍ:* This title is reminiscent of God's name given on Mount Sinai (Exod 3:14; cp. John 4:26; Isa 43:11-13; 48:12).

8:59 Jesus' audience finally understood his claim to divinity (8:58), and they were furious. They believed they had heard blasphemy and *picked up stones to throw at him,* which was the proper legal response (Lev 24:16). • *Jesus was hidden from them* because God had appointed a different time for his death (see note on 12:23; see also 7:30, 44; Luke 4:29-30).

9:1-41 At the Festival of Shelters (chs 7–8), Jesus claimed to be the light of the world (8:12). Now John tells about Jesus giving light, both physically and spiritually, to a blind man who lived in darkness (see 9:5). The story ends with a splendid reversal of roles: The blind man who was assumed to be in spiritual darkness could see God's light, whereas the Pharisees, who could see physically and were thought to be enlightened, were shown to be spiritually blind.

9:2 The *disciples* assumed that someone's sin—the man's or *his parents'*—had caused him to be *born blind.* Jesus corrected this common belief (9:3).

9:4 *We must quickly carry out the tasks assigned us by the one who sent us:* Other manuscripts read *I must quickly carry out the tasks assigned me by the one who sent me;* still others read *We must quickly carry out the tasks assigned us by the one who sent me.*

9:5 *I am the light of the world:* See note on 8:12.

9:6 During the NT era, *saliva* was used for medical purposes (see Mark 7:32-35; 8:22-25).

9:7 *Siloam,* a pool at the south end of the city of Jerusalem, was the source of water for the ceremonies at the Festival of Shelters. • *Siloam means "sent":* This phrase contained a double meaning: Jesus, who has been sent by God (4:34; 5:23, 37; 7:28; 8:26; 12:44; 14:24), told the blind man to wash in the pool called "sent."

But the beggar kept saying, "Yes, I am the same one!"

¹⁰They asked, "Who healed you? What happened?"

¹¹He told them, "The man they call Jesus made mud and spread it over my eyes and told me, 'Go to the pool of Siloam and wash yourself.' So I went and washed, and now I can see!"

¹²"Where is he now?" they asked.

"I don't know," he replied.

¹³Then they took the man who had been blind to the Pharisees, ¹⁴because it was on the Sabbath that Jesus had made the mud and healed him. ¹⁵The Pharisees asked the man all about it. So he told them, "He put the mud over my eyes, and when I washed it away, I could see!"

¹⁶Some of the Pharisees said, "This man Jesus is not from God, for he is working on the Sabbath." Others said, "But how could an ordinary sinner do such miraculous signs?" So there was a deep division of opinion among them.

¹⁷Then the Pharisees again questioned the man who had been blind and demanded, "What's your opinion about this man who healed you?"

The man replied, "I think he must be a prophet."

¹⁸The Jewish leaders still refused to believe the man had been blind and could now see, so they called in his parents. ¹⁹They asked them, "Is this your son? Was he born blind? If so, how can he now see?"

²⁰His parents replied, "We know this is our son and that he was born blind, ²¹but we don't know how he can see or who healed him. Ask him. He is old enough to speak for himself." ²²His parents said this because they were afraid of the Jewish leaders, who had announced that anyone saying Jesus was the Messiah would be expelled from the synagogue. ²³That's why they said, "He is old enough. Ask him."

²⁴So for the second time they called in the man who had been blind and told him, "God should get the glory for this, because we know this man Jesus is a sinner."

²⁵"I don't know whether he is a sinner," the man replied. "But I know this: I was blind, and now I can see!"

²⁶"But what did he do?" they asked. "How did he heal you?"

²⁷"Look!" the man exclaimed. "I told you once. Didn't you listen? Why do you want to hear it again? Do you want to become his disciples, too?"

²⁸Then they cursed him and said, "You are his disciple, but we are disciples of Moses! ²⁹We know God spoke to Moses, but we don't even know where this man comes from."

³⁰"Why, that's very strange!" the man replied. "He healed my eyes, and yet you don't know where he comes from? ³¹We know that God doesn't listen to sinners, but he is ready to hear those who worship him and do his will. ³²Ever since the world began, no one has been able to open the eyes of someone born blind. ³³If this man were not from God, he couldn't have done it."

³⁴"You were born a total sinner!" they answered. "Are you trying to teach us?" And they threw him out of the synagogue.

Spiritual Blindness

³⁵When Jesus heard what had happened, he found the man and asked, "Do you believe in the Son of Man?"

9:14
Luke 13:14
John 5:9

9:16
John 3:2; 7:43

9:17
Matt 21:11

9:22
Luke 6:22
John 7:13; 12:42;
16:2; 19:38
Acts 5:13

9:24
Josh 7:19

9:28
John 5:45

9:29
John 8:14

9:31
Job 27:8-9
Ps 34:15; 66:18;
145:19
Prov 15:29
Isa 1:15
Jer 11:11; 14:12
Mic 3:4
Zech 7:13

9:33
John 3:2

9:34
John 9:2

9:37
John 4:26

9:39
Luke 4:18

9:40
Rom 2:19

. . . .

9:11 The blind man identified *Jesus* and testified strongly about him. The man was healed of his physical infirmity, gained increasing spiritual insight (9:17, 33), and became Jesus' disciple (9:38; cp. 5:11-15).

9:13 The *Pharisees* (see 1:24) were arbiters of legal interpretation, so the community looked to them to explain this miracle. Rather than celebrate the healing, these religious leaders interrogated the man because Jesus had performed the miracle on the Sabbath (see 5:16-18).

9:17 The man had already identified his healer (9:11, 16). Now he made his own spiritual judgment, calling Jesus *a prophet*.

9:18 The Pharisees wanted to discount the miracle and hoped the man's *parents* would deny the healing.

9:20-22 *His parents* confirmed that their son had been *born blind*, but they hesitated to judge how he could see because they were *afraid* of the social consequences.

9:24 *God should get the glory for this:* Or *Give glory to God, not to Jesus;* Greek reads *Give glory to God.* Cp. Josh 7:19.

9:28-29 The Pharisees could not defeat the logic of the miraculous sign (9:24-25, 30-33), so they turned from reason and *cursed him* (see 9:34). • The harsh division between Jesus and the religious leaders was clear. They considered those who followed Jesus to have rejected *Moses* and Judaism.

9:30 The Jewish leaders did not *know* where Jesus came from. The man's astonishment was understandable—a healing like this was unprecedented. Jesus' works confirmed his origin as from God. Once his true identity was known, belief and discipleship should have followed, but the Jewish leaders were willfully blind.

9:32-33 Only God could do something such as *open the eyes of someone born blind.* By healing the man, Jesus offered the Jewish leaders an unquestionable sign that he was *from God* and was the Messiah (cp. Ps 146:8; Isa 35:5; 42:7).

9:34 Discipline such as being thrown *out of the synagogue* was not uncommon. It brought social isolation that might require the man's departure from the village. Such serious persecution was precisely what Jesus predicted for his followers (15:18-27; 16:2).

9:35-38 Jesus pressed the man who had been blind to understand the miracle and the identity of his healer. Immediately, the man expressed faith and gave

36The man answered, "Who is he, sir? I want to believe in him."

37"You have seen him," Jesus said, "and he is speaking to you!"

38"Yes, Lord, I believe!" the man said. And he worshiped Jesus.

39Then Jesus told him, "I entered this world to render judgment—to give sight to the blind and to show those who think they see that they are blind."

40Some Pharisees who were standing nearby heard him and asked, "Are you saying we're blind?"

41"If you were blind, you wouldn't be guilty," Jesus replied. "But you remain guilty because you claim you can see."

Jesus and the Festival of Dedication (10:1-42)
The Good Shepherd and His Sheep

10 "I tell you the truth, anyone who sneaks over the wall of a sheepfold, rather than going through the gate, must surely be a thief and a robber! 2But the one who enters through the gate is the shepherd of the sheep. 3The gatekeeper opens the gate for him, and the sheep recognize his voice and come to him. He calls his own sheep by name and leads them out. 4After he has gathered his own flock, he walks ahead of them, and they follow him because they know his voice. 5They won't follow a stranger; they will run from him because they don't know his voice."

6Those who heard Jesus use this illustration didn't understand what he meant, 7so he explained it to them: "I tell you the truth, I am the gate for the sheep. 8All who came before me were thieves and robbers. But the true sheep did not listen to them. 9Yes, I am the gate. Those who come in through me will be saved. They will come and go freely and will find good pastures. 10The thief's purpose is to steal and kill and destroy. My purpose is to give them a rich and satisfying life.

11"I am the good hshepherd. The good hshepherd sacrifices his life for the sheep. 12A hired hand will run when he sees a wolf

- -

Jesus reverence due only to God (9:38; cp. 20:28).

9:35 Son of Man: Some manuscripts read the Son of God. "Son of Man" is a title Jesus used for himself (1:51; 3:13, 14; 5:27; 6:27, 53, 62; 8:28). The Greek translates a Hebrew and Aramaic phrase meaning "human being." People were not completely sure what Jesus meant by it (see 12:34). However, it signifies Jesus' identity as both human and as the Messiah (cp. Dan 7:13-14).

9:38-39 Some manuscripts do not include "Yes, Lord, I believe!" the man said. And he worshiped Jesus. Then Jesus told him.

9:39 those who think they see: Literally those who see.

9:40-41 Are you saying we're blind? Jesus answered that those who claim to hold all religious truth will discover that they are blind, while those who recognize their spiritual poverty will find true sight. In the story, the blind man and his family frequently confessed that they did not know, while the Pharisees repeatedly stated their confidence and remained guilty because of their religious pride. If they had confessed their ignorance and admitted their spiritual blindness, they would be guiltless. Instead, their conscious and willful rejection of Jesus established their guilt.

10:1-42 Chapter 10 continues the series of festival sermons (see note on 5:1–10:42). Jesus now moves to Hanukkah (the Festival of Dedication), the timing of which is crucial to understanding the story (see note on 10:22).

10:1-21 This illustration of a shepherd and his sheep assumes a Middle Eastern understanding of shepherding and draws on OT tradition deeply embedded in first-century Jewish culture. God was the shepherd of Israel (Gen 49:24; Ps 23; 78:52-53; Isa 40:10-11). Spiritual and political leaders of Israel were also shepherds of God's people, the flock of God (Isa 56:9-12; Jer 23:1-4; Ezek 34). Jesus' sermon builds on the occasion of Hanukkah (see 10:22) to address the theme of shepherds, using this festival as an opportunity to reflect on Israel's leaders ("shepherds") in light of Ezek 34. Jesus presents himself as the only good shepherd (10:11-14).

10:1 A wilderness shepherd would build a sheepfold, a pen with low stone walls topped by thorny branches to hold his sheep at night and protect them from danger. • The pen had one gate (or opening in the wall) that was closed with branches. Any invasion of the pen was a threat to the flock. • A bad shepherd was like a thief and a robber. He exploited the sheep for his own interests and did not care for or nurture them. Bad shepherds took the sheep's milk and wool for themselves and butchered the sheep without providing for the animal's safety (Ezek 34:3; see Isa 56:11; Jer 23:1-4). This was Jesus' most stinging indictment of the Jewish leaders.

10:3 the sheep recognize his voice: The Middle Eastern shepherd is well known for having intimate knowledge of the sheep. Sheep are led with flute tunes, songs, or verbal commands.

10:4 A good shepherd always leads his sheep; he never drives them. When they recognize his voice, they trust his leadership and follow him.

10:7 I am: See note on 6:35. A good shepherd is known for guarding the sheep at the gate as a sentry.

10:8 Some manuscripts do not include before me.

10:9 will be saved (or will find safety): As gatekeeper, Jesus keeps away those who might harm his sheep, keeping his sheep inside the pen where they are safe.

10:10 Jesus' followers must be wary of bad shepherds who desire to steal and kill and destroy. As the Hanukkah story was told to the Jewish people (see note on 10:22), they were reminded about false religious leaders whose failures had led to the loss of God's Temple in Jerusalem.

10:11-14 I am: See note on 6:35. The good shepherd leads his sheep, finds food and water, and locates paths in the wilderness (see Ps 23). The good shepherd stands between his sheep and danger (10:11) and fights to protect them. The OT describes God as Israel's shepherd (Ps 23; 80:1; Isa 40:10-11). The leaders of God's people should shepherd their flock as God does (Ezek 34:23). However, the leaders of Israel in Jesus' time were bad shepherds.

10:11-13 Small villages often created communal flocks and employed a hired hand to tend the sheep. However, an employee lacked the commitment of a true shepherd. The wilderness of Judea

coming. He will abandon the sheep because they don't belong to him and he isn't their ⁱshepherd. And so the wolf attacks them and scatters the flock. ¹³The hired hand runs away because he's working only for the money and doesn't really care about the sheep.

¹⁴"I am the good shepherd; I know my own sheep, and they know me, ¹⁵just as my Father knows me and I know the Father. So I sacrifice my life for the sheep. ¹⁶I have other sheep, too, that are not in this sheepfold. I must bring them also. They will listen to my voice, and there will be one flock with one shepherd.

¹⁷"The Father loves me because I sacrifice my life so I may take it back again. ¹⁸No one can take my life from me. I sacrifice it voluntarily. For I have the authority to lay it down when I want to and also to take it up again. For this is what my Father has commanded."

¹⁹When he said these things, the people were again divided in their opinions about him. ²⁰Some said, "He's demon possessed and out of his mind. Why listen to a man like that?" ²¹Others said, "This doesn't sound like a man possessed by a demon! Can a demon open the eyes of the blind?"

Jesus at Hanukkah

²²It was now winter, and Jesus was in Jerusalem at the time of Hanukkah, the Festival of Dedication. ²³He was in the Temple, walking through the section known as Solomon's Colonnade. ²⁴The people surrounded him and asked, "How long are you going to keep us in suspense? If you are the Messiah, tell us plainly."

²⁵Jesus replied, "I have already told you, and you don't believe me. The proof is the work I do in my Father's name. ²⁶But you don't believe me because you are not my sheep. ²⁷My sheep listen to my voice; I know them, and they follow me. ²⁸I give them eternal life, and they will never perish. No one can snatch them away from me, ²⁹for my Father has given them to me, and he is more powerful than anyone else. No one can snatch them from the Father's hand. ³⁰The Father and I are one."

³¹Once again the people picked up

10:12
ⁱ*poimēn* (4166)
▸ John 21:16

10:14
2 Tim 2:19

10:15
Matt 11:27

10:16
Isa 56:8
Ezek 37:24
John 11:52
Eph 2:14-18

10:17-18
Phil 2:8-9
Heb 5:8; 7:16

10:23
Acts 3:11; 5:12

10:24
Luke 22:67

10:25
John 5:36; 10:38;
14:11

10:26
John 8:47

10:28
John 6:37, 39; 17:12

10:29
John 14:28
17:2, 6, 24

10:30
John 1:1; 10:38; 14:8-
11; 17:21-24

· ·

had many predators. When *a wolf* or other predators attacked, the hired hand would run rather than defend the sheep. Jesus will never do this; he will always stand between his sheep and danger.

10:14-17 *I sacrifice my life for the sheep:* Jesus was alluding to his crucifixion (ch 19).

10:15 The *Father* and the Son share a profound intimacy, which Jesus shares with his *sheep* through the Holy Spirit (14:23-31; 15:1-11).

10:16 *other sheep:* Believers outside Judaism would one day join Jesus' *sheepfold* (see 11:52). In Jesus' vision for his people, Jewish and Gentile believers from diverse cultures would become *one flock with one shepherd* (17:20-23).

10:18 *No one can take my life from me:* The Son's death was voluntary. Jesus was not a martyr or a victim. His decision to die was freely given in obedience and intimate relationship with his Father (see Acts 2:23-24). • Jesus' resurrection was not an afterthought in which God rescued his Son from tragedy. God could not be contained by a tomb, and since Jesus and the Father are one, Jesus possessed *the authority* to rise from death.

10:19-21 Jesus *divided* his audience yet again (see also 6:66-69; 7:43; 9:16), inspiring either opposition or faith. • *He's demon possessed:* Cp. 7:20; 8:48-49, 52. • *people:* Literally *Jewish people;* also in 10:24, 31.

10:22 *Hanukkah* was a *winter* festival that commemorated the rededication of the Temple after it had been defiled by Antiochus IV (175–163 BC). Two hundred years before Christ, Greek soldiers captured and pillaged the Jerusalem Temple, took its treasures and artifacts, and made it unusable for worship. In the winter of 165–164 BC, a Jewish army led by Judas Maccabeus reclaimed the Temple and rededicated it to the Lord. The Festival of Hanukkah ("dedication") marked this dedication (see *1 Maccabees* 3–4; *2 Maccabees* 8:1–10:8). During the festival, priests examined their commitment to service, using Ezek 34 as their principal text for reflection (also Jer 23:1-4; 25:32-38; Zech 11). At this Hanukkah celebration, Jesus used the shepherd theme from Ezek 34 to distinguish between himself as the good shepherd (10:11) and Israel's current religious leaders as bad shepherds (10:10, 12-13).

10:23 Massive covered colonnades surrounded the four sides of the central courtyard of the Temple. *Solomon's Colonnade,* on the east, provided shelter from winter weather.

10:24 The people who *surrounded* Jesus might have been seeking clarity, or they might have been hostile. In Luke 21:20 and Heb 11:30, the same word describes how Jerusalem and Jericho were surrounded before being destroyed; in Acts 14:20 it refers to Paul's disciples rallying around him after he was injured.

10:25-42 In Jesus' final public presentation of evidence about himself in this Gospel, he gives an exhaustive statement of his identity (10:30).

10:25 Jesus had already provided the Jewish people and their religious leaders with sufficient *proof* that he is the Son of God. The problem was not lack of information, but their unwillingness to *believe* him.

10:27-29 As the good shepherd, Jesus would die for his sheep and secure them from all predators and thieves (10:1, 8, 11; cp. Ezek 34:22-23). • The power of the *Father,* appearing in Christ, keeps his sheep safe. Believers cannot be taken from Jesus because no one is *more powerful* than he is. Their security is not sustained by their own efforts, but by Christ. • The word *snatch* implies violence (as in 6:15).

10:29 *for my Father has given them to me, and he is more powerful than anyone else:* Other manuscripts read *for what my Father has given me is more powerful than anything;* still others read *for regarding that which my Father has given me, he is greater than all.*

10:30 *The Father* and the Son are two separate persons with *one* purpose and nature (1:1, 14; 14:9; 20:28). This is the basis of Jesus' power to protect God's flock (10:28-29) and a stunning expression of Jesus' divinity.

10:31-33 The *people* realized Jesus' meaning (see 10:33) and wanted to

10:33
Lev 24:16
Matt 26:63-66
John 1:1, 18; 5:18;
20:28
Rom 9:5
Phil 2:6
Titus 2:13
2 Pet 1:1
1 Jn 5:20
ʲblasphēmia (0988)
  ▸ Eph 4:31
10:34
*Ps 82:6
10:36
John 5:17-20
10:42
John 2:23; 7:31; 8:30;
11:45; 12:11, 42
11:1
Matt 21:17
Luke 10:38
11:2
John 12:3
11:4
John 9:3
11:8
John 8:59; 10:31
ᵏrhabbi (4461)
  ▸ John 20:16
11:9
John 9:4
11:10
John 12:35
11:11
Dan 12:2
Matt 9:24; 27:52
Mark 5:39
Luke 8:52

stones to kill him. ³²Jesus said, "At my Father's direction I have done many good works. For which one are you going to stone me?"

³³They replied, "We're stoning you not for any good work, but for ʲblasphemy! You, a mere man, claim to be God."

³⁴Jesus replied, "It is written in your own Scriptures that God said to certain leaders of the people, 'I say, you are gods!' ³⁵And you know that the Scriptures cannot be altered. So if those people who received God's message were called 'gods,' ³⁶why do you call it blasphemy when I say, 'I am the Son of God'? After all, the Father set me apart and sent me into the world. ³⁷Don't believe me unless I carry out my Father's work. ³⁸But if I do his work, believe in the evidence of the miraculous works I have done, even if you don't believe me. Then you will know and understand that the Father is in me, and I am in the Father."

³⁹Once again they tried to arrest him, but he got away and left them. ⁴⁰He went beyond the Jordan River near the place where John was first baptizing and stayed there awhile. ⁴¹And many followed him. "John didn't perform miraculous signs," they remarked to one another, "but everything he said about this man has come true." ⁴²And many who were there believed in Jesus.

Foreshadowing Jesus' Death and Resurrection (11:1–12:50)
Lazarus: A Model of Jesus' Resurrection

11 A man named Lazarus was sick. He lived in Bethany with his sisters, Mary and Martha. ²This is the Mary who later poured the expensive perfume on the Lord's feet and wiped them with her hair. Her brother, Lazarus, was sick. ³So the two sisters sent a message to Jesus telling him, "Lord, your dear friend is very sick."

⁴But when Jesus heard about it he said, "Lazarus's sickness will not end in death. No, it happened for the glory of God so that the Son of God will receive glory from this." ⁵So although Jesus loved Martha, Mary, and Lazarus, ⁶he stayed where he was for the next two days. ⁷Finally, he said to his disciples, "Let's go back to Judea."

⁸But his disciples objected. "ᵏRabbi," they said, "only a few days ago the people in Judea were trying to stone you. Are you going there again?"

⁹Jesus replied, "There are twelve hours of daylight every day. During the day people can walk safely. They can see because they have the light of this world. ¹⁰But at night there is danger of stumbling because they have no light." ¹¹Then he said, "Our friend Lazarus has fallen asleep, but now I will go and wake him up."

. . . .

kill him. The problem was not Jesus' *good works,* but his claim to divinity (see 6:42, 60; 7:29-30). Committing *blasphemy* was punishable by stoning (Lev 24:23; see John 8:59).

10:34-36 *your own Scriptures:* Literally *your own law.* See Ps 82:6. • *I say, you are gods!* If the word *god* could be applied to people other than the Lord, then Jesus was not breaking the law by referring to himself in this way. Yet Jesus is not just any son of God; he is the *Son of God* who was *sent . . . into the world.*

10:38 Jesus' *miraculous works* should help true believers *know and understand* that the full reality of God dwells in Jesus.

10:40 His revelation to the Jewish leaders now complete, Jesus retired to the region *beyond the Jordan River* where John the Baptist had once worked and where Jesus was baptized.

10:41 *everything he said about this man has come true:* See 1:19-51; 3:22-36. The fulfillment of John the Baptist's predictions confirms both that he was a prophet and that what he said about Jesus was true.

10:42 This is a note of irony. While

Jesus found little faith among the religious leaders in the holy city of Jerusalem, in the desert he found *many who . . . believed.*

11:1-57 The raising of Lazarus foreshadows Jesus' own coming death and resurrection. Even the description of Lazarus' grave (11:38, 44) prefigures Jesus' grave (20:1, 7). Shortly after this event, Jesus was anointed for burial (12:3) and the hour of his glorification began (12:23).

11:1 In Hebrew, *Lazarus* is a shortened form of *Eleazar* ("God helps"). Among Jews in the first century, it was the fourth-most-common name for a man (see also Luke 16:19-31). • *Bethany* was a small village east of Jerusalem just over the Mount of Olives (11:18), where Jesus often stayed when he was in Jerusalem. Jesus would have traveled through Bethany on the way to Jerusalem because most Jews used a route going east from Jerusalem, down to Jericho, and north to Galilee. • *Mary and Martha* were sisters (Luke 10:38-42). Martha was probably older; she was the host in Luke's story and here represented the family. Mary later anointed Jesus with perfume (12:1-8).

11:2 *Mary who later poured the expensive perfume on the Lord's feet and wiped them with her hair:* This incident is recorded in ch 12.

11:3 The *two sisters* had a dilemma. They knew Jesus' power as a healer, but they also realized that his return to Judea would entail personal risk (11:8).

11:4 Jesus' response paralleled his words about the man born blind (9:1-5). Jesus already knew that Lazarus was dead (11:14); he was talking about Lazarus' resurrection (11:43), which would bring *glory* to *God.*

11:6 The trip from where Jesus was staying (see 10:40) to Jerusalem would have taken only one day, but Jesus followed his own sense of timing (2:4; 7:5-9) and would not be compelled by others.

11:8 The disciples were rightly worried about the risk (7:25; 8:37, 44, 59; 10:31, 39). • *people:* Literally *Jewish people;* also in 11:19, 31, 33, 36, 45, 54.

¹²The disciples said, "Lord, if he is sleeping, he will soon get better!" ¹³They thought Jesus meant Lazarus was simply sleeping, but Jesus meant Lazarus had died.

¹⁴So he told them plainly, "Lazarus is dead. ¹⁵And for your sakes, I'm glad I wasn't there, for now you will really believe. Come, let's go see him."

¹⁶Thomas, nicknamed the Twin, said to his fellow disciples, "Let's go, too—and die with Jesus."

¹⁷When Jesus arrived at Bethany, he was told that Lazarus had already been in his grave for four days. ¹⁸Bethany was only a few miles down the road from Jerusalem, ¹⁹and many of the people had come to console Martha and Mary in their loss. ²⁰When Martha got word that Jesus was coming, she went to meet him. But Mary stayed in the house. ²¹Martha said to Jesus, "Lord, if only you had been here, my brother would not have died. ²²But even now I know that God will give you whatever you ask."

²³Jesus told her, "Your brother will rise again."

²⁴"Yes," Martha said, "he will rise when everyone else ᵃrises, at the last day."

²⁵Jesus told her, "I am the resurrection and the life. Anyone who believes in me will live, even after dying. ²⁶Everyone who lives in me and believes in me will never ever die. Do you believe this, Martha?"

²⁷"Yes, Lord," she told him. "I have always believed you are the Messiah, the Son of God, the one who has come into the world from God." ²⁸Then she returned to Mary. She called Mary aside from the mourners and told her, "The Teacher is here and wants to see you." ²⁹So Mary immediately went to him.

³⁰Jesus had stayed outside the village, at the place where Martha met him. ³¹When the people who were at the house consoling Mary saw her leave so hastily, they assumed she was going to Lazarus's grave to weep. So they followed her there. ³²When Mary arrived and saw Jesus, she fell at his feet and said, "Lord, if only you had been here, my brother would not have died."

³³When Jesus saw her weeping and saw the other people wailing with her, a deep anger welled up within him, and he was deeply troubled. ³⁴"Where have you put him?" he asked them.

They told him, "Lord, come and see." ³⁵Then Jesus wept. ³⁶The people who were standing nearby said, "See how much he loved him!" ³⁷But some said, "This man healed a blind man. Couldn't he have kept Lazarus from dying?"

³⁸Jesus was still angry as he arrived at the tomb, a cave with a stone rolled across its entrance. ³⁹"Roll the stone aside," Jesus told them.

But Martha, the dead man's sister, protested, "Lord, he has been dead for four days. The smell will be terrible."

11:16
Matt 10:3
John 14:5; 20:24-28;
21:2
Acts 1:13

11:17
John 11:39

11:20
Luke 10:38-42

11:22
John 16:30

11:23-24
Dan 12:2
John 5:28-29
Acts 24:15
Phil 3:21
1 Thes 4:14

11:24
ᵃanastasis (0386)
▸ Acts 1:22

11:25
John 1:4; 3:36; 5:21;
6:39-40; 14:6
Col 1:18; 3:4
1 Jn 1:1-2; 5:10-11
Rev 1:17-18

11:26
John 8:51

11:27
Matt 16:16
John 6:14

11:35
Luke 19:41

11:37
John 9:6-7

11:39
John 11:17

· ·

11:16 *Thomas, nicknamed the Twin* (literally *Thomas, who was called Didymus*): See also 14:5; 20:24; 21:2; Mark 3:18. • *Let's go, too—and die:* Thomas knew that previous visits to Judea had been dangerous (5:18; 10:31, 39). Traveling to Jerusalem now would probably mean death for Jesus (cp. 11:49-50).

11:17 People were buried on the same day as their death. John noted that Lazarus had *been in his grave for four days,* so the miracle could not be construed as resuscitation.

11:18 *was only a few miles:* Greek *was about 15 stadia* [about 2.8 kilometers].

11:19 Life in NT times was lived publicly. Lazarus's large extended family, as well as the villagers, had arrived for a seven-day mourning period. To *console* the sisters *in their loss,* there was great wailing and crying (see 11:33 and note).

11:21 *Lord, if only you had been here:* Mary later repeated Martha's words (11:32), because both sisters knew Jesus' reputation as a healer. They concluded that Jesus would have healed Lazarus, but they did not imagine that Jesus would restore him from death.

11:22 *whatever you ask:* Martha thought that Jesus could still intervene in some way. Despite this, she objected when Jesus wanted to open the tomb (11:39); she wasn't thinking that Jesus would raise her brother from the dead.

11:24 *when everyone else rises, at the last day:* Martha misunderstood (cp. 11:11-13), thinking that Jesus was referring to the general resurrection of the dead at the end of time.

11:25 Jesus helped Martha to believe in him not simply as a healer, but as one who vanquishes death. • *I am the resurrection and the life* (some manuscripts do not include *and the life*): Victory over death is an aspect of living in association with Jesus. Although his followers are still mortal, they will enjoy eternal life after death. Regarding Jesus' *I am* statements, see the note on 6:35.

11:26-27 *Do you believe this?* Jesus was not asking if Martha believed he could bring Lazarus from the grave. Rather, did she believe that life itself is linked to Jesus? • *"Yes, Lord":* Even though the full implications were beyond her comprehension, she acknowledged that Jesus was indeed *the Messiah.* Yet she

was surprised at the power he held.

11:28-32 Mary now joined the scene on the edge of the village, repeating her sister's plaintive cry. She fell at Jesus' feet, not in worship but in desperate grief.

11:33 The loud *weeping* and *wailing* typified public displays of grief in this culture (Mark 5:38), as did beating one's chest (Luke 18:13). • *a deep anger welled up within him* (or *he was angry in his spirit*), *and he was deeply troubled:* The Greek word expresses human outrage, fury, and anger. Jesus was furious, not at Martha or Mary, but at the futility of this scene and the people's unbelief in light of the reality of the resurrection.

11:39 Lazarus was buried in a tomb cut from the rocky hillside; such tombs were common. The tomb was closed and opened for further burials with a rolling *stone* that covered the entrance. A central door led to a cave room where burial benches were carved in stone along the inner wall. Horizontal burial chambers were cut along the top edge of the benches. See the illustration on p. 1813.

11:41
Matt 11:25

11:42
John 12:30

11:43
Luke 7:14

11:47
Matt 26:3-5

11:49
Matt 26:3

11:50
John 18:13-14

11:51
Exod 28:30
Num 27:21

11:52
Isa 49:6
Luke 2:32
John 10:16
1 Jn 2:2

11:53
Matt 26:4

11:55
Exod 12:13
2 Chr 30:17-19
Matt 26:1-2
Mark 14:1

40Jesus responded, "Didn't I tell you that you would see God's glory if you believe?" 41So they rolled the stone aside. Then Jesus looked up to heaven and said, "Father, thank you for hearing me. 42You always hear me, but I said it out loud for the sake of all these people standing here, so that they will believe you sent me." 43Then Jesus shouted, "Lazarus, come out!" 44And the dead man came out, his hands and feet bound in graveclothes, his face wrapped in a headcloth. Jesus told them, "Unwrap him and let him go!"

The Plot to Kill Jesus

45Many of the people who were with Mary believed in Jesus when they saw this happen. 46But some went to the Pharisees and told them what Jesus had done. 47Then the leading priests and Pharisees called the high council together. "What are we going to do?" they asked each other. "This man certainly performs many miraculous signs. 48If we allow him to go on like this, soon everyone will believe in him. Then the Roman army will come and destroy both our Temple and our nation."

49Caiaphas, who was high priest at that time, said, "You don't know what you're talking about! 50You don't realize that it's better for you that one man should die for the people than for the whole nation to be destroyed."

51He did not say this on his own; as high priest at that time he was led to prophesy that Jesus would die for the entire nation. 52And not only for that nation, but to bring together and unite all the children of God scattered around the world.

53So from that time on, the Jewish leaders began to plot Jesus' death. 54As a result, Jesus stopped his public ministry among the people and left Jerusalem. He went to a place near the wilderness, to the village of Ephraim, and stayed there with his disciples.

55It was now almost time for the Jewish Passover celebration, and many people from all over the country arrived in Jerusalem several days early so they could go through the purification ceremony before Passover began. 56They kept looking for Jesus, but as they stood around in the

◀ **Jesus' Ministry in Judea (11:1–12:19).** Judea was a Roman prefecture under Pontius Pilate (see profile, p. 1691). John records much of Jesus' ministry in JERUSALEM (2:13–3:21; 5:1-47; 7:10–10:42; 12:12-50) and JUDEA (3:22; 11:1-44; 12:1-11). When the time came for Jesus' death, Jesus embarked on his final trip from Galilee to Jerusalem (see map, p. 1747). The events of 11:1–20:31 took place during Jesus' final period in and around Jerusalem.

11:50-51 *it's better . . . that one man should die:* Caiaphas's words were ironic. He meant that it was better for a revolutionary to die than to have the Romans crush the entire Jewish *nation*. But Caiaphas was correct in a way that he could not perceive. The salvation that Judaism needed had little to do with Rome; it would come through the cross of Christ. John notes that Caiaphas's inspiration was not *his own*, but came from God.

11:52 Christ's death was not for Israel only, but for all, including people of other cultures *scattered around the world* (10:16; 12:32).

11:53-54 When *the Jewish leaders began to plot Jesus' death,* Jesus made a judicious political move in response (11:54). • *Ephraim* was a village about twelve miles north of Jerusalem, where Jesus was safe from the Sanhedrin but close enough to walk to the upcoming Passover festival (11:55).

11:55-57 As crowds arrived in Jerusalem on pilgrimage for *Passover* (see 2:13), the city was buzzing with talk about Jesus and his miracle of raising Lazarus from the dead. People wondered if Jesus would be obedient to the law and come to the city to celebrate or play it safe in the countryside. The *priests and Pharisees* knew that Jesus was faithful to the law and would attend the festival, so they tried to make the city a trap for him.

11:45-46 As news of the miracle spread rapidly into the city of Jerusalem (12:9, 17), public opinion was again divided (6:66-69; 7:43; 9:16; 10:19; 11:37). Jesus' reputation as a healer and as one who could raise the dead was known in Galilee (see Matt 9:24-26; 10:8; 11:5). Now he had brought this power to Judea.

11:47 *the high council:* Greek *the Sanhedrin.*

11:48 The council's deliberations unveiled their fears that *everyone* would *believe in him.* If people believed that

the Messiah had come, the political implications would be threatening. The Romans viewed Jewish messiahs with suspicion, and the movement surrounding Jesus might inspire them to invade and destroy Jerusalem and its Temple. • *our Temple:* Or *our position;* Greek reads *our place.*

11:49 *Caiaphas* was the ruler of the high council from AD 18–36. He worked for ten years alongside Pontius Pilate, governor of Judea (AD 26–36; see 18:29), keeping the peace with Rome. • *at that time:* Literally *that year;* also in 11:51.

Temple, they said to each other, "What do you think? He won't come for Passover, will he?" [57]Meanwhile, the leading priests and Pharisees had publicly ordered that anyone seeing Jesus must report it immediately so they could arrest him.

Jesus Anointed at Bethany
John 12:1-11; cp. Matt 26:6-13 // Mark 14:3-9; cp. Luke 7:36-50

12 Six days before the Passover celebration began, Jesus arrived in Bethany, the home of Lazarus—the man he had raised from the dead. [2]A dinner was prepared in Jesus' honor. Martha served, and Lazarus was among those who ate with him. [3]Then Mary took a twelve-ounce jar of expensive perfume made from essence of nard, and she [b]anointed Jesus' feet with it, wiping his feet with her hair. The house was filled with the fragrance.

[4]But Judas Iscariot, the disciple who would soon betray him, said, [5]"That perfume was worth a year's wages. It should have been sold and the money given to the poor." [6]Not that he cared for the poor—he was a thief, and since he was in charge of the disciples' money, he often stole some for himself.

[7]Jesus replied, "Leave her alone. She did this in preparation for my burial. [8]You will always have the poor among you, but you will not always have me."

[9]When all the people heard of Jesus' arrival, they flocked to see him and also to see Lazarus, the man Jesus had raised from the dead. [10]Then the leading priests decided to kill Lazarus, too, [11]for it was because of him that many of the people had deserted them and [c]believed in Jesus.

Jesus' Messianic Entry into Jerusalem
John 12:12-19 // Matt 21:1-11 // Mark 11:1-11 // Luke 19:28-40

[12]The next day, the news that Jesus was on the way to Jerusalem swept through the city. A large crowd of Passover visitors [13]took palm branches and went down the road to meet him. They shouted,

"Praise God!
Blessings on the one who comes in the name of the LORD!
Hail to the King of Israel!"

[14]Jesus found a young donkey and rode on it, fulfilling the prophecy that said:

[15] "Don't be afraid, people of Jerusalem.
Look, your King is coming,
riding on a donkey's colt."

[16]His disciples didn't understand at the time that this was a fulfillment of prophecy.

Cross references (margin)

12:1-8
//Matt 26:6-13
//Mark 14:3-9

12:1
John 11:1

12:2
Luke 10:38-42

12:3
Luke 7:37-38
[b]aleiphō (0218)
> Jas 5:14

12:4
John 6:71

12:6
John 13:29

12:7
John 19:40

12:8
Deut 15:11

12:10
Luke 16:31

12:11
[c]pisteuō (4100)
> Acts 5:14

12:12-19
//Matt 21:1-11
//Mark 11:1-11
//Luke 19:28-38

12:13
Lev 23:40
*Ps 118:25-26
Zeph 3:15

12:15
Isa 35:4
*Zech 9:9

12:16
John 2:22; 7:39

12:1-50 Two stories build simultaneously. A growing number of people are praising Jesus (this climaxes in 12:12), and the authorities are increasingly determined to arrest him and put him to death. • John records three events that occurred just days prior to Passover (12:1-11, 12-19, 20-36). Then he explains why most of the people refused to believe and details Jesus' final public appeal (12:37-50).

12:1 Pilgrims from throughout Israel began arriving in Jerusalem the week *before the Passover.* The festival was on Thursday that year; Jesus arrived late the preceding Friday, just before the Sabbath.

12:2 *who ate:* Or *who reclined.* The typical posture for eating was to recline at a low table.

12:3 *Mary . . . anointed Jesus' feet:* Doing so was not awkward, because Jews reclined at formal meals, but it was certainly a dramatic gesture (cp. Matt 26:6-16; Mark 14:3-9). • *a twelve-ounce jar:* Greek *1 litra* [327 grams]. • *Nard,* a precious spice imported from North India, was sweet, red, and smelled like gladiola perfume. Twelve ounces of nard cost a year's wages (12:5). According to Mark, Mary also anointed Jesus' head (Mark 14:3), and the perfume

ran down and scented his garments (Mark 14:8). • *her hair:* Women never unveiled their hair in public (see Luke 7:38). Mary was acting with extravagant abandon and devotion.

12:5 *a year's wages:* Greek *300 denarii.* A denarius was equivalent to a laborer's full day's wage. Judas may have been exaggerating, but Mary's sacrifice was certainly very costly.

12:7 *Leave her alone:* Jesus' defense of Mary interpreted her deed. The nard was a *burial* spice for his death. Jesus was readied for burial as he moved toward the hour of glorification and death (see note on 12:23).

12:8 Jesus would never neglect *the poor,* but this opportunity to serve him was unparalleled.

12:9 *people:* Literally *Jewish people;* also in 12:11.

12:11 *had deserted them:* Or *had deserted their traditions;* literally *had deserted.*

12:12 *The next day* was Sunday (see 12:1). • *A large crowd* of pilgrims (many from Galilee) camped in this region. As Jesus followed the road to Jerusalem, they cheered him. This triumphal entry appears in all four Gospels (Matt 21:1-11; Mark 11:1-11; Luke 19:29-38).

12:13-14 *palm branches:* The date palm was a celebratory symbol of Jewish nationalism. • *meet him:* The Greek word commonly describes crowds greeting a returning, triumphant king. • *Praise God:* Greek *Hosanna,* an exclamation of praise adapted from a Hebrew expression that means "save now." • *Blessings on the one:* The crowd quoted Ps 118:25-26, with a greeting for those who came to Jerusalem. The phrase *Hail to the King of Israel* is not in the psalm (but see Zeph 3:15). Although the people saw Jesus as a national political liberator, he rejected this role (6:15).

12:14 By choosing *a young donkey* rather than a warhorse, Jesus calmed the frenzied crowd that was passionate for his kingship. He also fulfilled OT predictions regarding the Messiah (see Zech 9:9) and showed that his kingship was not that of a warrior. His gift is life, not conquest.

12:15 This verse is a quotation of Zech 9:9 • *people of Jerusalem:* Literally *daughter of Zion.*

12:16 The crowds and even the *disciples didn't understand* Jesus' true significance. When the disciples received the Holy Spirit following Jesus' glorification, they fully comprehended who Jesus was (see 2:22).

12:17
John 11:43-44

12:18
John 12:11; 19:37

12:21
John 1:43-44

12:23
John 13:32; 17:1

12:24
1 Cor 15:36

12:25
Matt 10:39
Luke 9:24; 17:33

12:26
John 14:3; 17:24

12:27
Ps 6:3
Matt 26:38
Mark 14:34

12:28
Matt 3:17; 17:5
Mark 1:11; 9:7
Luke 3:22; 9:35
2 Pet 1:17-18

12:31
John 14:30; 16:11
Eph 2:2

12:32
John 3:14; 6:44

12:34
Ps 89:4, 36; 110:4
Isa 9:7
Ezek 37:25
Dan 7:14

But after Jesus entered into his glory, they remembered what had happened and realized that these things had been written about him.

17Many in the crowd had seen Jesus call Lazarus from the tomb, raising him from the dead, and they were telling others about it. 18That was the reason so many went out to meet him—because they had heard about this miraculous sign. 19Then the Pharisees said to each other, "There's nothing we can do. Look, everyone has gone after him!"

Jesus Predicts His Death

20Some Greeks who had come to Jerusalem for the Passover celebration 21paid a visit to Philip, who was from Bethsaida in Galilee. They said, "Sir, we want to meet Jesus." 22Philip told Andrew about it, and they went together to ask Jesus.

23Jesus replied, "Now the time has come for the Son of Man to enter into his glory. 24I tell you the truth, unless a kernel of wheat is planted in the soil and dies, it remains alone. But its death will produce many new kernels—a plentiful harvest of new lives. 25Those who love their life in this world will

lose it. Those who care nothing for their life in this world will keep it for eternity. 26Anyone who wants to be my disciple must follow me, because my servants must be where I am. And the Father will honor anyone who serves me.

27"Now my soul is deeply troubled. Should I pray, 'Father, save me from this hour'? But this is the very reason I came! 28Father, bring glory to your name."

Then a voice spoke from heaven, saying, "I have already brought glory to my name, and I will do so again." 29When the crowd heard the voice, some thought it was thunder, while others declared an angel had spoken to him.

30Then Jesus told them, "The voice was for your benefit, not mine. 31The time for judging this world has come, when Satan, the ruler of this world, will be cast out. 32And when I am lifted up from the earth, I will draw everyone to myself." 33He said this to indicate how he was going to die.

34The crowd responded, "We understood from Scripture that the Messiah would live forever. How can you say the Son of Man

12:17-19 This scene describes the apex of Jesus' popularity.

12:17 *were telling others:* Literally *were testifying.*

12:19 *everyone:* Literally *the world.* The Pharisees' words were more significant than they realized. Jesus came to reach the world (3:17), and the Pharisees said that Jesus had accomplished his task.

12:20 Among the people drawn to Jesus (12:19) were *some Greeks,* God-fearing Gentiles who had come to Passover to worship. Jesus' mission was not simply to Israel but encompassed the entire world (10:16; 11:52). Following Jesus' resurrection, the church's mission was to go beyond Judea to Samaria, and ultimately to the ends of the earth (Matt 28:19; Acts 1:8).

12:21 The Greeks approached *Philip* because he had a Greek name and was no doubt Greek.

12:23 Jesus often said that *the time* (literally *the hour*) had not yet *come* (2:4; 7:30; 8:20), but now it had. The coming of the Greeks also marked the beginning of the key moment in Jesus' ministry—the time of his glorification. This occurred when Jesus' sacrificial work on the cross was completed (19:30), he rose from the dead (ch 20), he gave the Spirit (20:22), and he returned to his place of glory in heaven (17:5, 11). The connection with the Greeks who had come to Jerusalem (12:20) was significant: Jesus' ministry among the

Jews alone was finished and he now belonged to the wider world. • *Son of Man* is a title Jesus used for himself.

12:24 The central event of Jesus' glorification (12:23) was the cross. As with a *kernel . . . planted in the soil,* Jesus' *death* would bring abundant life.

12:25 For disciples, sacrifice and self-effacement are means of gaining the fullness of life provided by Jesus' sacrifice. Those who renounce the *world* will join Jesus in *eternity* and be honored by God just as Jesus is.

12:27 *my soul is deeply troubled:* John used the same term (Greek *tarassō*) to describe Jesus' strong emotion of agony before Lazarus' tomb (11:33; also 13:21). When Jesus stood before death, he could not be impassive. Jesus experienced genuine anguish, yet he remained strong in obedience to the Father's will (5:19-23; 6:37; 8:29, 38; 14:31).

12:28 *a voice spoke from heaven:* Cp. Matt 3:17; 17:5; Mark 1:11; 9:7; Luke 3:22; 9:35. • God had already *brought glory* to himself when Christ entered the world (1:14) and through Jesus' work, which showed God's power to the world. • *I will do so again:* The final display of glory would come at the cross (see 12:23; 17:1). In John, the cross is an event of *glory* as Christ was "lifted up" (12:32) and glorified there. Jesus was prepared for crucifixion like a king coming to his coronation; the cross was like a throne (see 19:19-22), and he was

buried like royalty. Jesus' time of glorification included the entire sequence from arrest through resurrection.

12:29 It was impossible for people to comprehend what was happening with Jesus, and many of his signs led to confusion and division in *the crowd.* Only later did his disciples understand (2:22; 12:16), when Jesus was glorified and the Spirit was given. Still, God's voice symbolized his validation of his Son before the world.

12:31-33 *The time for judging* does not occur only on Judgment Day; it began when the light penetrated the darkness and unmasked it (3:19; 5:24; 9:39). • *Satan, the ruler of this world,* is the architect of darkness, corrupter of the world, and promoter of death. Although Satan's final demise lies in the future, the work of Christ unraveled Satan's domain (see Luke 10:17-18; Mark 3:27). Christ is now enthroned as ruler in heaven (Acts 7:55-56; Eph 1:19-22).

12:32-34 *when I am lifted up from the earth* (see 3:14; 8:28): The crowd did not understand what Jesus meant. The Greek verb refers to being exalted (Matt 23:12) or honored (Luke 10:15). In John, the cross was not a place of shame and disgrace for Jesus, but the place where Jesus' true glory was shown.

12:34 *from Scripture:* Literally *from the law.* • Popular Judaism believed that *the Messiah would live forever* and triumph over his foes. Jesus' point of view seemed incomprehensible.

will die? Just who is this Son of Man, anyway?"

³⁵Jesus replied, "My light will shine for you just a little longer. Walk in the light while you can, so the darkness will not overtake you. Those who walk in the darkness cannot see where they are going. ³⁶Put your trust in the light while there is still time; then you will become children of the light."

After saying these things, Jesus went away and was hidden from them.

The Unbelief of the People

³⁷But despite all the miraculous signs Jesus had done, most of the people still did not believe in him. ³⁸This is exactly what Isaiah the prophet had predicted:

"LORD, who has believed our message?
    To whom has the LORD revealed his
    powerful arm?"

³⁹But the people couldn't believe, for as Isaiah also said,

⁴⁰ "The Lord has blinded their eyes
    and hardened their hearts—
so that their eyes cannot see,
    and their hearts cannot understand,
    and they cannot turn to me
    and have me heal them."

⁴¹Isaiah was referring to Jesus when he said this, because he saw the future and spoke of the Messiah's glory. ⁴²Many people did believe in him, however, including some of the Jewish leaders. But they wouldn't admit it for fear that the Pharisees would expel them from the synagogue. ⁴³For they loved human praise more than the praise of God.

⁴⁴Jesus shouted to the crowds, "If you trust me, you are trusting not only me, but also God who sent me. ⁴⁵For when you see me, you are seeing the one who sent me. ⁴⁶I have come as a light to shine in this dark world, so that all who put their trust in me will no longer remain in the dark. ⁴⁷I will not judge those who hear me but don't obey me, for I have come to save the world and not to judge it. ⁴⁸But all who reject me and my message will be judged on the day of judgment by the truth I have spoken. ⁴⁹I don't speak on my own authority. The Father who sent me has commanded me what to say and how to say it. ⁵⁰And I know his commands lead to eternal life; so I say whatever the Father tells me to say."

3. THE BOOK OF GLORY: THE WORD IS GLORIFIED (13:1–20:31)
The Passover Meal (13:1-30)
Jesus Washes His Disciples' Feet

13 Before the Passover celebration, Jesus knew that his hour had come to leave this world and return to his Father. He had loved his disciples during his ministry on earth, and now he loved them to the very end. ²It was time for supper, and the devil had already prompted Judas, son of Simon Iscariot, to betray Jesus. ³Jesus knew that the Father had given him authority over everything and that he had come from

12:35
John 8:12; 9:4; 12:46
12:36
John 8:59
Eph 5:8
1 Thes 5:5
12:38
*Isa 53:1
Rom 10:16
12:40
*Isa 6:10
Matt 13:14
12:41
Isa 6:1
12:42
John 7:13, 48; 9:22-23; 12:11
12:43
John 5:44
12:45
John 14:9
12:46
John 1:4; 3:19; 8:12; 9:5
12:47
John 3:17; 8:15
13:1
John 16:28; 17:1
13:2
Luke 22:3
John 6:70-71

. . . .

• **who is this Son of Man, anyway?** The Jews did not understand what sort of Messiah planned to die.

12:36 Jesus was **the light** (1:4, 7-9; 3:19-21; 8:12), and he urged the crowd to quickly make the choice to believe in him before it was too late. • They had the choice of becoming **children of the light** by rebirth through the power of God (1:12-13). • **Jesus . . . was hidden from them:** Jesus withdrew first from Judea (11:54) and then from this audience (12:36), and soon he would withdraw from the world (17:11).

12:37-38 Jesus' work was finished, yet **most of the people . . . did not believe in him.** His sermons before the world were complete and the signs had been displayed, but he was rejected (1:11). • The quotation is from Isa 53:1.

12:39-40 **The people couldn't believe:** John quotes Isa 6:10 to explain Israel's unbelief (see Matt 13:13-15; Mark 4:12; Luke 8:10; Acts 28:26-27). When revelation comes, we must believe. If we refuse, the light disappears (12:35-

36). When God's light departs from the world, the darkness closes over unbelieving hearts.

12:41 *Isaiah* had glimpsed *the Messiah's glory* and how the world would respond (see Isa 6:10).

12:42-43 *Many people did believe in him*, but they *wouldn't admit it*. However, to follow Jesus involves telling others about him despite the social consequences (1:35-51; 4:1-42).

12:44-50 Jesus makes a final appeal for belief. These verses summarize chs 1–12. Jesus was sent by the Father, the sole source of his ministry. Jesus is the light shining in darkness to bring salvation and eternal life to all who believe in him.

12:49-50 The greatest error is for people to see the light and reject it, thinking it has no connection with the *Father who sent* the light.

13:1–20:31 This section focuses on the sign of the cross, the great climax of Jesus' life, as well as the time Jesus spent preparing his disciples for it

(chs 13–17). Jesus is glorified through each event of these momentous days. Jesus' arrest, trial, crucifixion, and resurrection all evoke responses of awe. On the cross, Jesus is elevated in glory before the world (12:32).

13:1-38 The setting is Jesus' final Passover meal on Thursday evening, when Judas Iscariot betrays Jesus. John does not record the meal itself as the synoptic Gospels do (Matt 26:17-29; Mark 14:12-25; Luke 22:7-20; see also 1 Cor 11:23-26). John emphasizes other activities at the event, such as the foot washing (13:1-17), Judas's betrayal (13:18-30), and the prediction of Peter's denials (13:31-38).

13:1 *he loved them to the very end:* Or *he showed them the full extent of his love.*

13:2 *Judas . . . Iscariot,* who had refused to believe, was engulfed by darkness and had become Satan's pawn (see note on 12:39-40). • *the devil had already prompted Judas:* Or *the devil had already intended for Judas.*

13:4
Luke 12:37; 22:27

13:5
Luke 7:44
John 12:3

13:8
Ezek 36:25
1 Cor 6:11
Eph 5:26
Titus 3:5

13:10
John 15:3

13:11
John 6:64, 70-71; 13:2

13:13
1 Cor 12:3

13:14
Luke 22:27
1 Tim 5:10
1 Pet 5:5

13:15
Phil 2:5-7
1 Pet 5:3-5
1 Jn 2:6; 3:16

13:16
ᵈ*doulos* (1401)
▸ John 15:15

13:17
Jas 1:25

13:18
*Ps 41:9

13:20
Matt 10:40
Luke 10:16

13:21-30
//Matt 26:21-25
//Mark 14:18-21
//Luke 22:21-23

13:23
John 19:26

13:25
John 21:20

God and would return to God. ⁴So he got up from the table, took off his robe, wrapped a towel around his waist, ⁵and poured water into a basin. Then he began to wash the disciples' feet, drying them with the towel he had around him.

⁶When Jesus came to Simon Peter, Peter said to him, "Lord, are you going to wash my feet?"

⁷Jesus replied, "You don't understand now what I am doing, but someday you will."

⁸"No," Peter protested, "you will never ever wash my feet!"

Jesus replied, "Unless I wash you, you won't belong to me."

⁹Simon Peter exclaimed, "Then wash my hands and head as well, Lord, not just my feet!"

¹⁰Jesus replied, "A person who has bathed all over does not need to wash, except for the feet, to be entirely clean. And you disciples are clean, but not all of you." ¹¹For Jesus knew who would betray him. That is what he meant when he said, "Not all of you are clean."

¹²After washing their feet, he put on his robe again and sat down and asked, "Do you understand what I was doing? ¹³You call me 'Teacher' and 'Lord,' and you are right, because that's what I am. ¹⁴And since I, your

Lord and Teacher, have washed your feet, you ought to wash each other's feet. ¹⁵I have given you an example to follow. Do as I have done to you. ¹⁶I tell you the truth, ᵈslaves are not greater than their master. Nor is the messenger more important than the one who sends the message. ¹⁷Now that you know these things, God will bless you for doing them.

¹⁸"I am not saying these things to all of you; I know the ones I have chosen. But this fulfills the Scripture that says, 'The one who eats my food has turned against me.' ¹⁹I tell you this beforehand, so that when it happens you will believe that I AM the Messiah. ²⁰I tell you the truth, anyone who welcomes my messenger is welcoming me, and anyone who welcomes me is welcoming the Father who sent me."

Jesus Predicts Judas's Betrayal
John 13:21-30 // Matt 26:20-25 // Mark 14:17-21 // Luke 22:21-23

²¹Now Jesus was deeply troubled, and he exclaimed, "I tell you the truth, one of you will betray me!"

²²The disciples looked at each other, wondering whom he could mean. ²³The disciple Jesus loved was sitting next to Jesus at the table. ²⁴Simon Peter motioned to him to ask, "Who's he talking about?" ²⁵So that disciple

13:4-5 Foot washing, common in the Hellenistic and Jewish cultures as a daily routine and as a gesture of hospitality (see Luke 7:36-50), was a lowly, menial task reserved for servants. When Jesus *began to wash the disciples' feet,* he took the posture of a slave.

13:8 Based on the depth of his devotion to Jesus, it is understandable that *Peter protested.* But Jesus was not simply giving Peter a model of service; this was a symbolic pre-enactment of his greater act of sacrifice on the cross (13:7). Receiving Jesus' spiritual cleansing is a condition for discipleship, so if Peter could not accept this act, he could not be Jesus' disciple at all.

13:9 *wash my hands and head as well:* Peter misunderstood Jesus (cp. 2:19-20; 3:3-4). Peter thought that to have more water was to have more of Jesus. Only when Peter received the Spirit did everything become clear (e.g., see Acts 2:14-36).

13:10 Jesus referred to an ultimate cleansing through his sacrifice which makes *a person* clean *all over.* • Some manuscripts do not include *except for the feet.*

13:14-15 Jesus' acts of service, such as washing feet and dying on the cross, provided *an example* of personal sacri-

fice *to follow.* • *wash each other's feet:* Foot washing was so commonplace that Jesus might have intended a literal repetition of his act, or he might have seen it as symbolic. Either way, Jesus wants similar servanthood and sacrifice to characterize his followers.

13:16 *slaves are not greater than their master:* This proverb was popular and appears in many places (see also 15:20; Matt 10:24; Luke 6:40). Here, Jesus meant that the sacrifice modeled by the master should be seen in the life of the servant.

13:18 *I am not saying these things to all of you:* The subject of Judas's betrayal enters the story for the third time (13:2, 11). The matter weighed heavily on Jesus (13:21). • *I know the ones I have chosen:* The statement does not imply that Jesus chose only the eleven and that Judas was an outcast. Jesus chose Judas and gave him every opportunity to believe. He realized that Judas had embraced the darkness rather than the light (6:70). • *The one who eats my food has turned against me* (literally *has lifted his heel against me*): See Ps 41:9. Eating together was a cultural symbol of personal intimacy, which made Judas's betrayal all the more treacherous.

13:19 Judas's betrayal did not take Jesus unaware, and it should not shock his

disciples *when it happens.* • *that I AM the Messiah:* Or *that the 'I AM' has come;* or *that I am the LORD;* literally *that I am.* By using the phrase "I am," Jesus clearly equated himself with the God of the OT. See Exod 3:14.

13:21 For the third time, *Jesus was deeply troubled* (literally *was troubled in his spirit;* Greek *tarassō;* see 11:33; 12:27). The personal betrayal of Judas brought Jesus profound grief.

13:23 *The disciple Jesus loved* appears at the cross (19:26-27), at the tomb (20:2-9), and at the resurrection (21:1, 20-23). He is the author of this Gospel (21:24-25). Some scholars believe that Lazarus was in fact the disciple whom Jesus loved (see 11:3, 5, 36), but the person referred to here was among the twelve apostles, usually identified as the apostle John. • *was sitting next to Jesus at the table:* Literally *was reclining on Jesus' bosom.* They were probably reclining at a *triclinium,* a U-shaped table with couches. Guests reclined on the couches, while the center provided access to servers. The diners supported their bodies by their left elbows while using their right hands for eating. Feet were extended away from the table (cp. Luke 7:38).

13:25 Peter told "the disciple Jesus loved" (13:23), who was sitting next to leaned over to Jesus and asked, "Lord, who is it?"

²⁶Jesus responded, "It is the one to whom I give the bread I dip in the bowl." And when he had dipped it, he gave it to Judas, son of Simon Iscariot. ²⁷When Judas had eaten the bread, ᵉSatan entered into him. Then Jesus told him, "Hurry and do what you're going to do." ²⁸None of the others at the table knew what Jesus meant. ²⁹Since Judas was their treasurer, some thought Jesus was telling him to go and pay for the food or to give some money to the poor. ³⁰So Judas left at once, going out into the night.

Jesus' Final Farewell (13:31–17:26)
Jesus Predicts Peter's Denial
John 13:36-38; cp. Matt 26:31-35 // Mark 14:27-31; cp. Luke 22:31-34

³¹As soon as Judas left the room, Jesus said, "The time has come for the Son of Man to enter into his glory, and God will be glorified because of him. ³²And since God receives glory because of the Son, he will soon give glory to the Son. ³³Dear children,

I will be with you only a little longer. And as I told the Jewish leaders, you will search for me, but you can't come where I am going. ³⁴So now I am giving you a new commandment: Love each other. Just as I have loved you, you should love each other. ³⁵Your love for one another will prove to the world that you are my disciples."

³⁶Simon Peter asked, "Lord, where are you going?"

And Jesus replied, "You can't go with me now, but you will follow me later."

³⁷"But why can't I come now, Lord?" he asked. "I'm ready to die for you."

³⁸Jesus answered, "Die for me? I tell you the truth, Peter—before the rooster crows tomorrow morning, you will deny three times that you even know me.

Jesus, the Way to the Father
14 "Don't let your ᶠhearts be troubled. Trust in God, and trust also in me. ²There is more than enough room in my Father's home. If this were not so, would I have told you that I am going to prepare a

---

Jesus, to ask the betrayer's identity. As he reclined next to Jesus, he *leaned over to Jesus* and spoke privately.

13:26 Meals were eaten with flat *bread*, which diners would *dip* into a common *bowl*. When Jesus gave a morsel to Judas (cp. Ruth 2:14), the disciples might have thought Jesus was honoring him. They did not understand what was occurring. They even thought that Judas's departure (13:29) fulfilled an official duty for the feast! But Jesus was signaling to Judas that he understood Judas's plan and was not taken by surprise. Jesus' knowledge is profound and complete (see 1:48; 2:25).

13:27 When *Satan entered into* Judas (see Luke 22:3), he became an example of what happens to those who are consumed by the darkness. Satan uses such people as pawns in a wider struggle against the light. • *Hurry and do what you're going to do:* In issuing this command, Jesus once again showed that he was in control, not human beings or Satan (see note on 7:30).

13:28-29 *None of the others* suspected that something odd was happening. Passover evening was one of the only nights when the city gates were left open. The night was spent in prayer and meditation, *money* was given *to the poor*, and provisions were always needed for this complex meal.

13:30 *out into the night:* Judas's departure was emblematic: The darkness had swallowed him completely (see note on 13:2; cp. 3:19). Jesus, the light of the world, is the antithesis of the night.

13:31–17:26 The OT and later Jewish literature include numerous examples of farewells in which a dying person offers last words to intimate friends (see Gen 49:1-27; Deut 31–34; Josh 23–24; 1 Sam 12; 1 Chr 28–29). Such farewells used a standard form. The dying person, surrounded by his loved ones, comforted them and exhorted them to obey the law. He prayed and blessed them and often left behind some writings. In some cases, the departing person passed on his "spirit" to his followers or his successor (see Num 27:18; Deut 34:9; 2 Kgs 2:9-14). Each of these elements is present in Jesus' farewell. • This section is often called the Upper Room Discourse, since the meal was taken in an "upstairs room" (Luke 22:39).

13:31 *The time has come:* Judas's departure into the night marks a solemn divide in the plot of the Gospel. Jesus was left with his intimate friends as the hour of glory was dawning. This time was launched by Judas's betrayal, and it culminated in the resurrection. • *Son of Man* is a title Jesus used for himself.

13:32 Some manuscripts do not include *And since God receives glory because of the Son.*

13:33 Jesus addressed the apostles as his *children,* marking the start of his farewell address.

13:34-35 That the disciples were to love one another was not *a new commandment* (see Lev 19:18). However, that they were to love each other with the sort of love modeled by Jesus was dra-

matic. Jesus' love for God was expressed in perfect obedience (14:31); now this kind of love was his command—that disciples express their love for Jesus in committed obedience.

13:37 Peter claimed to be *ready to die* for Jesus, yet his denials are well known in the synoptic Gospels (Matt 26:32-34; Mark 14:27-30; Luke 22:31-34). Although Peter's verve and devotion failed, he was restored (21:15-19).

14:1-31 Jesus provided answers to his disciples' many spoken and unspoken concerns.

14:1 Jesus had himself been *troubled* (Greek *tarassō*) on three occasions (11:33; 12:27; 13:21). His confidence in God's power made it possible for him to face these crises. Faced with the upsetting words of 13:33, the disciples confronted similar feelings. • *Trust* (or *believe,* or *have faith*) *in God:* Only trusting God would help them through his hour of death.

14:2 *There is more than enough room in my Father's home* (or *There are many rooms in my Father's house*): God's house is the dwelling place where he resides (Rev 21:9–22:5). The word translated "room" is related to the Greek verb meaning "remain, abide, dwell." Jesus promises that his followers will have a place to "dwell" alongside him, wherever he is. Later, this "dwelling" becomes a place of "indwelling" as Jesus makes his home in his followers' hearts through the Spirit (14:23). • *If this were not so, would I have told you that I am going to prepare a place for*

14:3
John 14:10-11, 18-20;
16:16-22; 17:21-24

14:6
John 1:4, 14, 16; 8:32;
10:10; 11:25
Rom 5:2
Eph 2:18
Heb 10:20
1 Jn 5:20

14:7
John 6:46; 8:19
1 Jn 2:13

14:9
John 1:14, 18; 12:45
2 Cor 4:4
Col 1:15
Heb 1:3

14:10
John 5:19; 10:38;
17:11, 21-24

place for you? ³When everything is ready, I will come and get you, so that you will always be with me where I am. ⁴And you know the way to where I am going."

⁵"No, we don't know, Lord," Thomas said. "We have no idea where you are going, so how can we know the way?"

⁶Jesus told him, "I am the way, the truth, and the life. No one can come to the Father except through me. ⁷If you had really known me, you would know who my Father is. From now on, you do know him and have seen him!"

⁸Philip said, "Lord, show us the Father, and we will be satisfied."

⁹Jesus replied, "Have I been with you all this time, Philip, and yet you still don't know who I am? Anyone who has seen me has seen the Father! So why are you asking me to show him to you? ¹⁰Don't you believe that I am in the Father and the Father is in me? The words I speak are not my own, but my Father who lives in me does his work through me. ¹¹Just believe that I am in the Father and the Father is in me. Or at least believe because of the work you have seen me do.

¹²"I tell you the truth, anyone who believes in me will do the same works I have done, and even greater works, because I am

JOHN THE APOSTLE, SON OF ZEBEDEE (13:23-25)

John 18:15-16;
19:26-27; 20:2-10;
21:2, 7, 20-24
Matt 4:21-22; 10:2;
17:1; 20:20-24;
26:37-46
Mark 1:19-20, 29;
3:17; 5:37; 9:2, 38;
10:35-41; 13:3-4;
14:33-42
Luke 5:10; 6:14;
8:51; 9:28, 49, 54
Acts 1:13; 3:1-11;
4:1-22; 5:17-42;
8:14-25
Gal 2:9

John, brother of James and son of Zebedee, was one of the twelve apostles. Early tradition identifies him as the author of the Gospel of John, the Letters of John, and the book of Revelation.

John and his brother James were among those closest to Jesus (Mark 5:37; 9:2; 13:3; 14:33). His mother, Salome, might have been a sister of Mary, the mother of Jesus (cp. 19:25; Matt 27:56; Mark 15:40; 16:1). John's name usually occurs after James's, which suggests that John was younger. James and John were fishermen like their father (Matt 4:21; Mark 1:19). They fished with Peter and Andrew, another pair of brothers who became disciples (Luke 5:10). They were among the first whom Jesus called as disciples, and they left everything to follow him (Matt 4:22; Mark 1:20; Luke 5:11; cp. John 1:35-40). Jesus named them "Sons of Thunder" (Mark 3:17), which might imply that they were loud or short-tempered (cp. Luke 9:54). At one point, the two brothers evoked the indignation of the other disciples when they asked for special positions of privilege in the coming kingdom (Matt 20:20-28; Mark 10:35-45; cp. Luke 22:24-27).

Early tradition links John to five NT books: the Gospel of John, three Letters of John, and the book of Revelation. John is understood to be the unnamed "disciple Jesus loved" and "another disciple" (13:23-25; 18:15-16; 19:26-27; 20:2-10; 21:20-24). He was possibly the unnamed disciple of John the Baptist, who, together with Andrew, became an early follower of Jesus (1:35-40).

John's name occurs three times in Acts; each time he was working with Peter (Acts 3:1-11; 4:1-23; 8:14-25). Paul referred to him as one of the "pillars" of the church in Jerusalem (Gal 2:9).

The most widespread tradition about John's later life is that he moved to Ephesus, where he eventually became the bishop of Asia Minor, lived to an old age, and died peacefully in the company of friends. His Gospel provides the most profound portrait that we have of Jesus, and his letters provide one of the finest depictions of the Christian life (1 John).

you? Or *If this were not so, I would have told you that I am going to prepare a place for you.* Some manuscripts read *If this were not so, I would have told you. I am going to prepare a place for you.*

14:3 Some scholars believe that Jesus meant he would *come and get* his followers after the resurrection (14:18). Others think these words refer to Jesus' second coming. For the disciples, the more important coming was Jesus' return from the grave (ch 16).

14:6 *I am:* See note on 6:35. Access to the Father's presence is only through Jesus, who is *the way, the truth, and the life.* • The *way* to *the Father* is only

through Jesus. Other religions and philosophies propose different avenues to God, but Jesus asserted that he is the one exclusive path to God. • Jesus is the *truth* because God is truth. • God is the source of eternal *life.* At Lazarus's tomb, Jesus showed his divine power over life and death (11:25).

14:7 *If you had really known me, you would know who my Father is:* Some manuscripts read *If you have really known me, you will know who my Father is.*

14:8 *Philip* did not yet understand that in Jesus he was seeing the full embodiment of God (14:9).

14:9 *Anyone who has seen me has seen the Father!* Cp. 1:1-2. Jesus Christ is God-in-the-flesh (1:14), which explains his capacity to accomplish divine works. Jesus did not simply teach about God; in him God can be found. Jesus' remarkable statement echoed what he had said at Hanukkah: "The Father and I are one" (10:30). This claim is at the root of the world's opposition to Christ (5:18).

14:10 Jesus' claims were astonishing (10:30, 37-38). Yet true faith recognizes Jesus' union with God *the Father.*

14:12 Jesus promised that *anyone who believes* in him would perform great miracles and experience answers to

going to be with the Father. ¹³You can ask for anything in my name, and I will do it, so that the Son can bring glory to the Father. ¹⁴Yes, ask me for anything in my name, and I will do it!

Jesus Promises the Holy Spirit

¹⁵"If you love me, obey my commandments. ¹⁶And I will ask the Father, and he will give you another ᵍAdvocate, who will never leave you. ¹⁷He is the Holy Spirit, who leads into all truth. The world cannot receive him, because it isn't looking for him and doesn't recognize him. But you know him, because he lives with you now and later will be in you. ¹⁸No, I will not abandon you as orphans—I will come to you. ¹⁹Soon the world will no longer see me, but you will see me. Since I live, you also will live. ²⁰When I am

raised to life again, you will know that I am in my Father, and you are in me, and I am in you. ²¹Those who accept my commandments and obey them are the ones who love me. And because they love me, my Father will love them. And I will love them and reveal myself to each of them."

²²Judas (not Judas Iscariot, but the other disciple with that name) said to him, "Lord, why are you going to reveal yourself only to us and not to the world at large?"

²³Jesus replied, "All who love me will do what I say. My Father will love them, and we will come and make our home with each of them. ²⁴Anyone who doesn't love me will not obey me. And remember, my words are not my own. What I am telling you is from the Father who sent me. ²⁵I am telling

14:16
John 14:26; 15:26
Acts 1:4-5
ˢ*paraklētos* (3875)
› John 14:26

14:17
Rom 8:15-16
1 Jn 3:24

14:18
Rom 8:23; 9:4
2 Cor 4:9

14:20
John 10:38; 15:4-5;
16:16; 17:21-24

14:21
John 15:10; 16:27
1 Jn 2:5
2 Jn 1:6

14:22
Luke 6:16
Acts 10:41

14:23
Ps 91:1
Prov 8:17
John 15:10
Eph 3:17
1 Jn 4:16; 5:3
Rev 3:20; 21:3

Our Advocate (14:1–16:15)

1 Sam 2:25; 24:15
2 Sam 15:12
1 Kgs 12:6-14
1 Chr 27:32
Job 16:18-22
Isa 1:26; 9:6
Gal 3:19-20; 6:13
1 Tim 2:5
Heb 8:6; 9:15; 12:24
1 Jn 2:1

On four occasions, Jesus used an unusual word (Greek *paraklētos*, "called alongside," "advocate") to describe the Holy Spirit (14:16, 26; 15:26; 16:7). The same term occurs in Greek literature, where it refers to a legal advocate—someone who speaks in a person's defense and provides legal counsel. "Counselor" is a popular translation of this term, but the therapeutic connotations of this word in contemporary English are misleading; the older legal meaning of a lawyer providing advice or counsel is closer to the mark. "Comforter" is another popular translation, but this is also misleading; the older English meaning of someone who strengthens (an "encourager") is more accurate to the NT concept of *paraklētos*.

Jesus described the Spirit as *another* Advocate (14:16). Jesus, who is the first advocate (see 1 Jn 2:1), sent a second Advocate, the Holy Spirit. Every task of the Spirit in John 14–16 is a task Jesus undertook elsewhere in the Gospel. Jesus promised that the Holy Spirit would come to encourage, instruct, and strengthen his followers. In fact, the Spirit would sustain Jesus' own presence among his disciples. Five promises of the Spirit each indicate a different work that the Spirit does (14:16-17, 26; 15:26; 16:7, 13).

The Spirit became available to Jesus' disciples after his death (see 7:39; 20:22). The Spirit now continues the work of Jesus and his presence in the life of believers (14:16-24).

their prayers (see 1 Jn 5:14). These things would become possible when Jesus went to *the Father*, because he would send the Holy Spirit to empower the works (14:16). • The *greater works* will not outdo Jesus' work, but regular people empowered by the Spirit will be doing them. In the era of the Spirit, God promised to bring his Kingdom and power into the world in a way not seen before.

14:15 *If you love me:* Because Jesus loves the Father, he is obedient to what God directs him to say and do (12:49). If we love him, we will obey him, too (14:21, 23; 15:10, 14; see 1 Jn 2:3-4; 5:2). • *obey:* Other manuscripts read *you will obey;* still others read *you should obey.*

14:16 *another Advocate* (or *Comforter,* or *Encourager,* or *Counselor;* Greek reads *Paraclete;* also in 14:26): See "Our Advocate" at 14:1–16:15, above. The

Spirit continues Jesus' work by advising, defending, and protecting believers.

14:17 The *Holy Spirit, who leads into all truth* (literally *the Spirit of truth;* see also 15:26; 16:13), communicates the truth about God. The Spirit maintains Jesus' presence in the world, duplicating and sustaining Jesus' work. • *and later will be in you:* Some manuscripts read *and is in you.*

14:18 Jesus had already assured his followers that they would not be spiritual *orphans* and that he would return to them (14:1-4). While he is away, they will be filled with the Spirit, who will sustain them with his presence (14:12-17).

14:20 Jesus' resurrection (14:19) inaugurated his spiritual union with his disciples, which is parallel to the union he enjoys with the *Father* (see 15:4-5; 1 Jn 1:3).

14:22 Several men are named *Judas* in the NT. Judas, the brother of Jesus, (Mark 6:3) wrote the epistle of Jude. Judas, the son of James, whom John is referring to here, is listed as an apostle in Luke 6:16; he is elsewhere identified as Thaddaeus (Matt 10:3; Mark 3:18). • *Lord, why?* Judas posed an important question. If Jesus planned to return mightily from death, why not use the opportunity to *reveal* himself definitively to the *world* and validate his power and identity?

14:23-24 Jesus answered Judas's question, explaining that his coming would be a profound spiritual revelation beyond the world's grasp. • Jesus' coming would occur in three experiences: his resurrection, the coming of the Spirit, and his second coming. When he comes in the Spirit, he and the Father will reside within believers, making a *home with each of them* (see note on 14:2).

14:24
John 7:16; 14:10
14:26
John 1:33; 15:26;
16:7; 20:22
1 Jn 2:20, 27
ʰ*paráklētos* (3875)
  ▸ John 15:26
14:27
John 16:33; 20:19
Phil 4:7
Col 3:15
ⁱ*eirēnē* (1515)
  ▸ Acts 10:36
14:29
John 13:19
14:30
John 12:31
14:31
John 10:18; 12:49
15:1
Ps 80:8-11
Isa 5:1-7
ʲ*ampelos* (0288)
  ▸ John 15:5
15:5
ᵏ*ampelos* (0288)
  ▸ Jas 3:12
15:6
Matt 3:10
15:8
Gal 5:22-23

you these things now while I am still with you. ²⁶But when the Father sends the ʰAdvocate as my representative—that is, the Holy Spirit—he will teach you everything and will remind you of everything I have told you.

²⁷"I am leaving you with a gift—ⁱpeace of mind and heart. And the ⁱpeace I give is a gift the world cannot give. So don't be troubled or afraid. ²⁸Remember what I told you: I am going away, but I will come back to you again. If you really loved me, you would be happy that I am going to the Father, who is greater than I am. ²⁹I have told you these things before they happen so that when they do happen, you will believe.

³⁰"I don't have much more time to talk to you, because the ruler of this world approaches. He has no power over me, ³¹but I will do what the Father requires of me, so that the world will know that I love the Father. Come, let's be going.

Jesus, the True Vine of Israel

15 "I am the true ʲgrapevine, and my Father is the gardener. ²He cuts off every branch of mine that doesn't produce fruit, and he prunes the branches that do bear fruit so they will produce even more. ³You have already been pruned and purified by the message I have given you. ⁴Remain in me, and I will remain in you. For a branch cannot produce fruit if it is severed from the vine, and you cannot be fruitful unless you remain in me.

⁵"Yes, I am the ᵏvine; you are the branches. Those who remain in me, and I in them, will produce much fruit. For apart from me you can do nothing. ⁶Anyone who does not remain in me is thrown away like a useless branch and withers. Such branches are gathered into a pile to be burned. ⁷But if you remain in me and my words remain in you, you may ask for anything you want, and it will be granted! ⁸When you produce

Remaining in Christ (15:1-17)

John 6:56; 8:31
Exod 33:11; 34:28
Lev 8:35
Josh 7:11-12
1 Sam 16:22
2 Kgs 11:8
2 Chr 15:2
Ps 22:11, 19; 101:7
Dan 1:21; 2:49
Hag 2:5
Luke 15:31; 22:28
Phil 4:1
1 Jn 2:19, 27-28;
3:24
2 Jn 1:9
Rev 2:10; 13:10

One of Jesus' favorite words was *menō*, often translated "remain," "stay," or "abide." It describes a profound, intimate, and enduring relationship. For example, Jesus said, "You are truly my disciples if you remain faithful to [*menō en*, 'stay in'] my teachings" (8:31). The idea is that a disciple's life is fully formed by Jesus' word. Jesus described how the Son is in the Father and the Father is in the Son (14:10-11). Likewise, when we remain in Christ, the Son is in us and we are in the Father and the Son (17:21). Both the Father and the Son come and make their home within his disciples. This mutual indwelling is precisely what it means that the disciple remains in Christ. We cannot gain the permanence of our relationship by our own effort; this relationship is only made permanent by the gracious initiative of God indwelling our lives through his Spirit. This means commitment on the part of both God and the disciple. The mutual indwelling between God and the believer is not a fleeting or temporary commitment, but an enduring, permanent, and eternal relationship (see 1 Jn 2:14, 17).

14:26 Jesus promised to send *the Holy Spirit* (see also 14:16; 15:26; 16:7; 16:12-14). • The Spirit will *teach . . . everything,* recalling Jesus' words and clarifying their meaning. John experienced this power as he wrote his Gospel (2:22); Christians experience this work of the Spirit as they read the Scriptures.

14:27 The Jewish greeting *peace* (Hebrew *shalom*) captured the spirit of Jesus' work on earth to restore humanity's relationship with God (Isa 9:6-7; 52:7; 57:19; Rom 5:1). The resurrection (14:28) and the Spirit were instrumental in achieving this work.

14:28 *the Father, who is greater than I am:* Jesus is subordinate to the Father (see also 5:19-20), and yet is also one with the Father (10:30).

14:30 The events unfolding in Jerusalem that led to the cross were not controlled by *the ruler of this world,* meaning Satan. The cross was not an

accident, and Jesus was not a helpless victim. Rather, Jesus was obedient to God's plan.

15:1-27 Jesus prepared his disciples for his departure, instructing them to remain in close fellowship with him. The image of a grapevine illustrates both intimacy and fruitfulness. To sustain genuine spiritual life in the world, believers must remain intimately connected to Christ.

15:1 *I am:* See note on 6:35. The *grapevine* and the vineyard traditionally represented God's people, planted and tended by him in Israel (Ps 80:8-18; Isa 5:1-7; Jer 2:21; 12:10-11; Ezek 15:1-5; Hos 10:1-2). When Jesus used this image, he made an important departure: He declared that he is *the true grapevine,* and that a relationship with God requires attachment to him.

15:2-3 Gardeners cut away dead *branches* and trim healthy branches so

they will produce more *fruit.* Fruitfulness is the result of life-giving connection to the vine.

15:4 The term *remain* (Greek *menō*) is key to understanding 15:4-10. A growing disciple, in whom the Father and the Son live through the Spirit, must be continuously connected to Christ (see 14:16-25; 15:26).

15:6 *Anyone who does not remain* in Christ is separated from the vine and its life. A living branch produces clusters of grapes (15:5). Connection with the vine allows the life of Jesus to flow fruitfully through the disciple. Those who claim to be attached to Christ but yield no fruit are *useless* and will *be burned.*

15:7 Those whose lives are in harmony with Jesus *may ask for anything* because their prayers are controlled by his word. Their prayers will be answered and bring glory to God (14:10-13).

much fruit, you are my true disciples. This brings great glory to my Father.

9"I have loved you even as the Father has loved me. Remain in my [a]love. 10When you obey my commandments, you remain in my love, just as I obey my Father's commandments and remain in his love. 11I have told you these things so that you will be filled with my joy. Yes, your joy will overflow! 12This is my commandment: Love each other in the same way I have loved you. 13There is no greater [b]love than to lay down one's life for one's friends. 14You are my friends if you do what I command. 15I no longer call you [c]slaves, because a master doesn't confide in his [c]slaves. Now you are my friends, since I have told you everything the Father told me. 16You didn't choose me. I chose you. I appointed you to go and produce lasting fruit, so that the Father will give you whatever you ask for, using my name. 17This is my command: Love each other.

Jesus' Disciples and the World

18"If the world hates you, remember that it hated me first. 19The world would love you as one of its own if you belonged to it, but you are no longer part of the world. I chose you to come out of the world, so it hates you. 20Do you remember what I told you? 'A slave is not greater than the master.' Since they persecuted me, naturally they will persecute you. And if they had listened to me, they would listen to you. 21They will do all this to you because of me, for they have rejected the one who sent me. 22They would

not be guilty if I had not come and spoken to them. But now they have no excuse for their sin. 23Anyone who hates me also hates my Father. 24If I hadn't done such miraculous signs among them that no one else could do, they would not be guilty. But as it is, they have seen everything I did, yet they still hate me and my Father. 25This fulfills what is written in their Scriptures: 'They hated me without cause.'

26"But I will send you the [d]Advocate—the Spirit of truth. He will come to you from the Father and will testify all about me. 27And you must also testify about me because you have been with me from the beginning of my ministry.

16 "I have told you these things so that you won't abandon your faith. 2For you will be expelled from the synagogues, and the time is coming when those who kill you will think they are doing a holy service for God. 3This is because they have never known the Father or me. 4Yes, I'm telling you these things now, so that when they happen, you will remember my warning. I didn't tell you earlier because I was going to be with you for a while longer.

The Work of the Holy Spirit

5"But now I am going away to the one who sent me, and not one of you is asking where I am going. 6Instead, you grieve because of what I've told you. 7But in fact, it is best for you that I go away, because if I don't, the [e]Advocate won't come. If I do go away,

15:9
John 3:35
[a]agapē (0026)
▸John 15:13

15:10
John 14:15

15:11
John 17:13
1 Jn 1:4

15:12
John 13:34

15:13
John 10:11
Rom 5:6-8
[b]agapē (0026)
▸Rom 5:5

15:15
[c]doulos (1401)
▸Rom 1:1

15:16
Rom 1:13
1 Cor 3:12-14
Phil 1:22

15:18
John 7:7
1 Jn 3:13

15:19
John 17:14
1 Jn 4:5

15:21
Matt 5:11
1 Pet 4:14

15:22
John 9:41

15:24
John 5:36; 9:41

15:25
*Ps 35:19; 69:4

15:26
John 14:17
1 Jn 5:6-7
[d]paraklētos (3875)
▸John 16:7

15:27
John 21:24
1 Jn 1:2; 4:14

16:2
John 9:22
Acts 22:3-4

16:3
John 15:21

. . . .

15:8 *True disciples* will experience a transformed, fruit-bearing life because they live in a relationship of love with both Jesus and the Father (15:9-10).

15:10 Just as Jesus demonstrated his love for the Father by obeying his will (14:31), Jesus' disciples exhibit their love through obedience to him (13:34-35; 14:15; 1 Jn 2:5; 5:2-3).

15:12-13 *This is my commandment: Love each other:* See 13:34. • Jesus demonstrated his *love* by sacrificing his *life* at the cross.

15:14-16 Both Abraham and Moses were called *friends* of God (Exod 33:11; 2 Chr 20:7; Isa 41:8; Jas 2:23). This is the highest relationship possible between God and a person. Jesus chooses his friends (15:16), who demonstrate their friendship by obeying him.

15:15 The disciples of a rabbi were considered his servants or *slaves*. Jesus elevated his followers to a higher relationship as his *friends*.

15:18-27 Disciples must be like their

master in every respect, both in showing love and obedience and in experiencing the antagonism of those who oppose their message (15:20-21; see ch 9; 11:16). If the darkness is opposed to the light (1:5), and if Jesus' followers are bearers of that light in the world (1 Jn 1:7; 2:9), they should expect the world to hate them in the way it hated Jesus (see 17:14). Jesus' disciples share his separation from and conflict with the world.

15:20 *A slave is not greater than the master:* See note on 13:16. Jesus' disciples should mirror him in every way, even in his experience of persecution and martyrdom.

15:22-24 *But now they have no excuse:* Jesus' ministry provided both words (15:22) and works (15:24) as evidence that pointed to God. Once people have heard and seen him, they are accountable.

15:25 *in their Scriptures:* Literally *in their law.* Ps 35:19; 69:4. • *They hated me without cause:* This OT citation

reveals the unwarranted anger of those who belong to the darkness.

15:26 *But I will send you the Advocate* (or *Comforter,* or *Encourager,* or *Counselor;* Greek reads *Paraclete*)—*the Spirit of truth:* See notes on 14:16-17. Like a legal advocate, the Holy Spirit counsels and protects Jesus' followers.

15:27 Disciples are not alone when they *testify about* Christ (Matt 28:20). The Spirit accompanies them, providing the words to say (Matt 10:19-20).

16:1-2 Jesus had outlined the coming conflicts (15:18-25) so that the disciples would not *abandon* their *faith* (literally *be caused to stumble*). The greatest obstacle his disciples would face was to stumble and renounce their faith before their Jewish opponents (see Matt 23:34; Luke 6:22), especially during the dark days ahead (see 12:35; 1 Jn 2:9-11).

16:7 *the Advocate* (or *Comforter,* or *Encourager,* or *Counselor;* Greek reads *Paraclete*): The Spirit was a gift awaiting Jesus' departure and glorification (7:37-39; 14:16, 26; 15:26; 16:12-14).

16:4
John 13:19

16:5
John 7:33; 13:36

16:7
John 14:26; 15:26
ᵉ*paraklētos* (3875)
▸ 1 Jn 2:1

16:9
John 15:22

16:10
Acts 3:14; 7:52
Rom 1:17
1 Pet 3:18

16:11
John 12:31

16:13
John 14:17, 26

16:15
John 17:10

16:16
John 14:18-24

16:20
Mark 16:10
Luke 23:27
John 20:20

16:21
Isa 13:8; 21:3; 26:17
Acts 13:33
Col 1:18

16:22
Isa 66:14
John 20:20

16:23
John 14:20; 16:26

16:24
John 15:11

16:25
Ps 78:2
John 10:6

16:27
John 8:42; 14:21; 17:8

16:28
John 13:3

16:32
Zech 13:7
Matt 26:31, 56
John 8:29

16:33
John 14:27
Rom 5:1; 8:37
1 Jn 5:4

then I will send him to you. 8And when he comes, he will convict the world of its sin, and of God's righteousness, and of the coming judgment. 9The world's sin is that it refuses to believe in me. 10Righteousness is available because I go to the Father, and you will see me no more. 11Judgment will come because the ruler of this world has already been judged.

12"There is so much more I want to tell you, but you can't bear it now. 13When the Spirit of truth comes, he will guide you into all truth. He will not speak on his own but will tell you what he has heard. He will tell you about the future. 14He will bring me glory by telling you whatever he receives from me. 15All that belongs to the Father is mine; this is why I said, 'The Spirit will tell you whatever he receives from me.'

Sadness Will Be Turned to Joy

16"In a little while you won't see me anymore. But a little while after that, you will see me again."

17Some of the disciples asked each other, "What does he mean when he says, 'In a little while you won't see me, but then you will see me,' and 'I am going to the Father'? 18And what does he mean by 'a little while'? We don't understand."

19Jesus realized they wanted to ask him about it, so he said, "Are you asking yourselves what I meant? I said in a little while you won't see me, but a little while after that you will see me again. 20I tell you the truth, you will weep and mourn over what is going to happen to me, but the world will rejoice.

You will grieve, but your grief will suddenly turn to wonderful joy. 21It will be like a woman suffering the pains of labor. When her child is born, her anguish gives way to joy because she has brought a new baby into the world. 22So you have sorrow now, but I will see you again; then you will rejoice, and no one can rob you of that joy. 23At that time you won't need to ask me for anything. I tell you the truth, you will ask the Father directly, and he will grant your request because you use my name. 24You haven't done this before. Ask, using my name, and you will receive, and you will have abundant joy.

25"I have spoken of these matters in figures of speech, but soon I will stop speaking figuratively and will tell you plainly all about the Father. 26Then you will ask in my name. I'm not saying I will ask the Father on your behalf, 27for the Father himself loves you dearly because you love me and believe that I came from God. 28Yes, I came from the Father into the world, and now I will leave the world and return to the Father."

29Then his disciples said, "At last you are speaking plainly and not figuratively. 30Now we understand that you know everything, and there's no need to question you. From this we believe that you came from God."

31Jesus asked, "Do you finally believe? 32But the time is coming—indeed it's here now—when you will be scattered, each one going his own way, leaving me alone. Yet I am not alone because the Father is with me. 33I have told you all this so that you may have peace in me. Here on earth you

---

16:8-11 One of the Spirit's roles is to *convict the world*. Convict is a legal term: The world had conducted its trial of Jesus, examining the evidence for his case (his signs and claims). Now the world would stand trial before the Spirit, and its guilt would be proven.

16:8 The Spirit unveils to the world the real nature of *its sin*, the truth about *righteousness* found only in God, and *the coming judgment*, which has already dawned on the world as light penetrating the darkness.

16:11 *Judgment* of sinners had already begun, for the *ruler of this world*, Satan, had *already been judged* (see 12:31). The world thought it was judging Jesus, but the opposite occurred.

16:13 The *Spirit of truth* (see notes on 14:16-17), who conveys truth from God, guides the judgment of the world. • The Spirit says only *what he has heard* from the Father. The Father, Son, and Spirit work in perfect unity (16:15). The dis-

ciples could expect the Spirit to reveal things they had not heard before about the present and *the future* (see 14:26).

16:16-33 *a little while:* This refrain reassured the disciples that their separation from Jesus would be short lived.

16:16 Jesus reassured the disciples that his departure (on the cross) would be short and his return (in the resurrection) would be soon. When they saw him *again*, the disciples would experience overwhelming joy and intimacy with him in the Spirit.

16:20 At the crucifixion, *the world* thought it had won a victory over the light. The shock of the cross would cause the disciples to *weep and mourn*, but their sorrow would change to *joy* when Jesus defeated the grave (20:20).

16:21 *the pains of labor:* This metaphor symbolizes anguish that is followed by God's blessing and wonder (cp. Isa 21:2-3; 26:16-21; 66:7-10; Jer 13:21).

16:23-24 *Ask . . . and you will receive:* Two notable effects of the resurrection are the joy of understanding and the joy of successful prayer. The disciples would no longer experience the confusion described in 16:16-18.

16:25 Jesus spoke using *figures of speech*, which could only be interpreted with God's help (1 Cor 1:18-25). With the coming of the Spirit, the disciples would understand.

16:26-27 After Jesus' resurrection, the Spirit brought intimacy, allowing individual disciples to *ask the Father* to meet their needs. (14:23).

16:27 *from God:* Some manuscripts read *from the Father*.

16:33 *But take heart, because I have overcome the world:* "Such a saying as this is worthy to be carried from Rome to Jerusalem on one's knees" (Martin Luther). Jesus' final words did not chastise, but brought comfort. Jesus promised peace (14:27) and joy (16:20, 22).

will have many trials and sorrows. But take heart, because I have overcome the world."

Jesus' Final Prayer

17 After saying all these things, Jesus looked up to heaven and said, "Father, the hour has come. Glorify your Son so he can give glory back to you. ²For you have given him authority over everyone. He gives eternal life to each one you have given him. ³And this is the way to have eternal life—to know you, the only true God, and Jesus Christ, the one you sent to earth. ⁴I brought glory to you here on earth by completing the work you gave me to do. ⁵Now, Father, bring me into the glory we shared before the world began.

⁶"I have revealed you to the ones you gave me from this world. They were always yours. You gave them to me, and they have kept your word. ⁷Now they know that everything I have is a gift from you, ⁸for I have passed on to them the message you gave me. They accepted it and know that I came from you, and they believe you sent me.

⁹"My prayer is not for the world, but for those you have given me, because they belong to you. ¹⁰All who are mine belong to you, and you have given them to me, so they bring me glory. ¹¹Now I am departing from the world; they are staying in this world, but I am coming to you. Holy Father, you have given me your name; now protect them by the power of your name so that they will be united just as we are. ¹²During my time here, I protected them by the power of the name you gave me. I guarded them so that not one was lost, except the one headed for destruction, as the Scriptures foretold.

¹³"Now I am coming to you. I told them many things while I was with them in this world so they would be filled with my joy. ¹⁴I have given them your word. And the world hates them because they do not belong to the world, just as I do not belong to the world. ¹⁵I'm not asking you to take them out of the world, but to keep them safe from the evil one. ¹⁶They do not belong to this world any more than I do. ¹⁷Make them holy by your truth; teach them your word, which is truth. ¹⁸Just as you sent me into the world, I am sending them into the world. ¹⁹And I give myself as a holy sacrifice for them so they can be made holy by your truth.

17:1 John 13:31
17:2 Matt 28:18; John 6:37, 39
17:3 Phil 3:8; 1 Jn 5:20
17:5 John 1:1-2; 17:24; Phil 2:6
17:6 John 17:26
17:8 John 13:3; 16:30
17:9 1 Jn 5:19
17:10 John 16:15
17:11 John 10:30; 17:21; Gal 3:28
17:12 Ps 41:9; John 6:39
17:13 John 7:33; 15:11
17:14 John 15:18-19
17:15 1 Jn 5:18
17:17 John 15:3; Eph 5:25-26
17:18 John 20:21
17:19 Heb 2:11

Now he added that his disciples can discover peace even when surrounded by threats; they can be tranquil despite those who are hostile to their faith.

17:1-26 This chapter records Jesus' longest prayer, which is often called his "high priestly prayer." It provides an intimate glimpse into his heart. In this prayer, which closes the farewell that began at 13:31, Jesus expressed his own concerns to his Father (17:1-8) and then turned to concerns for the church and its future (17:9-26).

17:1 *Jesus looked up to heaven*, assuming the traditional Jewish posture for prayer (11:41; Ps 123:1). He probably also raised his hands (Exod 9:33; 17:11; Ps 28:2). Prayers like this were said aloud so that followers could hear (11:41-42; 12:27-30; also Matt 11:25-30; Luke 10:21-22). • *Father* was Jesus' usual way to address God, which he did six times in this prayer (see also 11:41; 12:27). This title—unusual in Judaism—reflected Jesus' intimacy with God. • This *hour* included Jesus' betrayal, arrest, torture, death, and resurrection (see note on 12:23). • *Glorify your Son:* In the Gospel of John, the cross is a place of honor. Jesus' oneness with the Father means that if the Son is glorified, the Father will also be glorified.

17:2 All *authority* has been placed in Jesus' hands (3:35); he can give *eternal life* as only God can (3:15; 5:21, 25-26).

17:3 *to know you:* The Hebrew idea of knowing encompassed experience and intimacy, which for Christians means love for God and obedience to him. • *sent to earth:* Jesus originated in heaven and was returning there (17:5), so he exercises divine authority as the agent of God.

17:4 Jesus' miracles displayed God's *glory* for the world to see (1:14). This task was finished; Jesus' life and obedience had glorified God.

17:5 Jesus prayed to return to the position he had with God *before the world began* (1:1).

17:6 This verse summarizes Christ's mission. He revealed the true person of God to the world, gathered up God's people into his flock, and instructed them in obedience. The result of this work is the church. • *have revealed you:* Literally *have revealed your name;* also in 17:26.

17:8 Jesus revealed himself widely to the world. Those who embraced his *message* became children of God (1:12; 11:52), and he revealed God's word to them.

17:9-19 Jesus prayed for his disciples, who must carry on after his departure.

17:10 Just as the Son brings glory to the Father (17:1, 4-5), the disciples *bring* the Son *glory* (17:22). The love and obedience that brought glory to God in Jesus' life become features of his disciples' lives.

17:11 *you have given me your name:* Some manuscripts read *you have given me these* [i.e., *these disciples*]. • Jesus' first concern for his disciples was that *they . . . be united* with an intimacy similar to the oneness shared by Jesus and the Father.

17:12-13 *I protected them by the power of the name you gave me:* Some manuscripts read *I protected those you gave me, by the power of your name.* • Until now, Jesus had *guarded* his followers. Now he was concerned for their strength and survival in his absence, because the world would be hostile toward them (15:18-27) and their mission of challenging the world by heralding the truth (16:8-11). After Jesus' departure, the Spirit would protect them (15:26) and bring them joy.

17:14 God's *word*, which Jesus had *given* his disciples, also provides a defense against the world. The Spirit would preserve and recall God's word in the church (14:26), equipping the church for its encounter with the world.

17:16-18 Being *holy* refers to purity gained by separation from the world, and living a life so aligned with God that it reflects his passions. Disciples are set apart by God, equipped by the Spirit, and readied by God's word to enter the world without being victimized by its darkness.

17:19 *I give myself as a holy sacrifice* (literally *I sanctify myself*): Priests and

17:20
John 17:9

17:21
John 10:38
Gal 3:28

17:22
John 17:11

17:23
John 16:27; 17:5

17:24
John 1:14; 12:26

17:25
Matt 11:27

17:26
John 15:9

18:1
2 Sam 15:23
Matt 26:36
Mark 14:32

18:3-11
//Matt 26:47-56
//Mark 14:43-50
//Luke 22:47-53

20"I am praying not only for these disciples but also for all who will ever believe in me through their message. 21I pray that they will all be one, just as you and I are one—as you are in me, Father, and I am in you. And may they be in us so that the world will believe you sent me.

22"I have given them the glory you gave me, so they may be one as we are one. 23I am in them and you are in me. May they experience such perfect unity that the world will know that you sent me and that you love them as much as you love me. 24Father, I want these whom you have given me to be with me where I am. Then they can see all the glory you gave me because you loved me even before the world began!

25"O righteous Father, the world doesn't know you, but I do; and these disciples know you sent me. 26I have revealed you to them, and I will continue to do so. Then your love for me will be in them, and I will be in them."

Jesus' Suffering and Death (18:1–19:42)
Jesus Is Betrayed and Arrested
John 18:1-12 // Matt 26:47-56 // Mark 14:43-52 // Luke 22:47-53

18 After saying these things, Jesus crossed the Kidron Valley with his disciples and entered a grove of olive trees. 2Judas, the betrayer, knew this place, because Jesus had often gone there with his disciples. 3The leading priests and

The World (17:5-26)

John 1:9-10; 3:16-
19; 7:7; 8:12; 12:47;
14:17-19, 27; 15:18-
19; 16:7-9, 20, 33
Gen 6:11-12
Ps 2:1-6; 9:8
Isa 61:11; 66:16
Matt 5:14; 13:38-40
Luke 16:8
Acts 17:31
1 Cor 1:20-28;
3:3; 6:2
2 Cor 5:19
Eph 2:2
Col 2:20
Jas 4:4
2 Pet 1:4; 2:20
1 Jn 2:15-16; 4:3-5
Rev 17:18; 19:19

One of the most frequently used words in John is "world" (Greek *kosmos*). In Greek-speaking Jewish thought, *kosmos* refers to the heavens and the earth as created by God (Gen 1; see also John 1:3, 10; 17:5, 24). John extends the concept to include the world of humanity (e.g., 1:10; 3:16).

Although it was created as good, the human world is hostile to God (1:10-11; 3:19-20; 12:37-41). It is controlled by a darkness that cannot comprehend the light and resists the light (3:19). The world is dead and needs life (6:33, 51), yet it hates the one who can save it (7:7). The world is under the dominion of Satan (12:31), who will one day be judged.

God loves the world of humanity, despite its hostility and rebellion against him. Jesus died to take away the sin of the world (1:29; 3:16-17). God's love for the world he created stands alongside his necessary judgment of the world (3:18-21, 36; 5:27-30; 12:47-48). Christ's followers experience this same tension in their mission. We are called into the world to bring the message of God's love, but we will experience conflict, because the world will be hostile to our message (see 14:27-31; 15:18-27; 17:13-26).

prophets were similarly set apart for service to God (Lev 8:30; Jer 1:5). Jesus recommitted himself to his mission, acknowledging that he was set apart for the purpose of the cross. The disciples would benefit because his death would enable them to experience new holiness in a deep attachment to God.

17:20 Jesus was *praying* for other sheep who were not yet in his flock (10:16). These are the believers through the centuries who have come to faith through the witness of Jesus' disciples.

17:21 For believers, becoming *one* with one another is an outgrowth of the union they enjoy with Jesus himself, a union modeled on the oneness of the Father and the Son. • *may they be in us:* Through the power of the Spirit, believers would experience a profound spiritual intimacy with the Father and the Son and be transformed (14:20, 23; 1 Jn 4:13). • Disciples of Jesus represent him, so their conduct and relationships with each other reflect the credibility of Christ in *the world.* When there is disunity, infighting, and intolerance, their

testimony to the world is unconvincing. When people observe the community of believers, they know that it represents Jesus; a unified, loving community convinces *the world* to *believe* (13:35; 1 Jn 3:11).

17:22 The community of believers should display the same *glory* that Jesus displayed from the Father.

17:23 *that the world will know:* If the church lives in the Spirit, reflects God's glory and love, and shows unity sustained by a shared knowledge of God, then its testimony will astonish *the world.*

17:24 *I want these . . . to be with me:* Some day, Jesus' followers will see Jesus' true glory, the true love that has existed in heaven since the beginning of time (17:5). Jesus was returning to heaven, and he yearned to see his disciples there so that they might glimpse what no words on earth can describe.

17:26 All who accept the Son and embrace the Father will experience the kind of *love* known only between the Father and the Son. • *I will be in*

them: Jesus wants to love his followers and indwell them with glory and joy unmatched by anything in the world.

18:1-40 After completing his farewell in the upper room (13:31–17:26), Jesus left the city and entered a garden just east of Jerusalem to pray. Here he was arrested, taken under guard into the city, and interrogated by the Jewish leaders. The climactic "time" that Jesus referred to repeatedly throughout the Gospel (see 2:4; note on 12:23) was now at hand.

18:1-2 *Jesus crossed the Kidron Valley,* a dry river valley (a *wadi*) outside Jerusalem's walls on the city's east edge. • The Garden of Gethsemane (Mark 14:32) was *a grove of olive trees* that grew along the west shoulder of the Mount of Olives (*gath shemaney* means "olive press" in Aramaic). Jesus liked this place and frequently prayed there (see 8:1; Luke 21:37; 22:39).

18:3 John's full description of the arresting party expands the picture from the other Gospels. The Temple authorities sent *Roman soldiers and Temple guards;* while the Temple guards made

Pharisees had given Judas a contingent of Roman soldiers and Temple guards to accompany him. Now with blazing torches, lanterns, and weapons, they arrived at the olive grove.

⁴Jesus fully realized all that was going to happen to him, so he stepped forward to meet them. "Who are you looking for?" he asked.

⁵"Jesus the Nazarene," they replied.

"I Aᴍ he," Jesus said. (Judas, who betrayed him, was standing with them.) ⁶As Jesus said "I Aᴍ he," they all drew back and fell to the ground! ⁷Once more he asked them, "Who are you looking for?"

And again they replied, "Jesus the Nazarene."

⁸"I told you that I Aᴍ he," Jesus said. "And since I am the one you want, let these others go." ⁹He did this to fulfill his own statement: "I did not lose a single one of those you have given me."

¹⁰Then Simon Peter drew a sword and slashed off the right ear of Malchus, the high priest's slave. ¹¹But Jesus said to Peter, "Put your sword back into its sheath. Shall I not drink from the cup of suffering the Father has given me?"

¹²So the soldiers, their commanding officer, and the Temple guards arrested Jesus and tied him up.

Peter's First Denial of Jesus
John 18:15-18 // Matt 26:69-70 // Mark 14:66-68 // Luke 22:54-57

¹³First they took him to Annas, the father-in-law of Caiaphas, the high priest at that time. ¹⁴Caiaphas was the one who had told the

18:4
John 6:64

18:9
John 6:39; 17:12

18:10
Luke 22:36, 38

18:11
Matt 20:22; 26:39
Mark 10:38; 14:36
Luke 22:42

18:12-15
//Matt 26:57-58
//Mark 14:53-54
//Luke 22:54

18:13
Luke 3:2
John 18:24

18:14
John 11:49-51

ANNAS AND CAIAPHAS (18:13-14, 19-24, 28)

John 11:49-53
Matt 26:3, 57-67
Mark 14:53-65
Luke 3:2
Acts 4:5-7

Annas and Caiaphas were both spoken of as high priests during the time of Jesus; they were instrumental in getting Jesus condemned to death.

Annas was the Jewish high priest about AD 6–15. Even after he was officially deposed by the Roman procurator of Judea, he retained considerable power and influence in the Jewish high council and was still spoken of as "high priest" fifteen to twenty years later (Luke 3:2; Acts 4:6)—perhaps because of the Jewish view that high priests retain their position for life. Five of his sons and his son-in-law Caiaphas became high priests after him. According to the Gospel of John, when Jesus was arrested, he was brought to Annas for his initial interrogation before he was turned over to Caiaphas for the official trial (18:13-24).

Caiaphas was the official Jewish high priest about AD 18–36. He worked closely with his powerful father-in-law, Annas. Caiaphas was the one who argued in the high council that it would be better for Jesus to be sacrificed than for the entire nation to be destroyed (11:49-50; cp. Matt 26:3-4). These prophetic words were given him by God because of his role as high priest (11:51-52). It was Caiaphas who tore his robes at Jesus' claim to be the Son of God (Matt 26:57, 65) and urged the high council to condemn him for blasphemy.

Not long after the execution of Jesus, the Jewish authorities became increasingly disturbed over the rapidly growing numbers of believers in Christ. Annas and Caiaphas also actively involved themselves in the interrogation of Peter and John over their healing a crippled beggar and their preaching about the resurrection of the dead (Acts 4:5-7).

the arrest, the Roman detachment stood by to prevent a riot. The Roman detachment was large enough to warrant a commander (18:12) and came armed, anticipating a struggle (18:10). Numerous men had claimed to be the Messiah, and often they had made politically explosive attempts to expel the Romans.

18:5 *Jesus the Nazarene:* Or *Jesus of Nazareth*; also in 18:7. • *I Aᴍ he* (or "*The 'I Aᴍ' is here*"; or "*I am the* Lᴏʀᴅ"; literally *I am*; also in 18:6, 8): Jesus identified himself by the divine name God had revealed to Moses on Mount Sinai (Exod 3:14; see also 4:26; 8:24, 58).

18:6 The soldiers and guards *all drew back* before the Lord (cp. Isa 6:5; Ezek 1:28; Dan 10:9; Acts 9:4; Rev 1:17). Even

Roman soldiers, who were trained not to fall, *fell to the ground* before Christ. Although they submitted to God, they didn't really understand what had occurred and proceeded with the arrest.

18:8 *I Aᴍ:* Jesus used God's divine name for the second time (see note on 18:5).

18:9 *his own statement:* See 6:39; 17:12. • *I did not lose a single one:* Jesus continued to be a good shepherd, offering his life for the sheep and protecting them from the wolves (10:11-15). From the beginning, however, Judas Iscariot had not been a true disciple of Jesus (17:12).

18:10-11 *Simon Peter drew a* short *sword* or a long knife that was generally worn with everyday garments. • The Hebrew name *Malchus* means "king," a

detail that John might have included for its wordplay on Jesus' true identity (see 18:36-37; 19:19). • *Put your sword back:* Jesus' mission was not to fight for his life, but to die for ours.

18:12-14 Jesus was bound by the soldiers and returned to Jerusalem. • *First they took him to Annas,* who had been the high priest and remained highly influential (five of his sons also became high priests). *Caiaphas,* his son-in-law, was the official *high priest at that time* (literally *that year*; see 18:24).

18:14 *one man should die for the people:* Caiaphas had previously made this political analysis (11:49-50). John points out the irony of this statement. Jesus' death did not bring Israel political salvation—it brought spiritual salvation to all who believe.

other Jewish leaders, "It's better that one man should die for the people."

15Simon Peter followed Jesus, as did another of the disciples. That other disciple was acquainted with the high priest, so he was allowed to enter the high priest's courtyard with Jesus. 16Peter had to stay outside the gate. Then the disciple who knew the high priest spoke to the woman watching at the gate, and she let Peter in. 17The woman asked Peter, "You're not one of that man's disciples, are you?"

"No," he said, "I am not."

18Because it was cold, the household servants and the guards had made a charcoal fire. They stood around it, warming themselves, and Peter stood with them, warming himself.

The High Priest Questions Jesus
John 18:19-24; cp. Matt 26:57-68 // Mark 14:53-65 // Luke 22:63-71

19Inside, the ᶠhigh priest began asking Jesus about his followers and what he had been teaching them. 20Jesus replied, "Everyone knows what I teach. I have preached regularly in the synagogues and the Temple, where the people gather. I have not spoken in secret. 21Why are you asking me this question? Ask those who heard me. They know what I said."

22Then one of the Temple guards standing nearby slapped Jesus across the face. "Is that the way to answer the high priest?" he demanded.

23Jesus replied, "If I said anything wrong, you must prove it. But if I'm speaking the truth, why are you beating me?"

24Then Annas bound Jesus and sent him to Caiaphas, the high priest.

Peter's Second and Third Denials
John 18:25-27 // Matt 26:71-75 // Mark 14:69-72 // Luke 22:58-65

25Meanwhile, as Simon Peter was standing by the fire warming himself, they asked him again, "You're not one of his disciples, are you?"

He denied it, saying, "No, I am not."

26But one of the household slaves of the high priest, a relative of the man whose ear Peter had cut off, asked, "Didn't I see you out there in the olive grove with Jesus?" 27Again Peter denied it. And immediately a rooster crowed.

Jesus' Trial before Pilate
John 18:28-38a // Matt 27:1-2, 11-14 // Mark 15:1-5 // Luke 23:1-5

28Jesus' trial before Caiaphas ended in the early hours of the morning. Then he was taken to the headquarters of the Roman

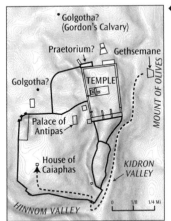

◀ Jesus' Trial and Crucifixion (John 18:1– 19:27; see also Matt 26:47–27:26; Mark 14:43–15:15; Luke 22:47–23:25). After Jesus was arrested in GETHSEMANE, he was taken to the HOUSE OF CAIAPHAS the high priest. There the Jewish leaders decided to send him to Pilate (at the PRAETORIUM) to sentence him to death (18:28). Pilate sent Jesus to Herod (at the PALACE OF ANTIPAS?), who questioned Jesus and sent him back (Luke 23:6-12). Then Pilate sentenced Jesus to be crucified (19:16). • Regarding the location of GOLGOTHA, see note on 19:17; see also illustration of Jerusalem in Jesus' time, p. 1753.

18:15 *That other disciple* is unnamed, but was probably the "disciple Jesus loved" (13:23)—John, the author of this Gospel.

18:16-17 During Jesus' interrogation by Annas (18:12-14, 19-24), *the woman watching at the gate* asked *Peter* if he was *one of that man's disciples.* In contrast to Jesus, who stood up to his questioners and denied nothing, Peter quickly denied his link to Jesus three times (18:17, 25, 27).

18:19 The *high priest began asking Jesus* questions, but his inquiry was contrary to Jewish legal procedure. In Jewish court, the priest did not ask questions directly of the defendant, but accumulated evidence from witnesses to establish guilt (see Num 35:30; Deut 17:6; 19:15; cp. Matt 18:16). If Jesus said anything incriminating, Annas would later use it to testify against him at Jesus' trial. He was attempting to follow Roman practice by making Jesus incriminate himself, rather than gathering evidence through witnesses as Jewish law demanded.

18:20-21 Jesus' sharp answer,

reminding Annas that everything was in the public record, unmasked the priest's attempt to follow Roman practice.

18:20 *people:* Literally *Jewish people;* also in 18:38.

18:22-23 When Jesus reminded Annas of correct judicial procedure, one of the *Temple guards* viewed it as insolence and *slapped Jesus.* However, Jesus knew the law and represented it truthfully. No witnesses were accusing him, and no evidence was being presented.

18:24 *Annas* was at an impasse—his probing had been unsuccessful. So he sent *Jesus* to *Caiaphas* to be prosecuted before the Sanhedrin, Jerusalem's judicial high council (see Mark 14:53–15:1).

18:25-27 *He denied it:* Peter's three denials were later echoed when Jesus invited him three times to reaffirm his love (21:15-17).

18:28 The trial before *Caiaphas* ended *in the early hours of the morning.* Since they did not have the power of capital punishment (18:31), the Sanhedrin needed to enlist Pilate, the Roman governor, to carry out an execution. • *the headquarters of the Roman governor:* Greek *the Praetorium;* also in 18:33. • *it would defile them:* They did not want to become ritually unclean by contact with Gentiles in Pilate's headquarters.

governor. His accusers didn't go inside because it would defile them, and they wouldn't be allowed to celebrate the Passover. ²⁹So Pilate, the governor, went out to them and asked, "What is your charge against this man?"

³⁰"We wouldn't have handed him over to you if he weren't a criminal!" they retorted.

³¹"Then take him away and judge him by your own law," Pilate told them.

"Only the Romans are permitted to execute someone," the Jewish leaders replied. ³²(This fulfilled Jesus' prediction about the way he would die.)

³³Then Pilate went back into his headquarters and called for Jesus to be brought to him. "Are you the king of the Jews?" he asked him.

³⁴Jesus replied, "Is this your own question, or did others tell you about me?"

³⁵"Am I a Jew?" Pilate retorted. "Your own people and their leading priests brought you to me for trial. Why? What have you done?"

³⁶Jesus answered, "My Kingdom is not an earthly kingdom. If it were, my followers would fight to keep me from being handed over to the Jewish leaders. But my Kingdom is not of this world."

³⁷Pilate said, "So you are a king?"

Jesus responded, "You say I am a king. Actually, I was born and came into the world to testify to the truth. All who love the truth recognize that what I say is true."

³⁸"What is truth?" Pilate asked.

Jesus Is Sentenced to Death
John 18:38b–19:16 // Matt 27:15-31 // Mark 15:6-20 // Luke 23:13-25

Then he went out again to the people and told them, "He is not guilty of any crime. ³⁹But you have a custom of asking me to release one prisoner each year at Passover. Would you like me to release this 'King of the Jews'?"

⁴⁰But they shouted back, "No! Not this man. We want Barabbas!" (Barabbas was a revolutionary.)

19 Then Pilate had Jesus flogged with a lead-tipped whip. ²The soldiers wove a crown of thorns and put it on his head, and they put a purple robe on him. ³"Hail! King of the Jews!" they mocked, as they slapped him across the face.

⁴Pilate went outside again and said to the people, "I am going to bring him out to you now, but understand clearly that I find him not guilty." ⁵Then Jesus came out wearing the crown of thorns and the purple robe. And Pilate said, "Look, here is the man!"

18:32
Matt 20:19
John 12:32-33

18:33
Luke 23:3
John 19:9

18:36
Matt 26:53
Luke 17:21
John 6:15

18:37
John 8:47
1 Jn 4:6

18:39–19:5
//Matt 27:15-31
//Mark 15:6-20
//Luke 23:13-25

19:1
Isa 50:6; 53:5

19:3
John 18:22

19:4
Luke 23:4
John 18:38

So Pilate, probably fearing a riot, went outside to meet them. • The *Passover* meal itself had occurred the night before (see 13:1; Mark 14:14-16). The following day, another meal began the weeklong Festival of Unleavened Bread (Lev 23:5-6).

18:29 *Pilate*, the fifth Roman *governor* of Judea, ruled the country from AD 26 to 36. He usually lived on the coast in Caesarea, but kept troops stationed in a fortress in Jerusalem where he appeared personally for major festivals. He was a brutal ruler whose atrocities against the Jews were legendary (e.g., Luke 13:1; Josephus, *War* 2.9.2-4).

18:31-32 Pilate found the charges unsatisfying and told the Sanhedrin, *judge him by your own law*. Pilate saw this as a Jewish squabble, which he refused to investigate. The Jewish leaders, however, insisted that an execution was necessary. • *fulfilled Jesus' prediction about the way he would die* (see 12:32-33): The Jews would have employed stoning; the Romans used crucifixion. If Pilate delivered Jesus' sentence, he would be crucified.

18:33 *Pilate* was personally responsible for capital crimes in which the interests and security of the Roman empire were at stake, so he began his formal legal inquiry. • *Are you the king of the*

Jews? To get the governor's attention, Caiaphas had charged that Jesus had urged people not to pay their taxes to the Roman government and had claimed to be a king (Luke 23:2). To Pilate, Jesus might have been just another Jewish terrorist–revolutionary (see Luke 23:18-19; Acts 5:36-37) with a head full of messianic notions and a band of well-armed followers.

18:34-35 Jesus' reply forced the governor to show the origin of his *question*. The Temple leadership was behind these charges. Pilate only wanted to know if Jesus was a rebel who might threaten Roman interests.

18:36-37 Jesus was willing to accept the title of *king*, but he made it clear that he did not govern an *earthly kingdom* that might rival Rome. Jesus' kingship is *not of this world*. Rather than being a political ruler, he rules through the devotion and obedience of his followers.

18:38-39 *What is truth?* Truth was not a foreign idea to Pilate, but he did not wait for an answer to his question because he did not believe there was one. • Pilate returned to the council members waiting outside and delivered his verdict: *not guilty*. Although he referred to Jesus as *"King of the Jews"* (see also 19:19), the title meant nothing more to Pilate than a mocking expression

of contempt. Pilate's offer of amnesty revealed his desire to let Jesus go.

18:40 Jesus was no threat to Rome, but *Barabbas was a revolutionary*, a violent man who took part in political uprisings (see Luke 23:19), with a proven capacity to challenge the Roman military occupation of Israel.

19:1-16 Jesus was also beaten after his sentencing (Mark 15:15), but here John records an earlier beating, which was likely Pilate's attempt to show that Jesus had been punished and could be released (19:4). When this failed, Pilate passed his sentence and handed Jesus over to the Jewish leaders for crucifixion (19:16).

19:2 The *crown of thorns* might have come from a date palm (cp. 12:13-14), whose thorns can exceed twelve inches. There are Greek coin images showing such crowns, with the stems woven and the thorns radiating upward above the crown. • The *purple robe* was probably a soldier's robe—dark red to complete the picture of mock royalty.

19:4-6 Pilate's intention was *to bring* Jesus *out* to display the marks of his punishment to sway the crowd to let him go. After being flogged with a lead-tipped whip, Jesus was bleeding profusely. • Pilate announced his verdict

19:6
John 18:31

19:7
Lev 24:16
Matt 26:63-66

19:11
Rom 13:1

19:12
Luke 23:2
Acts 17:7

19:13
Matt 27:19

19:16-27
//Matt 27:32-44
//Mark 15:21-32
//Luke 23:26-43

⁶When they saw him, the leading priests and Temple guards began shouting, "Crucify him! Crucify him!"

"Take him yourselves and crucify him," Pilate said. "I find him not guilty."

⁷The Jewish leaders replied, "By our law he ought to die because he called himself the Son of God."

⁸When Pilate heard this, he was more frightened than ever. ⁹He took Jesus back into the headquarters again and asked him, "Where are you from?" But Jesus gave no answer. ¹⁰"Why don't you talk to me?" Pilate demanded. "Don't you realize that I have the power to release you or crucify you?"

¹¹Then Jesus said, "You would have no power over me at all unless it were given to you from above. So the one who handed me over to you has the greater sin."

¹²Then Pilate tried to release him, but the Jewish leaders shouted, "If you release this man, you are no 'friend of Caesar.' Any-

one who declares himself a king is a rebel against Caesar."

¹³When they said this, Pilate brought Jesus out to them again. Then Pilate sat down on the judgment seat on the platform that is called the Stone Pavement (in Hebrew, *Gabbatha*). ¹⁴It was now about noon on the day of preparation for the Passover. And Pilate said to the people, "Look, here is your king!"

¹⁵"Away with him," they yelled. "Away with him! Crucify him!"

"What? Crucify your king?" Pilate asked.

"We have no king but Caesar," the leading priests shouted back.

¹⁶Then Pilate turned Jesus over to them to be crucified. So they took Jesus away.

The Crucifixion
John 19:17-24 // Matt 27:32-38 // Mark 15:21-27 // Luke 23:26-34

¹⁷Carrying the cross by himself, he went to the place called Place of the Skull (in

. . . .

of *not guilty* a second time, but he was met with a strident call for Jesus' death (19:6).

19:6 Pilate knew that a riot could happen when a man popular with the masses was executed, so he shifted responsibility to *crucify* Jesus to the *Temple* leaders.

19:7 During the trial before Caiaphas, the charge of blasphemy—calling *himself the Son of God*—was determined to be Jesus' true crime (see Mark 14:61-65). • The leaders had already tried pitting Roman imperial interests against Jesus (18:33), and would do so again (19:12). Now they challenged the governor on another level: Pilate must keep the peace by upholding local *law*, even when it was irrelevant to Rome. Claiming to be God's son was not illegal, because Israel's kings did this (Ps 2:7; 89:22-27). However, Jesus claimed to have the divine authority of God himself (see 5:18), which they saw as blasphemy.

19:8-9 *Pilate . . . was more frightened than ever:* He was superstitious, and the idea of gods appearing in the world was not uncommon (Acts 14:11). He sensed that more than a political fight was going on, so he asked Jesus, *Where are you from?* He did not mean Jesus' birthplace, but whether Jesus was a divine man who had descended from heaven. • *the headquarters:* Greek *the Praetorium*. • Why *Jesus gave no answer* is unclear. Perhaps it was because Pilate would not have been able to understand the answer—that true power comes only from God, and God had empowered Jesus (cp. 19:11).

19:10-11 *You would have no power over*

me: Although Pilate had *the power to . . . crucify* Jesus, it was only because God had given him this temporary power so Jesus could advance toward the cross (see 10:18).

19:12 Each time he had a conversation with Jesus, *Pilate tried to release him:* He kept trying, but his repeated efforts were fruitless. • *"Friend of Caesar"* is a technical term that refers to an ally of the emperor. It was an official title given to individuals such as senators who showed exceptional loyalty and service to the emperor. The Jewish leaders were implying that they would ruin Pilate's career by reporting that he was not working in Rome's interests. They probably knew that Pilate was also having a personal crisis. His patron in Rome, Sejanus (the chief administrator of the Empire under Tiberius Caesar), had fallen from favor and was executed in AD 31. Pilate had every reason to be afraid.

19:13 Pilate took the governor's *judgment seat* (Greek *bēma,* cp. Acts 25:6, "seat in court") to render his verdict. • The *Stone Pavement* was the platform holding the judgment seat; from there Pilate now spoke with the authority of his office.

19:14 *the day of preparation for the Passover* (or *the day of preparation during the Passover*): Here, Passover does not refer to the Jewish Passover meal, which had taken place the night before, but to the whole Festival of Unleavened Bread. It was now Friday, the day of preparation for the Passover Sabbath, which would begin at sundown (cp. Mark 15:42; Luke 23:54). • *people:* Literally *Jewish people;* also

in 19:20.

19:15 The final words of the priests, *"We have no king but Caesar,"* stood in direct contradiction to the OT understanding that God was Israel's king (cp. Judg 8:23; 1 Sam 8:7; 10:19). Jerusalem and its leaders were in the process of killing their true king (18:37) while paying homage to Caesar, the pagan king of Rome.

19:16 *Pilate turned Jesus over* to the Roman garrison, who prepared Jesus for crucifixion by a second flogging (Mark 15:15), which brought him near death. Bleeding profusely, his clothes soaked in blood, his thorn-laced crown now digging deeply into his head, and nearly in shock, Jesus was marched to a site outside the city.

19:17 The vertical beam (Latin *staticulum*) of *the cross* was generally kept at the crucifixion site, and the victim was forced to carry only the heavy crossbeam (Latin *patibulum*). • Crucifixions were public executions that took place near major roadways. They were designed to shock and warn the people. • *Place of the Skull* (Hebrew and Aramaic *Golgotha;* Latin *calvariae,* "Calvary"): See map on p. 1809. Most archaeologists agree that Jesus' crucifixion was at the site of the present-day Church of the Holy Sepulchre, located in the Christian Quarter of the old walled city of Jerusalem (see "First-Century Jerusalem," p. 1753). An alternate site, Gordon's Calvary (north of the Damascus Gate), is a model of what the scene possibly looked like, but it holds only a tomb from the 500s BC and therefore cannot be the authentic site of Jesus' crucifixion and burial.

Hebrew, *Golgotha*). [18]There they nailed him to the cross. Two others were crucified with him, one on either side, with Jesus between them. [19]And Pilate posted a sign on the cross that read, "Jesus of Nazareth, the King of the Jews." [20]The place where Jesus was crucified was near the city, and the sign was written in Hebrew, Latin, and Greek, so that many people could read it.

[21]Then the leading priests objected and said to Pilate, "Change it from 'The King of the Jews' to 'He said, I am King of the Jews.'"

[22]Pilate replied, "No, what I have written, I have written."

[23]When the soldiers had crucified Jesus, they divided his clothes among the four of them. They also took his robe, but it was seamless, woven in one piece from top to bottom. [24]So they said, "Rather than tearing it apart, let's throw dice for it." This fulfilled the Scripture that says, "They divided my garments among themselves and threw dice for my clothing." So that is what they did.

[25]Standing near the cross were Jesus' mother, and his mother's sister, Mary (the wife of Clopas), and Mary Magdalene. [26]When Jesus saw his mother standing there beside the disciple he loved, he said to her, "Dear woman, here is your son." [27]And he said to this disciple, "Here is your mother." And from then on this disciple took her into his home.

19:24
*Ps 22:18
19:25
Matt 27:55-56
Mark 15:40-41
Luke 8:2; 23:49
19:26
John 2:4; 13:23; 20:2;
21:7, 20

The Cross and Passover (19:17-36)

John 1:29, 36
Exod 12:1–13:16;
29:38-46
Num 9:1-14
Deut 16:1-8
2 Kgs 23:21-23
2 Chr 30:1-27
Ezra 6:19-21
Isa 53:7
Ezek 45:21-22
Matt 26:2, 17-19
Mark 14:17-31
Luke 22:14-30
Acts 8:32-35; 12:3-4
1 Cor 5:7-8
Heb 11:28
Rev 5:5-14

At the beginning of John's Gospel, John the Baptist introduced Jesus by calling him the "Lamb of God" (1:29, 36). This odd phrase might refer to the sacrificial lamb that was killed daily in the Temple (Exod 29:38-46) or to the sacrificial lamb of Isa 53:7 (cp. Acts 8:32-35; Rev 5:5-14). Both rituals of sacrifice spoke of rescue and forgiveness from sin.

However, this was not all that John had in mind. John presented Jesus as the Passover lamb whose death marks the central event of the Passover season (see Exod 12:46; Luke 22:7; 1 Cor 5:7). In the first century, Jews made a pilgrimage to Jerusalem each spring to celebrate the Passover and to reread the story of the Exodus (see Exod 12–15). When Israel was being rescued from Egypt, the blood of a lamb was sprinkled on the doorposts of each Jewish home in Egypt and saved those inside from death (Exod 12). Jews who came to Jerusalem to celebrate the Passover needed to supply a perfect young lamb for sacrifice. The animal could not be diseased or have broken bones.

Jesus used his final Passover meal to show that his sacrificial death would give new meaning to the festival (Mark 14:17-31). In John, the cross became an altar where Christ, the Passover lamb, was slain. Jesus' legs were not broken (19:33), fulfilling a Passover rule (19:36; Exod 12:46). Blood ran freely from his wound (19:34), showing that his life was being exchanged for others. Just as a lamb died to save the lives of Jewish families at the Passover in Egypt, so, too, this one death of the Son of God on the cross serves to bring salvation to the world.

19:18 None of the Gospel writers dwell on the details of being *nailed . . . to the cross* because they were well known and horrific. The soldiers used the cross as a means of torture; they wanted victims to survive for a while, in some cases for days. Because the Sabbath would begin at dusk (19:31), they expedited Jesus' crucifixion. Jesus had been thoroughly beaten with stone- or metal-tipped whips, so his back was thoroughly lacerated, and he was bleeding profusely.

19:19-22 *Pilate posted a sign on the cross:* It was customary for the Roman soldiers to provide a written public notice of the criminal's name and crimes. Perhaps as a final act of revenge against the Jewish high council, Pilate ordered that the sign should identify *Jesus of Nazareth* (or *Jesus the Nazarene*) as *the King of the Jews*. Jesus' kingship was posted in three languages for the whole world to understand.

19:23-24 As was their common practice, the Roman soldiers *divided his clothes*. The soldiers gambled for his valuable *robe*, which was *seamless*, rather than dividing it up. • *throw dice*: Literally *cast lots*. • *"They divided my garments among themselves and threw dice for my clothing":* See Ps 22:18.

19:25-26 This is the only reference to Jesus' *mother's sister* in the NT. She might have been the wife of Zebedee and the mother of James and John (cp. Matt 27:56), which would make Jesus and John cousins. If so, it would help explain why Jesus assigned the *disciple he loved* (John) to care for Mary (John's aunt). • *Mary (the wife of Clopas)* is only mentioned here. She might be the same person as Mary the mother of James and Joseph (cp. Matt 27:56). • Jesus had healed *Mary Magdalene*, a woman from the village of Magdala (Mark 16:9; Luke 8:2). • *Dear woman* was a formal and polite form of address (see 2:4).

19:27 *Here is your mother:* Jesus employed a Jewish family law that assigned the care of one person to another. The scene had an additional significance: The people who were present represented the new community of the church that was born at the cross. Jesus wanted them to care for each other in obedience to his command to love one another (13:34; 15:12, 17).

19:28-29 *I am thirsty:* See Ps 22:15; 69:21. • The *hyssop* bush had been

19:28-37
//Matt 27:45-56
//Mark 15:33-41
//Luke 23:44-49

19:28
*Ps 22:15; 69:21

19:30
Job 19:26-27

19:31
Deut 21:22-23

19:35
John 20:30-31; 21:24
1 Jn 1:1

19:36
*Exod 12:46
Num 9:12
*Ps 34:20

19:37
*Zech 12:10
Rev 1:7

19:38-42
//Matt 27:57-61
//Mark 15:42-47
//Luke 23:50-56

19:39
John 3:1-2; 7:50

The Death of Jesus

John 19:28-30// Matt 27:45-56 // Mark 15:33-41 //
Luke 23:44-49

28Jesus knew that his mission was now finished, and to fulfill Scripture he said, "I am thirsty." 29A jar of sour wine was sitting there, so they soaked a sponge in it, put it on a hyssop branch, and held it up to his lips. 30When Jesus had tasted it, he said, "It is finished!" Then he bowed his head and released his spirit.

31It was the day of preparation, and the Jewish leaders didn't want the bodies hanging there the next day, which was the Sabbath (and a very special Sabbath, because it was the Passover). So they asked Pilate to hasten their deaths by ordering that their legs be broken. Then their bodies could be taken down. 32So the soldiers came and broke the legs of the two men crucified with Jesus. 33But when they came to Jesus, they saw that he was already dead, so they didn't break his legs. 34One of the soldiers, however, pierced his side with a spear, and immediately blood and water flowed out. 35(This report is from an eyewitness giving an accurate account. He speaks the truth so that you also can believe.) 36These things happened in fulfillment of the Scriptures that say, "Not one of his bones will be broken," 37and "They will look on the one they pierced."

The Burial of Jesus

John 19:38-42 // Matt 27:57-61 // Mark 15:42-47 //
Luke 23:50-56

38Afterward Joseph of Arimathea, who had been a secret disciple of Jesus (because he feared the Jewish leaders), asked Pilate for permission to take down Jesus' body. When Pilate gave permission, Joseph came and took the body away. 39With him came

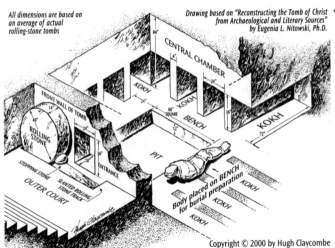

All dimensions are based on an average of actual rolling-stone tombs

Drawing based on "Reconstructing the Tomb of Christ from Archaeological and Literary Sources" by Eugenia L. Nitowski, Ph.D.

Copyright © 2000 by Hugh Claycombe

◀ **First-century Judean Tombs (John 19:41).** Joseph of Arimathea's tomb, where Jesus was buried (see Matt 27:57-60), was like other first-century Judean tombs. This drawing is based on sixty-one such "rolling-stone" tombs that have been discovered. These tombs, carved in limestone, were affordable only by wealthy families, and they were constructed according to the laws of Judaism (see *Mishnah Baba Batra* 6:8). After preparation for burial, bodies were placed in the KOKH (niche) which was then sealed with a rolling closure stone. Much later the dried bones were stored in ossuaries (stone boxes) within the tomb.

first letter (1 Jn 1:1-4) • *can believe:* Some manuscripts read *can continue to believe.*

19:36 *"Not one of his bones will be broken":* Exod 12:46; Num 9:12; Ps 34:20. The Passover lamb could have no broken bones; Jesus was the perfect Passover lamb (see also 1 Cor 5:7).

19:37 *"They will look on the one they pierced":* Zech 12:10 describes how Israel would look on a prophet or the Messiah and lament their own fatal lack of faith.

19:38 According to Luke, *Joseph of Arimathea* was a courageous man who was waiting for the Kingdom of God (Luke 23:50-51). He was a wealthy (Matt 27:57) and influential leader in Jerusalem and a member of the high council (Mark 15:43) who disagreed with the decision to kill Jesus. He asked Pilate for the favor of burying Jesus in his personal tomb. • Joseph was *a secret disciple* (cp. 12:42-43), but his bold deed brought him out in public support of Jesus.

used in Egypt to brush lamb's blood on the doorposts and lintels during the first Passover (Exod 12:22). Jesus is God's Passover lamb (1:29, 36), and his blood likewise saves.

19:30 Jesus called out in triumph and exhaustion that he had *finished* the work he set out to do. On the cross he was not a victim, but a servant doing God's bidding.

19:31-33 The Jewish authorities, eager to complete the crucifixion before Sabbath began at dusk, asked Pilate to break *the legs* of the men. Breaking the legs with a mallet was common: It promoted asphyxiation and hemorrhaging, because the victim could no longer push himself up to breathe.

19:34 To confirm that Jesus was dead,

a Roman soldier *pierced his side with a spear.* • *blood and water flowed out:* This has several levels of meaning: (1) The spear probably punctured Jesus' pericardium, the sac around the heart, releasing these fluids. (2) John might have been thinking of more Passover symbolism. The Passover lamb's blood had to flow as it died. (3) The living water, flowing from Jesus' side, reminds readers of earlier language that Jesus used to describe himself (see 7:37-39; "Living Water" at 4:10-14, p. 1777).

19:35 John was at the foot of the cross (19:26). He was not simply a collector of traditions about Jesus, but *an eyewitness giving an accurate account* of the events of Jesus' life (cp. 21:24). This same confidence can be seen in the opening of John's

Nicodemus, the man who had come to Jesus at night. He brought about seventy-five pounds of perfumed ointment made from myrrh and aloes. ⁴⁰Following Jewish burial custom, they wrapped Jesus' body with the spices in long sheets of linen cloth. ⁴¹The place of crucifixion was near a garden, where there was a new tomb, never used before. ⁴²And so, because it was the day of preparation for the Jewish Passover and since the tomb was close at hand, they laid Jesus there.

Jesus' Resurrection (20:1-31)
The Empty Tomb
John 20:1-10 // Matt 28:1-10 // Mark 16:1-8 // Luke 24:1-12

20 Early on Sunday morning, while it was still dark, Mary Magdalene came to the tomb and found that the stone had been rolled away from the entrance. ²She ran and found Simon Peter and the other disciple, the one whom Jesus loved. She said, "They have taken the Lord's body out of the tomb, and we don't know where they have put him!"

³Peter and the other disciple started out for the tomb. ⁴They were both running, but the other disciple outran Peter and reached the tomb first. ⁵He stooped and looked in and saw the linen wrappings lying there, but he didn't go in. ⁶Then Simon Peter arrived and went inside. He also noticed the linen wrappings lying there, ⁷while the cloth that had covered Jesus' head was folded up and lying apart from the other wrappings. ⁸Then the disciple who had reached the tomb first also went in, and he saw and believed—⁹for until then they still hadn't understood the Scriptures that said Jesus must rise from the dead. ¹⁰Then they went home.

Jesus Appears to Mary Magdalene
John 20:11-18; cp. Matt 28:8-10; Mark 16:9-11

¹¹Mary was standing outside the tomb crying, and as she wept, she stooped and looked in. ¹²She saw two white-robed angels, one sitting at the head and the other at the foot of the place where the body of Jesus had been lying. ¹³"Dear woman, why are you crying?" the angels asked her.

"Because they have taken away my Lord," she replied, "and I don't know where they have put him."

¹⁴She turned to leave and saw someone standing there. It was Jesus, but she didn't recognize him. ¹⁵"Dear woman, why are you crying?" Jesus asked her. "Who are you looking for?"

She thought he was the gardener. "Sir," she said, "if you have taken him away, tell me where you have put him, and I will go and get him."

¹⁶"Mary!" Jesus said.

She turned to him and cried out, "ᵍRab-boni!" (which is Hebrew for "Teacher").

19:39 *Nicodemus* (see 3:1; 7:50), a member of the high council, understood that these bodies had to be buried before the upcoming Sabbath (19:31, 42). His public support, as with Joseph of Arimathea, might indicate that he, too, was becoming a disciple (see note on 7:49-51). • *Myrrh* was a commonly used aromatic powder. • The *aloes* were fragrant powdered sandalwood often used as perfume. • *seventy-five pounds* (Greek *100 litras* [32.7 kilograms]): This enormous amount of spices was appropriate for royalty; Jesus, the king, was given a royal burial.

19:41 *a new tomb:* More than 900 first-century burial tombs have been discovered in Judea, carved into the limestone hills (see illustration, p. 1813).

19:42 *because it was the day of preparation for the Jewish Passover:* Literally *because of the Jewish day of preparation;* see note on 19:14. The Sabbath was approaching, so Joseph and Nicodemus (19:38-39) would return to complete the burial process later.

20:1 *Early on Sunday morning:* Literally *On the first day of the week.* As a devoted follower of Jesus (see Luke 8:1-3; Matt 27:55-56), *Mary Magdalene* arrived at the tomb to help complete Jesus' burial (see 19:42). • Many Judean tombs were sealed with a rolling *stone* (see illustration, p. 1813).

20:2 Mary Magdalene *ran and found Simon Peter.* Her natural assumption was that someone had robbed the tomb and perhaps stolen the body—which was not an uncommon occurrence.

20:3-10 The *other disciple* was probably John, "the disciple Jesus loved," the author of this Gospel (see 13:23). He and *Peter* validated Mary's testimony by examining the tomb for themselves. John arrived first, but Peter entered first.

20:6-7 What Peter and John found in the tomb was remarkable. The *linen wrappings* (19:40) were on the burial bench (see note on 19:41). Jews also used a facial *cloth* for burials (cp. 11:44), which was rolled, wrapped under the chin, and tied on the top of the head. The apostles found this face cloth *folded up* on the bench. John's inclusion of these details counters any suggestion that grave robbers had taken Jesus' body; such costly garments would have been stolen in a robbery.

20:8-9 *he saw and believed:* Despite not fully understanding, John knew that God had been at work, and he realized that Jesus was alive.

20:11-13 Although *two . . . angels* appeared inside the tomb, the riddle of Jesus' disappearance remained unsolved (see Luke 24:4). • *why are you crying?* Sorrow was not the appropriate response in this moment.

20:14-15 Jesus, whom Mary mistook for *the gardener,* repeated the angel's question and added, *Who are you looking for?* Jesus' question was to provoke Mary's thinking: At this point Mary was looking for the body of Jesus, but she was about to meet the living Christ. Was she truly ready to meet her Lord?

20:16 When Jesus called *Mary* by name, she recognized him immediately (see 10:3-4).

20:17 Mary thought that with the resurrection, Jesus would resume normal relations with his disciples. She was trying to *cling to* the joy she discovered in her resurrected Lord. But his fellowship with her would come in a new form (20:22). Jesus had *not yet ascended* to complete his return to the Father, but the process

19:40 Luke 24:12 John 20:5-7 · 20:1-8 //Matt 28:1-8 //Mark 16:1-8 //Luke 24:1-12 · 20:2 John 13:23 · 20:3 Luke 24:12 · 20:5 John 19:40 · 20:7 John 11:44 · 20:9 John 2:22 · 20:11-18 Mark 16:9-11 · 20:12 Mark 16:5 Luke 24:4 · 20:14 Mark 16:9 Luke 24:16 John 21:4 · 20:16 ᵍrhabbouni (4462) ▸Matt 23:7

20:17
Matt 28:10
John 16:28
Rom 8:29
Col 1:18
Heb 2:11

20:19-23
//Matt 28:16-20
//Luke 24:36-49

20:20
John 16:20-22; 19:34

20:21
Matt 28:19
John 17:18

20:22
John 7:37-39; 14:16-18, 26

20:24
John 11:16

¹⁷"Don't cling to me," Jesus said, "for I haven't yet ascended to the Father. But go find my brothers and tell them, 'I am ascending to my Father and your Father, to my God and your God.' "

¹⁸Mary Magdalene found the disciples and told them, "I have seen the Lord!" Then she gave them his message.

Jesus Appears to His Disciples
John 20:19-23 // Luke 24:35-49

¹⁹That Sunday evening the disciples were meeting behind locked doors because they were afraid of the Jewish leaders. Suddenly, Jesus was standing there among them! "Peace be with you," he said. ²⁰As he spoke, he showed them the wounds in his hands and his side. They were filled with joy when they saw the Lord! ²¹Again he said, "Peace be with you. As the Father has sent me, so I am sending you." ²²Then he breathed on them and said, "Receive the Holy Spirit. ²³If you forgive anyone's sins, they are forgiven. If you do not forgive them, they are not forgiven."

Jesus Appears to Thomas
²⁴One of the twelve disciples, Thomas (nicknamed the Twin), was not with the others

. . . .

THOMAS (20:24-28)

John 11:16; 14:5;
21:2
Matt 10:3
Mark 3:18
Luke 6:15
Acts 1:13

Thomas, also known as "the twin," was one of the twelve apostles (Matt 10:3; Mark 3:18; Luke 6:15; Acts 1:13). He is remembered for his unbelieving response to Jesus' resurrection.

Nothing is known of how Jesus first met and called Thomas to be his disciple. The only personal accounts of Thomas are found in the Gospel of John. Thomas voiced his willingness to follow Jesus, even if it meant death (11:16); he openly told Jesus that he didn't understand what he was saying (14:5); and he was one of the seven disciples who returned to fishing after the resurrection, when Jesus appeared to them (21:2).

When Jesus first appeared to his disciples after his death, Thomas was not present. When Thomas heard the report from the others, he did not believe it, insisting he would have to see the evidence of the crucifixion in Jesus' body with his own eyes and feel it with his own hands (20:19-23). A week later, when Jesus once again appeared to the disciples, he especially addressed Thomas, telling him to examine the marks of the nails and the spear in his body and challenging him to believe and not be skeptical. Thomas's response represents one of the strongest statements of Jesus' deity in the New Testament, and the culmination of the Gospel of John's portrayal of Jesus: "My Lord and my God!" (20:28).

Later tradition speaks of Thomas working as a missionary in the East: in Parthia (Eusebius), Persia (Jerome), and India (*Acts of Thomas*). The Mar Thoma church on the west coast of India traces its roots back to the early missionary work of Thomas. The historical reliability of these accounts is uncertain.

Thomas's name is unreliably linked to several later apocryphal writings: the *Acts of Thomas*, the *Infancy Gospel of Thomas*, the *Epistle to the Apostles*, the *Apocalypse of Thomas*, the *Book of Thomas the Athlete*, and especially the Coptic *Gospel of Thomas*, a Gnostic collection of Jesus' sayings.

. . . .

was underway. Before his final departure, he would give the Holy Spirit (20:22; see 14:15-21, 26; 15:26-27; 16:5-15).

20:18 Mary was the first eyewitness to see *the Lord* following his resurrection. She not only saw him, she heard him and touched him (see 1 Jn 1:1-4). This great privilege was given to a woman whose broken life had experienced healing (Luke 8:2). In Jewish culture this was astounding; a woman could not even be a witness in court. No Jew in this period would make up such a story.

20:19 *That Sunday evening:* Literally *In the evening of that day, the first day of the week.* • *meeting behind locked doors:* The disciples feared prosecution for following Jesus. • *Peace be with you:* This was a standard Jewish greeting (see also 3 Jn 1:15), but Jesus was doing more than just greeting his disciples: he was offering the Messiah's peace (see Isa

9:6; 52:7) and delivering the gift of his Kingdom (see 14:27; 16:33).

20:20 The reality of Jesus' resurrection was quite clear. Jesus *showed them the wounds* from the nails and the spear. He did not feign death, but conquered it. He was no phantom, but a real man with a real body. He had been dead, but was now alive. Jesus was fully human both in life (1:14) and in his resurrection.

20:21 *I am sending you:* God had sent Jesus into the world to establish his Kingdom, and now Jesus was sending his disciples to carry on his mission. Christ's emissaries carry the truth of Jesus' words to the world (cp. 17:18).

20:22 Jesus commissioned the disciples and then empowered them with *the Holy Spirit*. The Spirit had not been given previously because Jesus had not yet been glorified (7:39). The glorified Jesus, resplendent in his resurrected

body, poured the Spirit on his followers. This gift fulfilled many promises that the Spirit would be sent (14:16, 26; 15:26; 16:7, 13). It foreshadows the arrival of the Spirit's empowering presence at Pentecost (Acts 1:4-5; 2:1-47).

20:23 *If you forgive anyone's sins:* The ongoing work of Christ's followers parallels the work of Christ. Christ's followers do not distribute and withdraw God's forgiveness on a whim, but they follow Jesus' prompting through the Spirit (15:5), just as Jesus obeyed his Father (14:31).

20:24-25 *Thomas (nicknamed the Twin):* Literally *Thomas, who was called Didymus* (see also 11:16; 14:5). Thomas was absent when Jesus revealed himself. He remained skeptical despite the testimony of his friends, who had *seen the Lord.* Thomas demanded a concrete experience identical to theirs.

when Jesus came. ²⁵They told him, "We have seen the Lord!"

But he replied, "I won't believe it unless I see the nail wounds in his hands, put my fingers into them, and place my hand into the wound in his side."

²⁶Eight days later the disciples were together again, and this time Thomas was with them. The doors were locked; but suddenly, as before, Jesus was standing among them. "Peace be with you," he said. ²⁷Then he said to Thomas, "Put your finger here, and look at my hands. Put your hand into the wound in my side. Don't be faithless any longer. Believe!"

²⁸"My Lord and my God!" Thomas exclaimed.

²⁹Then Jesus told him, "You believe because you have seen me. ʰBlessed are those who believe without seeing me."

Purpose of the Book

³⁰The disciples saw Jesus do many other miraculous signs in addition to the ones recorded in this ⁱbook. ³¹But these are written so that you may continue to believe that Jesus is the Messiah, the Son of God, and that by believing in him you will have life by the power of his name.

4. EPILOGUE: THE WORD COMMISSIONS HIS FOLLOWERS (21:1-25)
The Miraculous Catch of Fish

21 Later, Jesus appeared again to the disciples beside the Sea of Galilee. This is how it happened. ²Several of the disciples were there—Simon Peter, Thomas (nicknamed the Twin), Nathanael from Cana in Galilee, the sons of Zebedee, and two other disciples.

³Simon Peter said, "I'm going fishing."

"We'll come, too," they all said. So they went out in the boat, but they caught nothing all night.

⁴At dawn Jesus was standing on the beach, but the disciples couldn't see who he was. ⁵He called out, "Fellows, have you caught any fish?"

"No," they replied.

⁶Then he said, "Throw out your net on the right-hand side of the boat, and you'll get some!" So they did, and they couldn't haul in the net because there were so many fish in it. ⁷Then the disciple Jesus loved said to Peter, "It's the Lord!" When Simon Peter heard that it was the Lord, he put on his tunic (for he had stripped for work), jumped into the water, and headed to shore. ⁸The others stayed with the boat and pulled the loaded net to the shore, for they were only about a hundred yards from shore. ⁹When they got there, they found breakfast waiting for them—fish cooking over a charcoal fire, and some bread.

¹⁰"Bring some of the fish you've just caught," Jesus said. ¹¹So Simon Peter went aboard and dragged the net to the shore. There were 153 large fish, and yet the net hadn't torn.

20:28
John 1:1, 18; 10:30; 14:9
Phil 2:6
Col 2:9
Titus 2:13
2 Pet 1:1
1 Jn 5:20

20:29
1 Pet 1:8
ʰ*makarios* (3107)
▸ Acts 20:35

20:30
John 21:25
ⁱ*biblion* (0975)
▸ John 21:25

20:31
John 3:15; 19:35
1 Jn 5:13

21:2
John 1:45-51; 11:16; 20:24

21:3
Luke 5:5

21:4
Luke 24:16
John 20:14

21:6
Luke 5:4-7

21:7
Matt 14:29
John 13:23

21:9
John 18:18

20:26-27 *Eight days later* was Sunday, one week after Jesus' resurrection (it was customary to include the current day when counting forward). Jesus' appearance on the following Sunday helps explain the disciples' meeting on "the Lord's Day" (see Rev 1:10). • *Peace be with you:* This scene was exactly like Jesus' first appearance (20:19-20). Jesus had already heard Thomas's complaint and now answered directly. • *Believe!* Jesus challenged Thomas to believe in the resurrection like the others.

20:28 *"My Lord and my God!"* This was not an astonished exclamation but a proclamation of heartfelt belief. It concludes John's study of Jesus' deity that has framed the whole book (see 1:1-18).

20:29 Jesus points to the generations of Christians who, through the testimony of others, would *believe without seeing.*

20:30-31 Many scholars view these words as the conclusion of John's Gospel, viewing ch 21 as an appendix. John's account is only a selection from Jesus' *many . . . miraculous signs.*

20:31 *that you may continue to believe:* Some manuscripts use the present tense, indicating that John wrote to encourage believers. Other manuscripts read *that you may come to believe,* suggesting that John wrote to stimulate new faith (cp. 1:7).

21:1-25 This final chapter adds an account about the resurrected Jesus in Galilee (21:1-14) and records the exchange between Peter and Jesus concerning Peter's love (21:15-23). The chapter ends by summarizing the authority and importance of John's eyewitness report (21:24-25).

21:1 *Sea of Galilee:* Greek *Sea of Tiberias,* another name for the Sea of Galilee (see 6:1).

21:2 *Several of the disciples* returned to fishing in the Sea of Galilee. This was not a sign that their faith had weakened—even rabbis who regularly preached kept practicing their occupations (see Acts 18:3; 20:34; 1 Cor 4:12). • *Thomas (nicknamed the Twin):* Literally *Thomas, who was called Didymus.* • *The sons of Zebedee* were James and John (see Matt 4:21).

21:3 Fishing was usually successful in the early hours of the morning.

However, this trip was useless and *they caught nothing all night.*

21:4-5 *Jesus was standing on the beach,* but the men did not recognize him (cp. 20:11-16; Luke 24:13-53). • *Fellows:* Literally *Children.*

21:6 *"Throw out your net on the right-hand side":* Casting a net into the sea at random was futile. But when *they did* as the stranger said, the immense catch was immediate (21:11).

21:7 *"It's the Lord!"* John recognized Jesus, probably remembering that a miracle like this had happened before (Luke 5:1-11). • Peter, who *had stripped* off his clothes while working, *put on his tunic* in order to meet the Lord.

21:8 *a hundred yards:* Greek *200 cubits* [90 meters].

21:9 Cooked *fish* and *bread* were the mainstays of the Galilean diet; Jesus provided the men with breakfast. The *charcoal fire* is reminiscent of the scene of Peter's denials (18:18).

21:11 This miracle showed generous provision (as in 2:1-12; 6:1-15). No symbolism attaches to the number *153.*

21:14
John 20:19, 26

21:15
Matt 26:33

21:16
Acts 20:28
Heb 13:20-21
1 Pet 5:2-3
ᶦpoimainō (4165)
▸ Acts 20:28

21:17
John 13:37-38; 16:30

21:19
John 13:36
2 Pet 1:14

21:20
John 13:23, 25

21:22
Matt 16:27

21:24
John 15:27; 19:35
1 Jn 1:1-3
3 Jn 1:12

21:25
John 20:30
ᵏbiblion (0975)
▸ 2 Tim 4:13

12"Now come and have some breakfast!" Jesus said. None of the disciples dared to ask him, "Who are you?" They knew it was the Lord. 13Then Jesus served them the bread and the fish. 14This was the third time Jesus had appeared to his disciples since he had been raised from the dead.

Peter's Restoration

15After breakfast Jesus asked Simon Peter, "Simon son of John, do you love me more than these?"

"Yes, Lord," Peter replied, "you know I love you."

"Then feed my lambs," Jesus told him.

16Jesus repeated the question: "Simon son of John, do you love me?"

"Yes, Lord," Peter said, "you know I love you."

"Then ᶦtake care of my sheep," Jesus said.

17A third time he asked him, "Simon son of John, do you love me?"

Peter was hurt that Jesus asked the question a third time. He said, "Lord, you know everything. You know that I love you."

Jesus said, "Then feed my sheep.

18"I tell you the truth, when you were young, you were able to do as you liked; you dressed yourself and went wherever you wanted to go. But when you are old, you will stretch out your hands, and others will dress you and take you where you don't want to go." 19Jesus said this to let him know by what kind of death he would glorify God. Then Jesus told him, "Follow me."

20Peter turned around and saw behind them the disciple Jesus loved—the one who had leaned over to Jesus during supper and asked, "Lord, who will betray you?" 21Peter asked Jesus, "What about him, Lord?"

22Jesus replied, "If I want him to remain alive until I return, what is that to you? As for you, follow me." 23So the rumor spread among the community of believers that this disciple wouldn't die. But that isn't what Jesus said at all. He only said, "If I want him to remain alive until I return, what is that to you?"

Concluding Remarks

24This disciple is the one who testifies to these events and has recorded them here. And we know that his account of these things is accurate.

25Jesus also did many other things. If they were all written down, I suppose the whole world could not contain the ᵏbooks that would be written.

21:12-13 None of the disciples dared to ask him, "Who are you?" Jesus' resurrected appearance was different. His offer of fish and bread removed all uncertainties (cp. 6:11; Luke 24:30).

21:14 This scene on the beach **was the third time Jesus had appeared** (see 20:11-23, 26-29).

21:15-17 do you love me? The three questions and affirmations mirror Peter's three denials (18:15-18, 25-27). Jesus invited Peter to reaffirm everything he had denied. • The Greek term translated **love** in Jesus' first two questions (agapaō) is different from the word in his third question (phileō). In each case, Peter answered with the second word (phileō). Most Greek scholars view the two words as synonyms in this situation. The focus of Jesus' exchange with Peter was not the quality of Peter's love, but Peter's commission to take care of Jesus' flock. Peter might be meditating on these events in 1 Pet 5:2-4.

21:15 more than these? Or more than these others do? Jesus was reminding Peter of his insistence that he would be more faithful and courageous than the others (13:37; Matt 26:33; Mark 14:29). He was urging Peter to examine himself.

21:17 feed my sheep: Jesus, who knows

all things (1:42; 2:25; 16:30), understood that despite Peter's terrible failing, he still had faith and commitment to Jesus. These words called Peter to nurture and protect Christ's followers.

21:18 you will stretch out your hands: Jesus was probably predicting crucifixion, which according to tradition is how Peter died. • **others** (some manuscripts read another one) **will dress you** (literally bind you): Jesus alludes to captivity, bondage, and even crucifixion—victims were often tied to the cross.

21:19 Peter's life was a ministry tending the flock of God, and his martyrdom was a **kind of death** that glorifies God. • **Follow me:** This might require suffering and death (see 13:16; 15:18-21).

21:20-22 "What about him, Lord?" Peter asked Jesus about the fate of John, wondering if he, too, would experience martyrdom. Jesus' answer was abrupt: It was not Peter's business to know how or when John would die. Peter's only task was to follow Jesus, which John was already doing. This episode forms the core of John's concept of discipleship: What matters most for the disciple of Jesus is to follow him and do his will, come what may.

21:23 Jesus' words to Peter **spread**,

causing some to conclude that John would not die until Jesus returned in his second coming. Jesus' rebuke to Peter (21:22) is repeated to answer that rumor. Those among **the community of believers** (literally the brothers) who believed this rumor were thus instructed to abandon any speculation about John. According to tradition, John died peacefully in Ephesus at an old age, surrounded by fellow believers.

21:24 This disciple is the one who testifies . . . and has recorded: John's Gospel is anchored in his personal experiences. It is not a story written from hearsay or speculation, but from the remembrance of a man who spent life-changing years with Jesus and recalled, with the help of the Holy Spirit (14:26), what Jesus said and did. • **we know:** This account of the life of Christ was not speculation or weak reminiscence. Rather, it was based on the confident knowledge of reliable eyewitness accounts.

21:25 the whole world could not contain the books: John ends his Gospel acknowledging that the story he has described is larger than anything he can imagine or fully communicate. Though it is glorious for us to read, John's account pales in comparison to the glory of the person it describes.

INTRODUCTION TO THE
NEW LIVING TRANSLATION

Translation Philosophy and Methodology

English Bible translations tend to be governed by one of two general translation theories. The first theory has been called "formal-equivalence," "literal," or "word-for-word" translation. According to this theory, the translator attempts to render each word of the original language into English and seeks to preserve the original syntax and sentence structure as much as possible in translation. The second theory has been called "dynamic-equivalence," "functional-equivalence," or "thought-for-thought" translation. The goal of this translation theory is to produce in English the closest natural equivalent of the message expressed by the original-language text, both in meaning and in style.

Both of these translation theories have their strengths. A formal-equivalence translation preserves aspects of the original text—including ancient idioms, term consistency, and original-language syntax—that are valuable for scholars and professional study. It allows a reader to trace formal elements of the original-language text through the English translation. A dynamic-equivalence translation, on the other hand, focuses on translating the message of the original-language text. It ensures that the meaning of the text is readily apparent to the contemporary reader. This allows the message to come through with immediacy, without requiring the reader to struggle with foreign idioms and awkward syntax. It also facilitates serious study of the text's message and clarity in both devotional and public reading.

The pure application of either of these translation philosophies would create translations at opposite ends of the translation spectrum. But in reality, all translations contain a mixture of these two philosophies. A purely formal-equivalence translation would be unintelligible in English, and a purely dynamic-equivalence translation would risk being unfaithful to the original. That is why translations shaped by dynamic-equivalence theory are usually quite literal when the original text is relatively clear, and the translations shaped by formal-equivalence theory are sometimes quite dynamic when the original text is obscure.

The translators of the New Living Translation set out to render the message of the original texts of Scripture into clear, contemporary English. As they did so, they kept the concerns of both formal-equivalence and dynamic-equivalence in mind. On the one hand, they translated as simply and literally as possible when that approach yielded an accurate, clear, and natural English text. Many words and phrases were rendered literally and consistently into English, preserving essential literary and rhetorical devices, ancient metaphors, and word choices that give structure to the text and provide echoes of meaning from one passage to the next.

On the other hand, the translators rendered the message more dynamically when the literal rendering was hard to understand, was misleading, or yielded archaic or foreign wording. They clarified difficult metaphors and terms to aid in the reader's understanding. The translators first struggled with the meaning of the words and phrases in the ancient context; then they rendered the message into clear, natural English. Their goal was to be both faithful to the ancient texts and eminently readable. The result is a translation that is both exegetically accurate and idiomatically powerful.

Translation Process and Team

To produce an accurate translation of the Bible into contemporary English, the translation team needed the skills necessary to enter into the thought patterns of the ancient authors and then to render their ideas, connotations, and effects into clear, contemporary English. To begin this process, qualified biblical scholars were needed to interpret the meaning of the original text and to check it against our base English translation. In order to guard against personal and theological biases, the scholars needed to represent a diverse group of evangelicals who would employ the best exegetical tools. Then to work alongside the scholars, skilled English stylists were needed to shape the text into clear, contemporary English.

With these concerns in mind, the Bible Translation Committee recruited teams of scholars that represented a broad spectrum of denominations, theological perspectives, and backgrounds within the worldwide evangelical community. (These scholars are listed at the end of this introduction.) Each book of the Bible was assigned to three different scholars with proven expertise in the book or group of books to be reviewed. Each of these scholars made a thorough review of a base translation and submitted suggested revisions to the appropriate Senior Translator. The Senior Translator then reviewed and summarized these suggestions and proposed a first-draft revision of the base text. This draft served as the basis for several additional phases of exegetical and stylistic committee review. Then the Bible Translation Committee jointly reviewed and approved every verse of the final translation.

Throughout the translation and editing process, the Senior Translators and their scholar teams were given a chance to review the editing done by the team of stylists. This ensured that exegetical errors would not be introduced late in the process and that the entire Bible Translation Committee was happy with the final result. By choosing a team of qualified scholars and skilled stylists and by setting up a process that allowed their interaction throughout the process, the New Living Translation has been refined to preserve the essential formal elements of the original biblical texts, while also creating a clear, understandable English text.

The New Living Translation was first published in 1996. Shortly after its initial publication, the Bible Translation Committee began a process of further committee review and translation refinement. The purpose of this continued revision was to increase the level of precision without sacrificing the text's easy-to-understand quality. This second-edition text was completed in 2004, and an additional update with minor changes was subsequently introduced in 2007. This printing of the New Living Translation reflects the updated 2007 text.

Written to Be Read Aloud
It is evident in Scripture that the biblical documents were written to be read aloud, often in public worship (see Nehemiah 8; Luke 4:16-20; 1 Timothy 4:13; Revelation 1:3). It is still the case today that more people will hear the Bible read aloud in church than are likely to read it for themselves. Therefore, a new translation must communicate with clarity and power when it is read publicly. Clarity was a primary goal for the NLT translators, not only to facilitate private reading and understanding, but also to ensure that it would be excellent for public reading and make an immediate and powerful impact on any listener.

The Texts behind the
New Living Translation
The Old Testament translators used the Masoretic Text of the Hebrew Bible as represented in *Biblia Hebraica Stuttgartensia* (1977), with its extensive system of textual notes; this is an update of Rudolf Kittel's *Biblia Hebraica* (Stuttgart, 1937). The translators also further compared the Dead Sea Scrolls, the Septuagint and other Greek manuscripts, the Samaritan Pentateuch, the Syriac Peshitta, the Latin Vulgate, and any other versions or manuscripts that shed light on the meaning of difficult passages.

The New Testament translators used the two standard editions of the Greek New Testament: the *Greek New Testament,* published by the United Bible Societies (UBS, fourth revised edition, 1993), and *Novum Testamentum Graece,* edited by Nestle and Aland (NA, twenty-seventh edition, 1993). These two editions, which have the same text but differ in punctuation and textual notes, represent, for the most part, the best in modern textual scholarship. However, in cases where strong textual or other scholarly evidence supported the decision, the translators sometimes chose to differ from the UBS and NA Greek texts and followed variant readings found in other ancient witnesses. Significant textual variants of this sort are always noted in the textual notes of the New Living Translation.

Translation Issues
The translators have made a conscious effort to provide a text that can be easily understood by the typical reader of modern English. To this end, we sought to use only vocabulary and language structures in common use today. We avoided using language likely to become quickly dated or that reflects only a narrow subdialect of English, with the goal of making the New Living Translation as broadly useful and timeless as possible.

But our concern for readability goes beyond the concerns of vocabulary and sentence structure. We are also concerned about historical and cultural barriers to understanding the Bible, and we have sought to translate terms shrouded in history and culture in ways that can be immediately understood. To this end:

• We have converted ancient weights and measures (for example, "ephah" [a unit of dry volume] or "cubit" [a unit of length]) to modern English (American) equivalents, since the ancient measures are not generally meaningful to today's readers. Then in the textual footnotes we offer the literal Hebrew, Aramaic, or Greek measures, along with modern metric equivalents.

• Instead of translating ancient currency values literally, we have expressed them in common terms that communicate the message. For example, in the Old Testament, "ten shekels of silver" becomes "ten pieces of silver" to convey the intended message. In the New Testament, we have often translated the "denarius" as "the normal daily wage" to facilitate understanding. Then a footnote offers: "Greek *a denarius,* the payment for a full day's wage." In general, we give a clear English rendering and then state the literal Hebrew, Aramaic, or Greek in a textual footnote.

• Since the names of Hebrew months are unknown to most contemporary readers, and since the Hebrew lunar calendar fluctuates from year to year in relation to the solar calendar used today, we have looked for clear ways to communicate the time of year the Hebrew months (such as Abib) refer to. When an expanded or interpretive rendering is given in the text, a textual note gives the literal rendering. Where it is possible to define a specific ancient date in terms of our modern calendar, we use modern dates in the text. A textual footnote then gives the literal Hebrew date and states the rationale for our rendering. For example, Ezra 6:15 pinpoints the date when the postexilic Temple was completed in Jerusalem: "the third day of the month Adar." This was during the sixth year of King Darius's reign (that is, 515 B.C.). We have translated that date as March 12, with a footnote giving the Hebrew and identifying the year as 515 B.C.

• Since ancient references to the time of day differ from our modern methods of denoting time, we have used renderings that are instantly understandable to the modern reader. Accordingly, we have rendered specific times of day by using approximate equivalents in terms of our common "o'clock" system. On occasion, translations such as "at dawn the next morning" or "as the sun was setting" have been used when the biblical reference is more general.

- When the meaning of a proper name (or a wordplay inherent in a proper name) is relevant to the message of the text, its meaning is often illuminated with a textual footnote. For example, in Exodus 2:10 the text reads: "The princess named him Moses, for she explained, 'I lifted him out of the water.'" The accompanying footnote reads: "*Moses* sounds like a Hebrew term that means 'to lift out.'"

Sometimes, when the actual meaning of a name is clear, that meaning is included in parentheses within the text itself. For example, the text at Genesis 16:11 reads: "You are to name him Ishmael *(which means 'God hears')*, for the LORD has heard your cry of distress." Since the original hearers and readers would have instantly understood the meaning of the name "Ishmael," we have provided modern readers with the same information so they can experience the text in a similar way.

- Many words and phrases carry a great deal of cultural meaning that was obvious to the original readers but needs explanation in our own culture. For example, the phrase "they beat their breasts" (Luke 23:48) in ancient times meant that people were very upset, often in mourning. In our translation we chose to translate this phrase dynamically for clarity: "They went home *in deep sorrow.*" Then we included a footnote with the literal Greek, which reads: "Greek *went home beating their breasts.*" In other similar cases, however, we have sometimes chosen to illuminate the existing literal expression to make it immediately understandable. For example, here we might have expanded the literal Greek phrase to read: "They went home beating their breasts *in sorrow.*" If we had done this,

we would not have included a textual footnote, since the literal Greek clearly appears in translation.

- Metaphorical language is sometimes difficult for contemporary readers to understand, so at times we have chosen to translate or illuminate the meaning of a metaphor. For example, the ancient poet writes, "Your neck is *like* the tower of David" (Song of Songs 4:4). We have rendered it "Your neck is *as beautiful as* the tower of David" to clarify the intended positive meaning of the simile. Another example comes in Ecclesiastes 12:3, which can be literally rendered: "Remember him . . . when the grinding women cease because they are few, and the women who look through the windows see dimly." We have rendered it: "Remember him before your teeth—your few remaining servants—stop grinding; and before your eyes—the women looking through the windows— see dimly." We clarified such metaphors only when we believed a typical reader might be confused by the literal text.

- When the content of the original language text is poetic in character, we have rendered it in English poetic form. We sought to break lines in ways that clarify and highlight the relationships between phrases of the text. Hebrew poetry often uses parallelism, a literary form where a second phrase (or in some instances a third or fourth) echoes the initial phrase in some way. In Hebrew parallelism, the subsequent parallel phrases continue, while also furthering and sharpening, the thought expressed in the initial line or phrase. Whenever possible, we sought to represent these parallel phrases in natural poetic English.

- The Greek term *hoi Ioudaioi* is literally translated "the Jews" in many English translations. In the Gospel of John, however, this term doesn't always refer to the Jewish people generally. In some contexts, it refers more particularly to the Jewish religious leaders. We have attempted to capture the meaning in these different contexts by using terms such as "the people" (with a

footnote: Greek *the Jewish people*) or "the religious leaders," where appropriate.

- One challenge we faced was how to translate accurately the ancient biblical text that was originally written in a context where male-oriented terms were used to refer to humanity generally. We needed to respect the nature of the ancient context while also trying to make the translation clear to a modern audience that tends to read male-oriented language as applying only to males. Often the original text, though using masculine nouns and pronouns, clearly intends that the message be applied to both men and women. A typical example is found in the New Testament letters, where the believers are called "brothers" (*adelphoi*). Yet it is clear from the content of these letters that they were addressed to all the believers— male and female. Thus, we have usually translated this Greek word as "brothers and sisters" in order to represent the historical situation more accurately.

We have also been sensitive to passages where the text applies generally to human beings or to the human condition. In some instances we have used plural pronouns (they, them) in place of the masculine singular (he, him). For example, a traditional rendering of Proverbs 22:6 is: "Train up a child in the way he should go, and when he is old he will not turn from it." We have rendered it: "Direct your children onto the right path, and when they are older, they will not leave it." At times, we have also replaced third person pronouns with the second person to ensure clarity. A traditional rendering of Proverbs 26:27 is: "He who digs a pit will fall into it, and he who rolls a stone, it will come back on him." We have rendered it: "If you set a trap for others, you will get caught in it yourself. If you roll a boulder down on others, it will crush you instead."

We should emphasize, however, that all masculine nouns and pronouns used to represent God (for example, "Father") have been maintained without exception. All decisions of this kind have been driven by the concern to reflect accurately the intended meaning of the original texts of Scripture.

Lexical Consistency in Terminology
For the sake of clarity, we have translated certain original-language terms consistently, especially within synoptic passages and for commonly repeated rhetorical phrases, and within certain word categories such as divine names and non-theological technical terminology (e.g., liturgical, legal, cultural, zoological, and botanical terms). For theological terms, we have allowed a greater semantic range of acceptable English words or phrases for a single Hebrew or Greek word. We have avoided some theological terms that are not readily understood by many modern readers. For example, we avoided using words such as "justification" and "sanctification," which are carryovers from Latin translations. In place of these words, we have provided renderings such as "made right with God" and "made holy."

The Spelling of Proper Names
Many individuals in the Bible, especially the Old Testament, are known by more than one name (e.g., Uzziah/Azariah). For the sake of clarity, we have tried to use a single spelling for any one individual, footnoting the literal spelling whenever we differ from it. This is especially helpful in delineating the kings of Israel and Judah. King Joash/Jehoash of Israel has been consistently called Jehoash, while King Joash/Jehoash of Judah is called Joash. A similar distinction has been used to distinguish between Joram/Jehoram of Israel and Joram/Jehoram of Judah. All such decisions were made with the goal of clarifying the text for the reader. When the ancient biblical writers clearly had a theological purpose in their choice of a variant name (e.g., Esh-baal/Ishbosheth), the different names have been maintained with an explanatory footnote.

For the names Jacob and Israel, which are used interchangeably for both the individual patriarch and the nation, we generally render it

"Israel" when it refers to the nation and "Jacob" when it refers to the individual. When our rendering of the name differs from the underlying Hebrew text, we provide a textual footnote, which includes this explanation: "The names 'Jacob' and 'Israel' are often interchanged throughout the Old Testament, referring sometimes to the individual patriarch and sometimes to the nation."

The Rendering of Divine Names
All appearances of *'el, 'elohim,* or *'eloah* have been translated "God," except where the context demands the translation "god(s)." We have generally rendered the tetragrammaton (*YHWH*) consistently as "the LORD," utilizing a form with small capitals that is common among English translations. This will distinguish it from the name *'adonai,* which we render "Lord." When *'adonai* and *YHWH* appear together, we have rendered it "Sovereign LORD." This also distinguishes *'adonai YHWH* from cases where *YHWH* appears with *'elohim,* which is rendered "LORD God." When *YH* (the short form of *YHWH*) and *YHWH* appear together, we have rendered it "LORD GOD." When *YHWH* appears with the term *tseba'oth,* we have rendered it "LORD of Heaven's Armies" to translate the meaning of the name. In a few cases, we have utilized the transliteration, *Yahweh,* when the personal character of the name is being invoked in contrast to another divine name or the name of some other god (for example, see Exodus 3:15; 6:2-3).

In the New Testament, the Greek word *christos* has been translated as "Messiah" when the context assumes a Jewish audience. When a Gentile audience can be assumed, *christos* has been translated as "Christ." The Greek word *kurios* is consistently translated "Lord," except that it is translated "LORD" wherever the New Testament text explicitly quotes from the Old Testament, and the text there has it in small capitals.

Textual Footnotes
The New Living Translation provides several kinds of textual footnotes, all included within the study notes in this edition:

- When for the sake of clarity the NLT renders a difficult or potentially confusing phrase dynamically, we generally give the literal rendering in a textual footnote. This allows the reader to see the literal source of our dynamic rendering and how our transation relates to other more literal translations. These notes are prefaced with "literally." For example, in Acts 2:42 we translated the literal "breaking of bread" (from the Greek) as "the Lord's Supper" to clarify that this verse refers to the ceremonial practice of the church rather than just an ordinary meal. Then we attached a footnote to "the Lord's Supper," which reads: "Literally *the breaking of bread.*"

- Textual footnotes are also used to show alternative renderings, prefaced with the word "Or." These normally occur for passages where an aspect of the meaning is debated. On occasion, we also provide notes on words or phrases that represent a departure from long-standing tradition. These notes are prefaced with "Traditionally rendered." For example, the footnote to the translation "serious skin disease" at Leviticus 13:2 says: "Traditionally rendered *leprosy.* The Hebrew word used throughout this passage is used to describe various skin diseases."

- When our translators follow a textual variant that differs significantly from our standard Hebrew or Greek texts (listed earlier), we document that difference with a footnote. We also footnote cases when the NLT excludes a passage that is included in the Greek text known as the *Textus Receptus* (and familiar to readers through its translation in the King James Version). In such cases, we offer a translation of the excluded text in a footnote, even though it is generally recognized as a later addition to the Greek text and not part of the original Greek New Testament.

- All Old Testament passages that are quoted in the New Testament are identified by a textual footnote at the New Testament location. When the New Testament clearly quotes from the Greek translation of the Old Testament, and when it differs significantly in wording from the Hebrew text, we also place a textual footnote at the Old Testament location. This note includes a rendering of the Greek version, along with a cross-reference to the New Testament passage(s) where it is cited (for example, see notes on Proverbs 3:12; Psalms 8:2; 53:3).

- Some textual footnotes provide cultural and historical information on places, things, and people in the Bible that are probably obscure to modern readers. Such notes should aid the reader in understanding the message of the text. For example, in Acts 12:1, "King Herod" is named in this translation as "King Herod Agrippa" and is identified in a footnote as being "the nephew of Herod Antipas and a grandson of Herod the Great."

- When the meaning of a proper name (or a wordplay inherent in a proper name) is relevant to the meaning of the text, it is either illuminated with a textual footnote or included within parentheses in the text itself. For example, the footnote concerning the name "Eve" at Genesis

3:20 reads: "*Eve* sounds like a Hebrew term that means 'to give life.' " This wordplay in the Hebrew illuminates the meaning of the text, which goes on to say that Eve "would be the mother of all who live."

Cross-References
There are a number of different cross-referencing tools that appear in New Living Translation Bibles, and they offer different levels of help in this regard. All straight-text Bibles include the standard set of textual footnotes that include cross-references connecting New Testament texts to their related Old Testament sources. (See more on this above.)

Many NLT Bibles include an additional short cross-reference system that sets key cross-references at the end of paragraphs and then marks the associated verses with a cross symbol. This space-efficient system, while not being obtrusive, offers many important key connections between passages. Larger study editions include a full-column cross-reference system. This system allows space for a more comprehensive listing of cross-references.

As we submit this translation for publication, we recognize that any translation of the Scriptures is subject to limitations and imperfections. Anyone who has attempted to communicate the richness of God's Word into another language will realize it is impossible to make a perfect translation. Recognizing these limitations, we sought God's guidance and wisdom throughout this project. Now we pray that he will accept our efforts and use this translation for the benefit of the church and of all people.

We pray that the New Living Translation will overcome some of the barriers of history, culture, and language that have kept people from reading and understanding God's Word. We hope that readers unfamiliar with the Bible will find the words clear and easy to understand and that readers well versed in the Scriptures will gain a fresh perspective. We pray that readers will gain insight and wisdom for living, but most of all that they will meet the God of the Bible and be forever changed by knowing him.

THE BIBLE TRANSLATION
COMMITTEE, *October 2007*

BIBLE TRANSLATION TEAM
Holy Bible, New Living Translation

PENTATEUCH
Daniel I. Block, Senior Translator
Wheaton College

GENESIS
Allen Ross, *Beeson Divinity School, Samford University*
Gordon Wenham, *Trinity Theological College, Bristol*

EXODUS
Robert Bergen, *Hannibal-LaGrange College*
Daniel I. Block, *Wheaton College*
Eugene Carpenter, *Bethel College, Mishawaka, Indiana*

LEVITICUS
David Baker, *Ashland Theological Seminary*
Victor Hamilton, *Asbury College*

Kenneth Mathews, *Beeson Divinity School, Samford University*

NUMBERS
Dale A. Brueggemann, *Assemblies of God Division of Foreign Missions*
R. K. Harrison (deceased), *Wycliffe College*
Paul R. House, *Wheaton College*
Gerald L. Mattingly, *Johnson Bible College*

DEUTERONOMY
J. Gordon McConville, *University of Gloucester*
Eugene H. Merrill, *Dallas Theological Seminary*
John A. Thompson (deceased), *University of Melbourne*

HISTORICAL BOOKS
Barry J. Beitzel, Senior Translator
Trinity Evangelical Divinity School

JOSHUA, JUDGES
Carl E. Armerding, *Schloss Mittersill Study Centre*
Barry J. Beitzel, *Trinity Evangelical Divinity School*
Lawson Stone, *Asbury Theological Seminary*

1 & 2 SAMUEL
Robert Gordon, *Cambridge University*
V. Philips Long, *Regent College*
J. Robert Vannoy, *Biblical Theological Seminary*

1 & 2 KINGS
Bill T. Arnold, *Asbury Theological Seminary*

William H. Barnes, *North Central University*
Frederic W. Bush, *Fuller Theological Seminary*

1 & 2 CHRONICLES
Raymond B. Dillard (deceased), *Westminster Theological Seminary*
David A. Dorsey, *Evangelical School of Theology*
Terry Eves, *Erskine College*

RUTH, EZRA—ESTHER
William C. Williams, *Vanguard University*
H. G. M. Williamson, *Oxford University*

WISDOM BOOKS
Tremper Longman III, Senior Translator
Westmont College

JOB
August Konkel, *Providence Theological Seminary*
Tremper Longman III, *Westmont College*
Al Wolters, *Redeemer College*

PSALMS 1–75
Mark D. Futato, *Reformed Theological Seminary*
Douglas Green, *Westminster Theological Seminary*
Richard Pratt, *Reformed Theological Seminary*

PSALMS 76–150
David M. Howard Jr., *Bethel Theological Seminary*
Raymond C. Ortlund Jr., *Trinity Evangelical Divinity School*
Willem VanGemeren, *Trinity Evangelical Divinity School*

PROVERBS
Ted Hildebrandt, *Gordon College*
Richard Schultz, *Wheaton College*
Raymond C. Van Leeuwen, *Eastern College*

ECCLESIASTES, SONG OF SONGS
Daniel C. Fredericks, *Belhaven College*
David Hubbard (deceased), *Fuller Theological Seminary*
Tremper Longman III, *Westmont College*

PROPHETS
John N. Oswalt, Senior Translator
Wesley Biblical Seminary

ISAIAH
John N. Oswalt, *Wesley Biblical Seminary*
Gary Smith, *Midwestern Baptist Theological Seminary*
John Walton, *Wheaton College*

JEREMIAH, LAMENTATIONS
G. Herbert Livingston, *Asbury Theological Seminary*
Elmer A. Martens, *Mennonite Brethren Biblical Seminary*

EZEKIEL
Daniel I. Block, *Wheaton College*
David H. Engelhard, *Calvin Theological Seminary*
David Thompson, *Asbury Theological Seminary*

DANIEL, HAGGAI—MALACHI
Joyce Baldwin Caine (deceased), *Trinity College, Bristol*
Douglas Gropp, *Catholic University of America*
Roy Hayden, *Oral Roberts School of Theology*
Andrew Hill, *Wheaton College*
Tremper Longman III, *Westmont College*

HOSEA—ZEPHANIAH
Joseph Coleson, *Nazarene Theological Seminary*
Roy Hayden, *Oral Roberts School of Theology*
Andrew Hill, *Wheaton College*
Richard Patterson, *Liberty University*

GOSPELS AND ACTS
Grant R. Osborne, Senior Translator
Trinity Evangelical Divinity School

MATTHEW
Craig Blomberg, *Denver Seminary*
Donald A. Hagner, *Fuller Theological Seminary*
David Turner, *Grand Rapids Baptist Seminary*

MARK
Robert Guelich (deceased), *Fuller Theological Seminary*
George Guthrie, *Union University*
Grant R. Osborne, *Trinity Evangelical Divinity School*

LUKE
Darrell Bock, *Dallas Theological Seminary*
Scot McKnight, *North Park University*
Robert Stein, *The Southern Baptist Theological Seminary*

JOHN
Gary M. Burge, *Wheaton College*
Philip W. Comfort, *Coastal Carolina University*
Marianne Meye Thompson, *Fuller Theological Seminary*

ACTS
D. A. Carson, *Trinity Evangelical Divinity School*
William J. Larkin, *Columbia International University*

Roger Mohrlang, *Whitworth University*

LETTERS AND REVELATION
Norman R. Ericson, Senior Translator
Wheaton College

ROMANS, GALATIANS
Gerald Borchert, *Northern Baptist Theological Seminary*
Douglas J. Moo, *Wheaton College*
Thomas R. Schreiner, *The Southern Baptist Theological Seminary*

1 & 2 CORINTHIANS
Joseph Alexanian, *Trinity International University*
Linda Belleville, *Bethel College, Mishawaka, Indiana*
Douglas A. Oss, *Central Bible College*
Robert Sloan, *Baylor University*

EPHESIANS—PHILEMON
Harold W. Hoehner, *Dallas Theological Seminary*
Moises Silva, *Gordon-Conwell Theological Seminary*
Klyne Snodgrass, *North Park Theological Seminary*

HEBREWS, JAMES, 1 & 2 PETER, JUDE
Peter Davids, *Schloss Mittersill Study Centre*
Norman R. Ericson, *Wheaton College*
William Lane (deceased), *Seattle Pacific University*
J. Ramsey Michaels, *S. W. Missouri State University*

1–3 JOHN, REVELATION
Greg Beale, *Wheaton College*
Robert Mounce, *Whitworth University*
M. Robert Mulholland Jr., *Asbury Theological Seminary*

SPECIAL REVIEWERS
F. F. Bruce (deceased), *University of Manchester*
Kenneth N. Taylor (deceased), *Translator, The Living Bible*

COORDINATING TEAM
Mark D. Taylor, *Director and Chief Stylist*
Ronald A. Beers, *Executive Director and Stylist*
Mark R. Norton, *Managing Editor and O.T. Coordinating Editor*
Philip W. Comfort, *N.T. Coordinating Editor*
Daniel W. Taylor, *Bethel University, Senior Stylist*

CONTRIBUTORS

EDITORS

GENERAL EDITOR
Sean A. Harrison

EXECUTIVE EDITOR
Mark D. Taylor

CONTENT EDITORS
David P. Barrett
G. Patrick LaCosse
Bradley J. Lewis
Henry M. Whitney III
Keith Williams

STYLISTIC EDITOR
Linda Schlafer

COPY EDITORS
Keith Williams, Coordinator
Leanne Roberts, Proofreading
  Coordinator
Paul Adams
Jason Driesbach
Adam Graber
Annette Hayward
Judy Modica
Jonathan Schindler
Caleb Sjogren
Cindy Szponder
Lisa Voth
Matthew Wolf

GENERAL REVIEWERS

GENESIS—DEUTERONOMY
Daniel I. Block

JOSHUA—ESTHER, MAPS
Barry J. Beitzel

JOB—SONG OF SONGS
Tremper Longman III

ISAIAH—MALACHI
John N. Oswalt

MATTHEW—ACTS
Grant R. Osborne

ROMANS—REVELATION
Norman R. Ericson

CONTRIBUTING SCHOLARS

GENESIS
Andrew Schmutzer
Allen P. Ross

EXODUS
John N. Oswalt

LEVITICUS
William C. Williams

NUMBERS
Gerald L. Mattingly

DEUTERONOMY
Eugene H. Merrill

JOSHUA
Joseph Coleson

JUDGES
Carl E. Armerding

RUTH
Joseph Coleson
Sean A. Harrison

1 & 2 SAMUEL
Victor P. Hamilton

1 & 2 KINGS
Richard D. Patterson

1 & 2 CHRONICLES
August Konkel

EZRA, NEHEMIAH, ESTHER
Gary V. Smith

JOB
Dale A. Brueggemann

PSALMS
Willem VanGemeren

PROVERBS
Tremper Longman III

ECCLESIASTES
Sean A. Harrison
Daniel C. Fredericks

SONG OF SONGS
Daniel C. Fredericks
Tremper Longman III

ISAIAH
Willem VanGemeren

JEREMIAH, LAMENTATIONS
G. Herbert Livingston

EZEKIEL
Iain Duguid

DANIEL
Gene Carpenter

HOSEA, JOEL
Owen Dickens

AMOS
William C. Williams

OBADIAH
Carl E. Armerding

JONAH
G. Patrick LaCosse

MICAH
Eugene Carpenter

NAHUM, HABAKKUK, ZEPHANIAH
Richard D. Patterson

HAGGAI, ZECHARIAH, MALACHI
Andrew Hill

MATTHEW
Scot McKnight

MARK
Robert Stein

LUKE
Mark Strauss

JOHN
Gary M. Burge

ACTS
Allison Trites

ROMANS
Douglas J. Moo

1 CORINTHIANS
Roger Mohrlang

2 CORINTHIANS
Ralph P. Martin

GALATIANS
Sean A. Harrison

EPHESIANS, PHILIPPIANS,
PHILEMON
Roger Mohrlang

COLOSSIANS
Douglas J. Moo

1 & 2 THESSALONIANS
Gene L. Green

1 & 2 TIMOTHY, TITUS
Jon Laansma

HEBREWS
George Guthrie

JAMES
Norman R. Ericson

1 & 2 PETER, JUDE
Douglas J. Moo

1–3 JOHN
Philip W. Comfort

REVELATION
Gerald Borchert

OLD TESTAMENT PROFILES
Tremper Longman III

NEW TESTAMENT PROFILES
Roger Mohrlang

ARTICLES
Daniel I. Block
Eugene Carpenter
Philip W. Comfort
Iain Duguid
Sean A. Harrison
Tremper Longman III
Douglas J. Moo
Grant R. Osborne

Richard D. Patterson
Daniel H. Williams
William C. Williams

WORD STUDY SYSTEM
James A. Swanson
Keith Williams

SPECIAL REVIEWER
Kenneth N. Taylor (deceased)

BIBLE PUBLISHING TEAM
PUBLISHER
Douglas R. Knox

ASSOCIATE PUBLISHER
Blaine A. Smith

ACQUISITIONS DIRECTOR
Kevin O'Brien

ACQUISITIONS EDITOR
Kim Johnson

OTHER SERVICES
GRAPHIC DESIGNERS
Timothy R. Botts (Interior)
Julie Chen (Cover)

CARTOGRAPHY
David P. Barrett

ILLUSTRATORS
Hugh Claycombe
Luke Daab
Sean A. Harrison

TYPESETTING
Joel Bartlett (The Livingstone
    Corporation)
Gwen Elliott

PROOFREADING
Peachtree Editorial Services

INDEXING
Karen Schmitt
    (Schmitt Indexing)

Many thanks to all who have had a hand
in the creation of this study Bible,
and most of all to the Lord of heaven and earth,
who gave us his word and Spirit so generously.